OPENING STRATEGIES

TEACHER'S BOOK

Brian Abbs
Ingrid Freebairn

STRATEGIES 1

Longman

Contents

Introduction

1 The target learner
 – who the course is for and where it can be used
2 The overall aims
 – what the course tries to do
3 The needs of beginners
 – how the course relates to the student
4 The rationale behind the syllabus
 – how the course is constructed
5 The methodology
 – how the material is taught
6 The grammar
 – how the course develops knowledge of the language system
7 The vocabulary
 – how the course presents vocabulary
8 The teacher
 – how the teacher approaches the course
9 Authenticity
 – how the course relates to the real world
10 The setting and characters
 – what the course is about

Description of the course

1 The Students' Book
2 The Teacher's Book
3 The recorded materials
4 The Workbook
5 The Test booklet

General teaching procedures

1 Presenting a function
2 Presenting a structure
3 Presenting vocabulary
4 Speech work
5 Pair work
6 Group work
7 Blackboard/OHP work
8 Substitution tables
9 Charts
10 Communicative tasks
11 Pictures
12 Correction
13 Use of L1 in monolingual classes
14 Testing and assessment

Course specific procedures

1 Presentation dialogues
2 Sets: language boxes and practice materials
3 Open dialogue
4 Roleplay
5 Listening activity
6 Reading texts
7 Writing tasks
8 Oral exercises
9 Grammatical summary boxes
10 Homework and homework correction
11 Student reference materials

Practical organisation and preparation

1 Classroom management
2 Timing
3 Sequencing
4 Lesson preparation
5 Notes
6 Classroom equipment
7 Student study materials
8 Abbreviations used in the teacher's notes
9 Classroom language

Unit surveys and teaching notes

Unit 1   Arrival
Unit 2   Pleased to meet you
Unit 3   I like London
Unit 4   Coffee or tea?
Unit 5   Consolidation
Unit 6   Getting around
Unit 7   Sunday in the park
Unit 8   At the Kennedy's
Unit 9   An evening out
Unit 10 Consolidation
Unit 11 Shopping
Unit 12 Back from Cambridge
Unit 13 Trouble at the hotel
Unit 14 Success!
Unit 15 Consolidation

Tests   Description, administration, key and tapescript

Indexes

1 Grammatical summary
2 How to say it
3 Active words and expressions (in alphabetical order)
4 Useful word groups
5 Selected further reading

Introduction

1 The target learner
– who the course is for and where it can be used

Opening Strategies is designed for young adults and adults, in small or large classes in secondary schools, colleges and universities, and in language and adult education institutes. It is suitable for:

      complete beginners – people who are learning English for the first time;

or false beginners – people who have tried to learn some English before, either in classes or with self-study material, but who want to start afresh from the beginning;

or mixed ability groups – people who are either beginners or false beginners.

2 The overall aims
– what the course tries to do

The main aims of this course of integrated language learning materials are to:

a) show students how to communicate in a wide range of situations

b) train students to speak simply and accurately and to develop basic skills in listening, reading and writing

c) harness students' enthusiasm and motivation by showing them that they are learning and saying something useful from the start

3 The needs of beginners
– how the course relates to the student

From the outset, Opening Strategies establishes purposes for communication by means of activities which involve the learner's personal identity and experience, knowledge of the world and his/her reactions to everyday affairs and situations.

But in order to communicate effectively there must be thorough practice of the foreign language system. Both purpose and ability have to be developed: this is the central tenet of a communicative course such as Opening Strategies.

Opening Strategies attempts to satisfy the needs of beginners in the following ways:

a) It shows how the language can be used immediately for a purpose, because the syllabus is based primarily on functional objectives and communicative events in situations.

b) It makes language learning objectives explicit so that the learner knows what to say and how to say it, to whom and when and where to say it. This explicitness of the material is evident at four levels – within each exercise, within each 'set' of work, within each unit and within the framework of the whole course.

c) It provides thorough and consistent practice of selected grammatical realisations of each function in clearly organised steps. This practice gives confidence, after which the learner is invited to try out newly-acquired linguistic knowledge in controlled and then freer situations.

d) It uses a classroom methodology which combines teacher-initiated practice and controlled pair work to establish accuracy, with more learner-centred interaction in pair work and group tasks to establish fluency.

e) It enables the learner to test hypotheses about language use in creative language activities such as open dialogues, roleplay, acting, games and communicative tasks.

f) It integrates the skills from the beginning: it encourages the learner to take the initiating role in speech exchanges and conversations, to write in sequence, to listen to and extract information in different ways and to read for and organise information. It develops these skills by using realistic spoken and written language and authentic realia – tickets, advertisements, graphics, timetables and maps.

g) It presents real people in a contemporary society – in this case Britain – and although set in London (at an international conference), it introduces people from all over the world.

4 The rationale behind the syllabus
– how the course is constructed

Opening Strategies is built on a communicative syllabus, one that selects items from inventories of language uses or functions, notions or conceptual areas such as Number, Time, Distance and Location, and topic areas such as Food and Drink, Travel and Shopping. These are matched with selected grammatical and lexical realisations. This language is then graded according to principles of linguistic complexity, usefulness relating to learner needs, transferability into real life and experience, and generalisability.

As well as following the above principles, the sequence of materials in Opening Strategies is organised according to the natural development of communicative events which occur when people arrive in a new place or foreign country and conduct the business of their daily lives, e.g. meeting people, making friends, finding their way around, shopping, making arrangements, doing business and relaxing.

The final selection and grading of all linguistic items is then adjusted according to classroom experience and commonsense ideas about students' needs and interests.

In the overall design of Opening Strategies, the central components of language – function, notion, topic and form – are interlocking and set within the four skills. Notional and topic areas appear as set titles, e.g. Names, Numbers, Countries and nationalities, Places, and Food, drink and money. Functions are shown in the list of contents in the Students' Book and are given with their selected realisations and linguistic structures in the Teacher's Book, e.g. *Order food and drink (function): Can I have two coffees, please? (realisation): Modal verb: can [request] (structure)*. Skills are signposted with clear headings: Listening, Reading, and Writing.

For the rich source of inventories of language notions, topic areas, functions, structures and skills from which the syllabus of Opening Strategies is constructed, we must acknowledge our debt to many books published in Europe in recent years. The ideas in these books – some of which are listed below* – have changed and enriched language teaching.

5 The methodology
– how the material is taught

Recent articles on communicative language teaching have suggested different ways of improving the methodology in order to make a communicative syllabus 'truly communicative'. These suggest that mechanical language learning exercises such as pattern practice, substitution tables and oral drills should be avoided. Preferably, they argue, the learner should be presented with a series of tasks or problem-solving activities which involve genuine information gaps.

In Opening Strategies these valuable insights have influenced the activities in the consolidation units where the tasks require a combination of communicative language and skills.

In the main teaching units, the methodological approach moves in three stages:

(i) pre-communicative**
This stage presents language in contexts through realistic dialogues, controlled practice in model utterances followed by further practice in controlled contexts using simultaneous pair-work exchanges.

(ii) communicative
The second stage provides practical communicative activities which give the learner a purpose for relating the language in focus to personal situations, experience and knowledge of the world. These activities also act as test situations for the learner to try out newly-acquired linguistic knowledge across a range of skills.

(iii) analysis
The final stage isolates the linguistic system in tables or paradigms so that the learner has access to the system from which to generate language in contexts other than those provided in the materials.

6 The grammar
– how the course develops knowledge of the language system

The organisation of Opening Strategies is based initially on notional/functional categories of language. What students need to express through the language is seen as the first criterion for selecting, grading and organising the language presented in the course.

*These include:
> Industrial English, T.C. Jupp and S. Hodlin, Heinemann Educational (1975).
> Notional Syllabuses, D.A. Wilkins, Oxford University Press (1976).
> The Threshold Level, J.A. van Ek with L.G. Alexander, Longman (1976).
> Communicative Syllabus Design, John Munby, Cambridge University Press (1978).

**We have taken this term from Communicative Language Teaching – An Introduction, William Littlewood, Cambridge University Press (1981).

Also essential is a knowledge of the grammatical system if students are to have access to a 'core grammar' from which to generate their own language. Therefore, in Opening Strategies, a careful structural grading runs parallel to the functional progression. There is two-way access to the language – from a functional and from a grammatical viewpoint – so that the learner knows what grammatical forms are being taught and to what uses they can be put. Opening Strategies also integrates personal factors (who we are and whom we are addressing) and the situational factors (where we are) with the grammatical system so that appropriate and meaningful communication can be developed.

7 The vocabulary
– how the course presents vocabulary

Learners must have access to a wide range of words: communication cannot take place without an adequate repertoire of content words.

However, a general course for beginners has to make a distinction between words that the learner needs and wants to know, and words which can be learned and retrieved at any one time. Opening Strategies, in order to provide stimulating contexts as the basis for communication, includes many words which students do not need to learn – they need only to recognise them.

Students should be told that not every word printed in the Students' Book needs to be learnt. However, they must also be responsible for their own word store; and certain selected key words will have to be learnt. They should feel free to ask the meaning of words not listed for active learning and should have access to a good bilingual dictionary.

In Opening Strategies, the policy for selecting vocabulary for active learning and use is as follows: words have been selected which either occur among general service word lists and which have a high frequency value, or are generic, e.g. vegetable (but not bean or pea), meat (but not lamb or beef).

Vocabulary is presented mainly through dialogues and practice material. It is also introduced, where appropriate, in reading texts and other parts of the unit material. Wherever 'active' words occur, they are extracted and highlighted at the appropriate point in the teaching notes which follow. They are also printed in word groups unit-by-unit in the end pages of the Students' Book.

'Non-active' words which give life, style and texture to the practice work in the sets do not need to come immediately into the learner's active repertoire, e.g. Can you windsurf/waterski? in the set which teaches can (ability) with reference to different sports and skills. These words are not essential learning items even if some students may want to learn them.

Many words appear first for recognition and are taken up actively in a later unit when they are more relevant, e.g. sometimes occurs in the dialogue in Unit 7 but is listed for active learning in Unit 8 when it reappears with the remaining adverbs of frequency under the set title of 'Routines'.

On average, there are eight new active words or expressions for the student to learn per 40-minute lesson. Teachers can add to the lists of active words when needed according to their teaching situations and their students' needs, interests and backgrounds. (There is an index of selected word fields at the back of this Teacher's Book, page 129.)

8 The teacher
– how the teacher approaches the course

There are four distinct roles for the teacher to play in the teaching of this material. One is the familiar, traditional role of *language instructor*. Here, the teacher presents and explains the new language, controls the practice, and evaluates and corrects the performance. This dominant role is necessary at certain stages if the students are to have the guidance to carry out the freer, communicative activities, and the confidence to handle the new language.

The second role is that of *classroom manager*: the teacher, in conjunction with the book, selects and coordinates the activities to form a coherent lesson. The teacher also organises and supervises the pair work and group work and intervenes and provides help where necessary.

The third role is that of *silent observer*, in which the teacher sets up activities and allows students to proceed without intervention. This non-participatory role allows learners to develop their own learning strategies. At the same time, it requires the teacher to be on the alert and to monitor the students' performance in order to check errors and develop ideas for follow-up in future lessons.

The fourth role is that of *peer-member of the group*. Here, the teacher joins in the activities on an equal basis. By doing this, the teacher promotes an atmosphere of relaxation and cooperation and by joining in, can promote the value of the learning task.

These roles are central to the methodological approach of Opening Strategies. They are fluctuating and overlapping parts of a whole teaching personality. Together with the materials, they allow the learners' communicative ability to develop.

9 Authenticity
– how the course relates to the real world

Opening Strategies takes fictitious characters and sets them in authentic places in a real city. The places where they meet and carry out their daily lives exist in real life. Great care has been taken in the choice of locations for the photographs so that the characters and the settings come to life and provide living context for the language, topics and events which occur. Moreover, the photographs offer cultural and socio-cultural information about the life and people of Britain.

The listening passages in the teaching units are mostly scripted to ease listening comprehension. Authentic recordings are included in the consolidation units and later teaching units to bridge the gap between controlled, edited language and spontaneous, authentic speech.

All the 'realia' is authentic and is taken from newspapers, magazines and other printed material.

Other reading passages are adapted and linguistically controlled. They present issues and situations relevant to contemporary society, such as the lack of facilities in small towns, unemployment, and studying or working away from home.

10 The setting and characters
– what the course is about

Opening Strategies is about a group of people who meet at an international video conference at the World Trade Centre at St Katherine's Dock near the Tower of London. The dock and its old warehouses no longer serve their original purpose. They have been converted into shops, apartments, pubs, restaurants and a conference centre so that they now function as a busy complex for business and leisure. Overlooking the River Thames and St Katherine's Dock is the newly built Tower Hotel which, among other things, provides accommodation for people attending the World Trade Centre. This is the setting in which our characters meet. They then travel to other parts of London and to other parts of Britain.

The lives of the characters outside the conference play an important part in the book. Vince, for example, has a wife and family in Los Angeles, and we see details of their lives there. Diana has a husband and daughter in Manchester; she also has a friend in London whom she meets to go to a concert. The interweaving of the characters' personal lives provides the reason for writing, telephoning and finding out information and adds to the depth and texture of the materials. The network of human relationships provides many points of identification for the learners and gives contexts for them to develop ideas relating to their own lives and experience.

There is also a story. This does not play a major part in the development of the language of the book: it acts merely to give sequence to the units, momentum to the action and motives for the behaviour of the people we meet.

Description of the course

The course consists of
– a Students' Book
– a Teacher's Book
– a set of recorded material (on cassette)
– a Workbook
– a Test booklet

1 The Students' Book

The Students' Book is divided into 15 units. Twelve of these are teaching units and three are consolidation units. Each teaching unit consists of:
(i)   Presentation dialogues
(ii) Sets (of classroom exercises)
(iii) Skills practice material

(iv) Oral exercises
(v) Grammatical summary
Consolidation units are Units 5, 10 and 15.
Indexes of reference material are included at the back of the Students' Book.

(i) Presentation dialogues

In all the teaching units, the language in focus is presented through dialogue. The dialogue is divided into three or more short parts, followed by check questions and sets of practice material.

(ii) Sets

The purpose of the set titles is to orientate the students to the practice work which follows, using language which is readily understandable, e.g. Unit 4 Set 1 Food, drink and money; Unit 6 Set 1 Past events. The sets practise and develop language in three distinct moves:
1 isolation of the language to be taught
2 controlled practice in appropriate contexts
3 transfer of language to the students' own experience
Most of the set exercises are oral, although simple guided writing practice is often incorporated, or suggested in the teacher's notes.

(iii) Skills practice material

The skills material integrates speaking, listening, reading and writing skills, while at the same time representing language previously practised in the sets in different contexts. Speaking practice takes place through open dialogues and roleplay exercises; the listening passages are specially written realistic conversations or monologues where listening for information is the target skill; the reading passages are mainly factual/descriptive paragraphs or letters for language consolidation; writing tasks are always controlled and in most cases consist of modelled writing with the students substituting information about themselves and their lives.

(iv) Oral exercises

The oral exercises provide intensive practice of selected structures from the unit in communicative exchanges. A model exchange and prompts for all the following exchanges are printed in the Students' Book so that the students can do the exercises in pairs if a language laboratory is not available.

Some exercises are labelled 'open'. This means that the students are free to introduce their own ideas and information within the framework of a suggested model. Examples of suggested responses are printed in *italics* in the tapescripts for the oral exercises in this book. All the oral exercises can be used for additional writing practice in class or for homework.

(v) Grammatical summary

On the final page of each unit is a summary of the grammatical items contained in the unit. These items are displayed in tables. They serve as a useful aid not only for analysis of the system but also for revision.

Consolidation units

Units 5 and 10 bring together and revise the language presented in the previous units. They are divided into four parts: the first part is a communicative task to promote spoken fluency; the second part is devoted to consolidation of listening and reading skills, the third part concentrates on tasks related to authentic reading texts and realia; the fourth part is a language review in the form of a test. Unit 15 ends the book with a game, reading followed by language work and discussion, and two authentic interviews with students studying in Britain.

Indexes

These consist of:
(i)   active words and expressions listed unit-by-unit
(ii) the structural content of each unit
(iii) tables of basic grammatical systems
(iv) a list of useful irregular verbs and their principle parts
The indexes can be used by the students for reference and revision.

2 The Teacher's Book

This consists of:
Introduction
Description of the course
General teaching procedures
Course specific procedures
Practical organisation and preparation
Detailed unit-by-unit teaching notes, with a tapescript of the recorded material at the appropriate point. The notes for each unit are preceded by a detailed analysis of the composition of each unit (unit summaries).
Tests: description, administration, key and tapescript.
Indexes:
1 Grammatical summary
   – an index of all the grammatical items presented in the course
2 How to say it
   – a list of all the speech functions used in the course. These are categorised under notional titles listed in alphabetical order
3 Active words and expressions
   – these are listed in alphabetical order with the unit reference for when they first appear
4 Useful word groups
   – adjectives and their opposites; countries and nationalities; word fields
5 Selected further reading

3 The recorded materials

All of these, which are available on cassette, are recorded by British and American native speakers. They follow the order in which they occur in the Students' Book. Tapescripts for all of them are printed at the appropriate points in this Teacher's Book. They consist of:

(i) Presentation dialogues

These are recorded first in parts, corresponding to the parts in the Students' Book, at a slightly slower than normal speed, without any extraneous sound effects. Each part is then paused for students to listen and repeat. At the end, the complete dialogue, combining all parts, is recorded at natural speed with full sound effects.

(ii) Open dialogues

These are recorded with pauses for the students to give their own responses.

(iii) Listening texts

These are mainly scripted but some practice in listening to authentic English is given in the consolidation units and in some teaching units towards the end of the course. All the listening practice is task-related and special instructions for each appears in the detailed teaching notes for each unit.

(iv) Oral exercises

These are recorded so that the student can complete three steps: listen, speak and check performance against a model utterance. The conversation is always rounded off with an answer if the model utterance is a question, e.g. Unit 3 Oral exercise 2: *Ask if Diana likes classical music.* s: *Does Diana like classical music? (Does Diana like classical music?) Yes, she does.* With open exercises usually only the first frame has a model utterance.

(v) Tests

The listening passages which make up the listening skills section of the Opening Strategies Tests (Section D) can be found on the cassettes at the end of Units 5, 10 and 15. Tapescripts of these passages are printed in the Tests section of this Teacher's Book.

4 The Workbook

The Workbook consists of 15 units providing additional practice of structures and vocabulary introduced in the corresponding unit of the Students' Book. The main characters and situations are re-introduced and the exercises include completing dialogues, writing dialogues and letters, various comprehension and gap filling exercises and different types of word puzzle. These exercises can be worked through in class or can be given to the students as homework.

5 The Test booklet

The Test booklet contains three short assessment tests which are designed to be used after Units 5, 10 and 15. Each test is divided into eight sections: the first three sections (Part One) cover structure and vocabulary; the remaining five sections (Part Two) cover the communicative use of language. A full description of these along with notes on administration, a key and tapescript of the listening comprehension passages are given in the Tests section of this Teacher's Book, page 109.

General teaching procedures

1 Presenting a function

When presenting a particular function or language use, it is advisable to avoid using descriptive labels, e.g. (using L1) *Today we are going to learn how to make informal introductions.* Apart from this method being restricted to the teaching of monolingual groups, it is more motivating and more memorable to contextualise the situation first, and use the descriptive labels after-

wards as an instructional device. For example, when teaching the language of introductions, the teacher can select two students and bring them to the front of the class. T: *Juan, this is Ann-Marie. Ann-Marie, this is Juan.* The teacher then encourages the students to say *Hello* and perhaps shake hands. T: (to the class) *Now you introduce each other. Pierre, introduce Maria and Kurt.* etc. In this way, the situation is clear and the metalanguage (the descriptive label) is absorbed unconsciously.

2 Presenting a structure

When a language function is presented in context, the students have two tasks. The first is to draw conclusions about the situation (Who is speaking, to whom, when and where?) The second is to absorb the language. Because there is so much for the students to take in at one time, the teacher needs to repeat the utterance two or three times. Only when the students have heard the language correctly, can they be expected to repeat it correctly. Repetition in chorus is a step towards individual production and is a great help for students as a confidence builder. They can practise in a group forming the sounds before they have to produce the language individually. After choral repetition, individual students can be asked to repeat the utterance so that the teacher can monitor individual performances.

The teacher will need to vary the elements that make up an utterance, e.g. Unit 7 (Present continuous tense) T: *What's he doing? He's doing yoga. What's she doing? She's jogging. What are they doing? They're sailing model boats.* These examples, with the change of personal pronouns and accompanying verb *to be*, show the students how the tense is formed with different structural components. It is essential that students practise manipulating different structural elements in controlled contexts before they can be expected to transfer the language in different contexts.

3 Presenting vocabulary

In Opening Strategies, vocabulary is presented in a context either in a dialogue or text, or in groups of words for input in a language exercise. They are not always accompanied by pictures so that the teacher has to use other methods to teach meaning. These may be:

a) showing real objects
b) drawing on the blackboard or showing pictures from magazines
c) miming
d) giving examples
e) explaining in simple English
f) explaining in L1
g) translating

The choice of method will depend on the type of word. Simple, everyday objects like *chair, window, book,* etc. can be pointed to; physical objects like *cat, house, tree* can be drawn on the blackboard or pictures of them can be shown; verbs of motion can be mimed; adjectives can be illustrated by example, e.g. *red, big, heavy.* Abstract nouns and culturally-specific words are most easily translated or explained using L1 where possible. If there is no common L1, examples can sometimes help, as can a bilingual dictionary. The key active words to be learnt in each unit of Opening Strategies are listed unit-by-unit at the back of the Students' Book.

4 Speech work

Whenever new language is being presented for active use, the students should repeat the language chorally and individually using the tape as a model where possible. When sentence stress and intonation cause problems, the back-chaining method is effective. Here the teacher asks the students to repeat the utterance in parts, starting from the end and building up towards the beginning, e.g. T: *Listen please: What time does the train leave? Say after me: train leave?... does the train leave?... What time does the train leave?* The important point to remember is to keep the intonation pattern constant each time. Students will find it easier to imitate the whole pattern if they start from the end. Chaining from the beginning to the end, i.e. forward-chaining, is less effective.

5 Pair work

The exercises in the sets instruct the students to work in pairs simultaneously. An advantage of pair work is the extensive practice that can be done by all the students in a short space of time. Also, pair work relieves the boredom which arises when students are made to listen to their colleagues doing exercises in turn.

The procedure is as follows. The teacher divides the class into pairs and labels each member of each pair A and B. Students work in pairs following the model in the exercise first A-B, then changing parts to B-A. All the pairs are active at the same time. The teacher goes round and monitors the performance of as many pairs as possible, correcting where necessary. Correction should not occur every time a mistake is heard; it should be given with discretion so as not to inhibit the students who are using new language for the first time. (See note 12, Correction, in this section on page ix.)

If there is an uneven number in the class, the teacher can either make a group of three or take part him/herself as a member of a pair. If this is a permanent situation, it is important that not always the same student is the odd-man-out. Pairs should in any case be rearranged regularly to avoid boredom.

6 Group work

For certain types of task in Opening Strategies, e.g. for roleplays, special projects and short discussions, students are asked to work in groups. Because many teachers have large classes of over twenty students and find it practically impossible to rearrange their classrooms, group work is only suggested judiciously. However, many teachers may wish to use groups for other activities and should feel free to do so. A good arrangement for any size class, instead of the traditional horse-shoe shape, is into sets of group tables. If a permanent group seating arrangement is set up from the beginning, the teacher can still use the arrangement for whole class teaching as well as pair and group work, and no time is wasted rearranging the tables and chairs. Different ways of making up groups can be used for the sake of variety. Several points are worth remembering when setting up group work: always give clear instructions for what you want the students to do; give a time limit for the task and warn the students a minute or so before the time is up; appoint a secretary if the task requires it and tell the secretaries how you want them to record the work; when the group work has begun, take a back-seat position and interfere as little as possible. (See section 8, The teacher, in Introduction page v.)

Recording and reporting back can take different forms:

a) One member of each group acts as secretary for the group, takes notes during the discussion and reports back orally to the whole class.

b) All members of the group take notes and write a written report.

c) Cross-group reporting.

The procedure for cross-grouping is as follows. In an imaginary class of fifteen students, the students first form groups of five, each member of the group being allotted a letter: A, B, C, D or E. After a limited period of discussion, the groups re-form. All the A's go to one group, all the B's to another and so on until there are five new groups of three students in each. The role of each student in the cross-groups is to report the answers or give a summary of the opinions of his or her original group. (See diagram.)

Cross-group reporting

(1) Divide 15 students into 3 groups to work			(2) Re-form into 5 groups to report
Group 1	Group 2	Group 3	
A	A	A	→ 1
B	B	B	→ 2
C	C	C	→ 3
D	D	D	→ 4
E	E	E	→ 5

The advantage of this kind of work is that, firstly, each student carries the individual responsibility of reporting the original group's deliberations and therefore must be an active listener and note-taker as well as a speaker; secondly, everyone must say something in the cross-group reporting session.

The teacher can sit in on the first working groups and the cross-groups, noting mistakes or issues which can be taken up and discussed with the whole class after the discussions are concluded.

7 Blackboard/overhead projector (OHP) work

The blackboard or OHP can be used for several purposes: focussing the attention of the class; making quick illustrations; writing up language examples after they have been presented; making substitution tables, and so on. It is important to write neatly and carefully and arrange the information clearly, e.g. one area for new words, another for important language patterns and substitution tables, another for temporary jottings, drawings, games and so on.

Words and structures are more memorable if they are seen to be written, even though they may already appear printed in the Students' Book. Variety and movement can be created in the classroom by asking students to come up to the blackboard/OHP occasionally and write words or sentences or draw pictures.

8 Substitution tables

Substitution tables are systematically presented in the Students' Book but can be made up by the teacher and students together on the blackboard using more relevant vocabulary when appropriate.

Substitution tables allow the students to see the system behind the language they are using. Once the students are familiar with the way the tables work, i.e. the function of the vertical and horizontal lines, and which are the static and which are the variable elements, useful intensive practice can be achieved by asking students to make sentences from the table. The emphasis at this pre-communicative phase, is to practise manipulating the forms. This stage is also useful for concentrating on the stress and intonation of the sentences. The teacher can conduct the whole class, groups or individuals by pointing to a key word and getting them to make grammatical sentences from the table, e.g. the teacher points to *He*:

I	am	leaving	
He She	is	having a party	tomorrow.
We	are	going home	

and the students have a choice of three sentences to make but each must start with *He is.*

9 Charts

Charts provide material for intensive language practice or for comprehension work after listening or reading passages. (For examples of each see Unit 4 Set 2 Exercise 1 and Unit 4 Listening and Reading.)

The procedure for each is different. When a chart is used for language practice, it is important to present new vocabulary first and give clear examples of what the students are required to do before setting them to work. In some cases, e.g. Unit 8 Set 1, the chart is completed and language practice consists of using the information given in the chart in the way suggested in the model, e.g. *Doug always goes to work by . . . . He never . . . .* In other cases, e.g. in Unit 4 Set 2 the chart is a list of spare time activities with two columns at the side marked 'You' and 'Your partner'. In cases like this, the chart is presented in the form of a questionnaire, e.g. *Do you like going to the cinema/reading?* etc. The students answer the questions about themselves first, noting down their answers, and then ask the partners the same questions noting down

their answers in the column as well. They can now talk about and report back the information, using the language structure in focus, e.g. *Maria likes going to the cinema but she doesn't like watching television.*

In comprehension work, the headings in the chart act as a guide to processing the text. Answers are usually one-word or in note-form, thus only testing comprehension, not a combination of comprehension and structural accuracy.

The value of charts is to enable the students to conduct their own learning and consequently reduce teacher talking time.

10 Communicative tasks

Communicative tasks which resemble real-life situations motivate the learner to use the language creatively. Communicative tasks ('information gap exercises') are one way of bridging the gap between pre-communicative practice and real-life situations. These tasks require the students not only to use a wide range of language but also to think and to make choices.

The principle behind them is that student A has access to information which student B has not got, and that student B has a problem to solve which requires knowing some or all of that information.

Many exercises in the Students' Book can be adapted to communicative tasks if the teacher wishes. Either student A can be instructed to mask the information while he/she puts the questions to student B, or the teacher can photocopy the different pieces of information and distribute them separately to all the A's and the B's in the pairs.

11 Pictures

The pictures which appear in the Students' Book consist of three main types:
1 photographs of the characters in settings relevant to the dialogue contexts
2 illustrations as direct input for practice work
3 photographs and illustrations to accompany texts and exercises

In Opening Strategies, the pictures have more than a decorative purpose. When accompanying a dialogue, they provide the context, they bring characters and settings to life and they give cultural information about life in Britain. Photographs and illustrations accompanying texts and exercises have a predictive value and are an important aid to comprehension.

Occasionally pictures can act as the basis for additional language work on description.

12 Correction

There is no hard and fast rule for correction. In the controlled practice stage, where the emphasis is on correct production, correction should perhaps take place as soon as possible after the mistake has been made (although not in mid-sentence). In the freer stage, for example in roleplays, open dialogues and discussions, where the emphasis is more on successful communication, students should not be interrupted during the

action. Mistakes can be noted down while listening to different pairs or groups in action, and dealt with afterwards. This can be done in several ways:
a) by discussing with the whole class general mistakes which several students have made
b) by noting down one or two important mistakes from each student and going through them systematically with the whole class listening
c) (if the class is small) by noting down each student's mistakes on a separate piece of paper and handing the piece of paper back to the student afterwards. The students can then think about the mistakes and correct them orally or in writing. If they keep these pieces of paper, they can refer to them later and see if the same mistakes keep occurring. This can be especially useful for revision purposes

13 Use of L1 in monolingual classes

The main reason for suggesting use of the mother tongue at an elementary level is to save time when giving instructions, scene-setting for dialogues and roleplay, and explaining passive vocabulary, thereby gaining time for intensive practice.

The mother tongue can also be used to advantage in explaining cultural points which arise from the pictures, dialogues and texts, and occasionally in discussions with the students about their progress, their feelings about the material and similar topics which fall outside the lesson but which can give the teacher valuable feedback.

There is of course an enormous amount to be gained by the students in hearing as much English as possible in all sorts of situations, especially when the students are unlikely to hear or use it outside the classroom. *It is therefore essential to phase out the use of the mother tongue as soon as possible.* Instructions which form a recognisable pattern can quite soon be given in English as can explanations of vocabulary and even simple explanations of cultural points.

The teacher's aim, by the end of Opening Strategies, is to be able to conduct the entire lesson successfully and efficiently in English.

14 Testing and assessment

There is a Test booklet accompanying Opening Strategies containing three tests to be used after Units 5, 10 and 15. For guidance on administering and marking the tests, see the Tests section on page 109 of this book. However, the teacher should integrate testing into the general teaching programme. At the beginning of each new unit the teacher can check the meaning of all active words from the previous unit and do question and answer, or stimulus and response work to revise important structures. In classes with a first language in common, translation can be used to good effect as a quick testing device.

The consolidation units, 5 and 10, contain classroom activities for general revision and a test of the main language items from the previous four units.

Students' assessment of their own progress can be achieved by means of a questionnaire at various intervals during the course. Multiple-choice questions can give the teacher valuable feedback on his/her own teaching as well as an insight into the students' reactions to the material and their own progress.

Course specific procedures

1 Presentation dialogues

The presentation dialogues centre round the four main characters and in each unit are divided into self-contained parts. Their purpose is to set all the language in context.

Suggested procedure (after Unit 1):
a) Revise what the students know about the characters and what they are doing. If you like, replay the complete version of the preceding dialogue.
b) Refer students to the photographs and ask them to describe what they can see. Relate this to the context of the dialogue.
c) Present any new vocabulary which the students may find difficult and highlight or explain the active words and expressions.
d) Ask students to look at the true/false statements or the comprehension questions which usually follow each dialogue part. These will help focus their listening and reading of the dialogue.
e) Play the appropriate section of the tape (or read the dialogue with as much expression as possible). Stop the tape at certain intervals if you wish.
f) The students correct the true/false statements or answer the questions. Refer back to the dialogue and go through it, helping the students with any new or difficult expressions, or points of cultural background.
g) Play the tape again.
h) Play the 'paused' version of the dialogue for the students to listen to and repeat. Alternatively, transfer this activity to the language laboratory.
i) Students read the dialogue in parts and/or act it in pairs or groups.
j) When each dialogue part has been presented and practised in this way, play the complete, linked version without pausing the tape.

2 Sets: language boxes and practice materials

If the teacher prefers to do the set exercises before the presentation material (see note 3, Sequencing, page xiii), the functions on which the sets are based will have to be presented without reference to their use and context in the presentation dialogue. In any case, it is always advisable to give extra examples of new functions in contexts which are immediately relevant to the students and their surroundings.

Each set has, in principle, a theme of its own. It should form a complete and uninterrupted teaching unit if possible. These set exercises represent the basic language practice needed before attempting the skills activities.

Each set exercise is introduced by a language box containing a model – usually taken from the dialogue – of the language to be practised. Teachers can refer the students back to its use in the dialogue by replaying the part of the tape which contains that particular utterance to remind the students of the context. Some teachers may prefer to make the context initially more relevant to the students before referring to the model utterance. In the early units all model utterances should be repeated chorally and individually (see note 2, Presenting a structure, page vii). Later on, however, especially when the boxes contain longer, more complex examples, the students can be asked to study the box silently.

3 Open dialogue

The open dialogue is centred on one or more of the functions practised in the unit. The students should be encouraged to give 'true' answers, using the correct structure or situational phrase where applicable. A practice model should be given so that students know what is expected of them.

a) Set the situation clearly.
b) Ask one student to read the printed side of the dialogue (or read it yourself in the early units). Give the response yourself.
c) Change parts with the student. This time, you read the printed part, the student responds. Make sure that the student's responses are true, as he/she may think that he/she has to say the same as you.
d) Practise the same exchange with another student giving the responses. This should establish that more than one answer is possible.
e) Divide the students into pairs and ask them to practise the dialogue, changing parts afterwards. Go round and listen. This last activity may be carried out in the language laboratory if one is available.

4 Roleplay

The roleplay exercises invite the students to take roles in situations which they will find easy to identify with. In most cases they are asked to be themselves in a specific situation. Only on few occasions are they required to take on a different persona. The language required to conduct the roleplay satisfactorily is a combination of important language functions from the unit. The instructions give a clear outline of the roles and the situation in simple English but the teacher may choose to set the scene using the L1 when possible. Examples should always be given of the type of language expected of the students before asking them to start. The roleplays can be practised simultaneously in groups and one or two groups can be asked to perform in front of the rest of the class afterwards.

Sometimes roleplay in pairs is guided by a chain of cues like: 1 *Greet your friend*: 2 *Ask your friend to come in*, etc. In these roleplays the teacher should develop the language for each cue with the whole class before the students work in pairs.

5 Listening activity

The instructions for activities which accompany the listening passage appear in the Students' Book and help the students to focus their attention on the important facts to be drawn from the passage.

a) Play the tape to yourself or read the tapescript before the lesson.
b) Check what questions or activities accompany the passage.
c) Present any new 'key' words for general comprehension of the passage.
d) Play the tape through without stopping.
e) Prepare the students for the activity, making sure they know what to do. (Stages d) and e) may be reversed.)
f) Play the tape again stopping in relevant places. Do not stop to explain the meaning of all new words and expressions.
g) Check the answers.

Stage f) could be done in the language laboratory. The students can stop the tape as often as they like. In real life, of course, one does not have the opportunity to listen again to something one did not understand at a first hearing. The teacher should control the number of times that students listen to a given passage. As the course progresses, students should decrease the number of times they go over the listening passage. Classroom practice is in this context preferable. It also prevents the student from stopping the tape himself when he meets a language item which is not immediately recognisable.

6 Reading texts

The reading texts in the teaching units have been specially written so that they: a) bring together and consolidate structural and lexical items from the unit; b) introduce extra vocabulary for active use; c) introduce the students gradually to the use of coordinating devices for linked writing.

The texts are always accompanied by questions or some form of comprehension check so that essential vocabulary and structures can be retrieved. In most cases the texts serve as a model for writing.

The reading texts in the consolidation units consist of texts and realia from authentic sources. The teacher should use the questions and accompanying tasks to guide the students, so that the 'passive' vocabulary which inevitably occurs in authentic texts, does not deflect from the purpose of the exercise and slow up the work in hand.

7 Writing tasks

The course includes many suggestions for simple writing activities, ranging from controlled sentence writing to descriptive and narrative paragraphs and letters. All of these are preceded by a model for guidance.

Extended writing activities set for homework should be prepared in class. The students need time to organise their thoughts, to ask for help over suitable words and expressions and perhaps guidance in starting the first few lines. Short writing activities can be done in class to vary the pace of the lesson.

8 Oral exercises

These exercises can be used in the language laboratory or in the classroom. Many teachers with access to a laboratory will want to prepare the students in class first to enable them to use the laboratory time as effectively as possible.

It is advisable first to play the tape of the example exchanges in order to demonstrate how the exercise works and to provide a good model for stress and intonation. After these initial examples, the exercises can be done in these ways:
a) Teacher plays the tape or reads the tapescript of the stimuli and asks the class to respond chorally, followed by individual repetition or vice versa.
b) Students work in pairs following the model exchange giving both stimulus and response between them (all the stimuli are printed in the Students' Book for this purpose).
c) A combination of a) and b): the teacher works T-S first, then instructs students to work in pairs on the same exercises.
d) Half the class gives the stimulus (chorally) and the other half gives the response (chorally). This arrangement can be used occasionally for variety.
e) For additional consolidation work, students can be asked to write out the responses for homework.

These exercises not only consolidate structures and vocabulary but also give consistent practice in pronunciation, stress and intonation. Teachers should therefore consider the oral exercises as an integral and important part of the basic language practice for each unit.

The open oral exercises that encourage students to answer as they wish should be treated slightly differently. After playing a model exchange on the tape, the teacher should work tape-T, or S-T first, so as to give the students the idea of the sort of responses that are acceptable. After this they can do the exercise in pairs.

9 Grammatical summary boxes

The tables at the end of each unit give an overview of the system behind the language the students have learnt to use. Teachers can use the tables for extra pattern practice at the end of each unit and to encourage the students to make their own hypotheses to test in other contexts.

10 Homework and homework correction

Suggestions for homework are included in the detailed teacher's notes at the end of each unit. As a unit is designed to cover several lessons, teachers will want to spread the homework load between the lessons.

To give the students maximum talking time in class, it is generally recommended that written work be set for homework. Some writing in class can nevertheless be useful for varying the tempo of the lesson and giving the students a change of activity after intensive oral practice.

In principle, all homework should be prepared in class beforehand, especially the freer writing activities where the students may need help in advance over new vocabulary and expressions.

Correction of homework
Suggestions:
a) Collect in written work, mark and give back. Marking can be done with symbols that you and the class agree on, e.g. *sp* = spelling mistake *gr* = grammar mistake *v* = vocabulary mistake *w.o.* = word order mistake *exp* = wrong expression or not the best way of expressing what the student means. Students are then forced to think about their mistakes in a different and more constructive way than if the right version is written in above their mistakes.
b) Ask the students to exchange their homework with their partner. They then correct each other's work as far as possible, either writing in the correct version or marking with a symbol. Students then hand each other's work back and do any necessary corrections while you go round and help.
c) Ask a few students to read their work out loud to the rest of the class. The other students listen for mistakes and help to correct them. As most of the writing is controlled, there should not be too many mistakes. Many of the mistakes will, in any case, be common to other students who are listening and these students will then have an opportunity of correcting their own mistakes on the spot.

After this oral check some teachers may like to collect in all the written work and check that the students have made the necessary corrections in class.
d) Written answers to comprehension questions and fill-in exercises can be checked orally in a chain round the class, or by showing a key on an overhead transparency and asking students to correct their own work.

11 Student reference materials

These consist of the following:
a) (at the end of each unit) tables of the grammatical items which have been presented and practised in the unit
b) (at the end of the Students' Book)
   – lists of active words and expressions to be learnt. These are presented unit-by-unit
   – lists of language form/focus presented unit-by-unit
   – a list of selected grammatical systems
   – a selection of irregular verbs and their principle parts

It is essential to refer students to these reference materials before they start work with the course and to refer to them at appropriate intervals.

Practical organisation and preparation

1 Classroom management

Teachers with many years of experience will know that, while allowing for individual personality traits, certain recognisable 'types' of student tend to appear regularly in classes, regardless of level, nationality, sex or age. It is important to know how to handle the different types of student.

(i) The dominant type: answers all the questions even out of turn; asks questions repeatedly; talks a lot to the teacher; takes charge in group work; leads the discussion, and talks more than the others.
Suggestions:
a) pair a dominant type with another one for pair work
b) group dominant students together for group work
c) do not ask too many open questions to the class – direct the questions at particular students and gesture to the dominant students to keep quiet if they try to answer
d) if necessary, enlist their support out of class and tell them that you would like them to help in the class to get the quieter students to speak
e) use postponing tactics in class discussions, e.g. 'That's very interesting – let's talk about it in the break . . .'

(ii) The quiet type: in contrast with the dominant student, the quiet type speaks only when spoken to; is afraid of making mistakes; keeps silent in group discussions and never takes the initiative.
Suggestions:
a) put with similar types for pair and group work (Do not pair with a dominant student in the hope that this will bring them out – it doesn't.)
b) ask simple direct questions which you know they can answer
c) encourage and praise whenever possible
d) give initiating roles in roleplay work
e) make sure you do not miss them out when doing T-S work

(iii) The fast learner: is not necessarily dominant, but gets everything right first time; makes very few mistakes and always finishes pair work and other exercises before anyone else.
Suggestions:
a) set extra, more challenging work so that they are fully stretched
b) pair them occasionally with weaker students and ask them specially to help the other students
c) assert different standards of accuracy and fluency for them so that you are correcting them as often as the others – this will benefit them and make the rest of the class feel more secure

(iv) The slow learner: takes a long time to grasp new language; often makes mistakes; tends to ignore correction; takes a long time to complete oral and written exercises; seems to forget language learnt from one lesson to the next.
Suggestions:
a) gear your presentation and explanation to the slow learners – the others will benefit from thorough teaching and plenty of repetition
b) never make them feel stupid – praise and encourage when possible
c) pair or group them with other students of the same

standard or with a kind, cooperative member of the class who will help the slower learner
d) always make your instructions very clear and ask them simple uncomplicated questions
e) set aside extra time to explain and go through with these students
f) make them repeat the right answer when corrected, and ask them to write out corrected sentences from their written homework

2 Timing

Between 90 and 120 hours should be sufficient to complete the course. Each teaching unit will take from six to eight hours. This implies at least three double teaching periods (one hour = an academic hour of approximately 45–60 minutes), including an hour in the language laboratory.

3 Sequencing

The material is arranged in much the same way in each unit, e.g. Unit 4:
Presentation dialogue Part 1
Set 1
Presentation dialogue Part 2
Set 2
Set 3
Presentation dialogue Part 3
Set 4
Open dialogue
Roleplay
Listening
Reading
Writing
Oral exercises
Grammar summary
Slight variations occur in the number of dialogue parts and how the sets are distributed, but the order is the same in principle.

Some teachers may wish to vary the pace and pattern of a lesson by choosing a different sequence: they may, for example, prefer to start with the set work and then move back to the presentation material to revise and re-contextualise the language practised in the sets.

If no language laboratory is available, the oral exercises are best practised in sections: the students practise those that relate to each set after the set work has been completed. For best results, work on the oral exercises should *precede* work on the skills material, as they will ensure adequate practice of the necessary language.

4 Lesson preparation

Clearly organised lesson plans are central to the repertoire of the professional teacher. Most teachers will need to adapt the existing materials and notes to suit their own classes. A file of supplementary teacher's notes and lesson plans should be kept alongside the Teacher's Book.

Before teaching any unit or part of a unit, the teacher should look at the summary of the main teaching points which precedes the unit. This indicates:

a) the topic or situational areas involved
b) the new functions to be learnt
c) the structural exponents of the functions
d) the active vocabulary to be learnt at each stage of the unit

The teacher should then turn to the relevant pages in the Students' Book and the corresponding pages of detailed notes in the Teacher's Book and work through the lesson mentally. This will give the teacher an opportunity to decide on the best sequencing (see last section), to make adjustments to suit the students and to prepare any material on an overhead transparency that might be useful during the course of the lesson. The transcript of the recorded material should be read carefully so that the teacher can prepare the students for the listening activities.

5 Notes

Notes to texts, dialogues and realia occur frequently in the Teacher's Book. These explain cultural points, names, places, and idiomatic words and expressions not likely to occur in a dictionary. They are primarily for teacher reference when the students feel the need for special explanation or translation. However, students can often work out the meaning of unfamiliar words and expressions from the context and should always be encouraged to do so. If such explanations are needed, they should come after, and not before, the reading of the text.

6 Classroom equipment

Essential pieces of equipment are a black (or white) board and a tape recorder. Useful but not essential are an overhead projector, a flannel board, a teacher's kit of useful objects like a toy clock, telephone, etc., a collection of laminated magazine illustrations or flashcards for vocabulary presentation and a pinboard to display students' work, special notices, interesting pictures and articles, etc.

7 Student study materials

Teachers should make sure at the start of the course that the students are equipped with:
– a sensible-sized notebook (possibly A-4 size), and a pen, a pencil and an eraser.
– a bilingual dictionary

A good monolingual dictionary (e.g. *Longman Dictionary of Contemporary English*) is useful: a few copies for the whole class could be kept permanently in the classroom and shared by students when required.

Where sets of books are to be used by other classes, students should be asked to copy out sentences or charts from the book, rather than fill in words in pencil.

Check that they lay their work out clearly and correctly. It is a good idea to get the students into the habit of writing legibly at all times, and to use margins and paragraph indentations when writing compositions or letters.

As students are asked to work in pairs and groups frequently throughout the course, they should be encouraged to tackle language problems on their own, either by asking each other for help or by using a dictionary.

8 Abbreviations used in the teacher's notes

T	Teacher
S	Student
L1	Native language
L2	First foreign language or second language
SB	Students' Book
TB	Teacher's Book
T-S	Teacher to Student: The teacher asks a question or makes a statement and the student answers or responds.
S-T	Student to Teacher: The student asks a question or makes a statement and the teacher answers or responds.
S1-S2, S2-S3	Student to Student: One student asks another student a question. The second student answers. Then the second student asks a third student a similar question and so on, in the form of a chain. It is better if the chain does not always follow the order of seating in the classroom, in case the students 'switch off' until it is their time to perform.
e.g.	for example
i.e.	that is (explanatory)
c.f.	compare with
etc.	etcetera
opp.	the opposite of (+ word)
=	means the same as
SSR	Suggested Students' Response
OHP	Overhead projector
BB	Blackboard
Ex	Exercise
HW	Homework

9 Classroom language

The following should be given in English by the teacher.*
(Could you) listen   (please)
(Please) listen to this/to the cassette
repeat after the tape/in the pauses
say it loudly (I can't hear you)
say it together/after me
say it again/once more
say it like this
do it again
try it again
look here/at this/at the blackboard/at this picture
look at exercise .../page .../index .../the map of Britain
read this aloud/silently/to your partner
read the dialogue/letter/text/on page ...
write this in your notebooks
do exercise ... for homework
copy this sentence in your notebooks/this chart and fill it in

*For a more detailed account of classroom language see *Teaching English through English*, Jane Willis, Longman (1981).

spell it
work in pairs/groups/on your own
get into groups of 3, 4, 5, *etc.*
change parts/groups
stand up
sit down/over there/next to Julio

come to the front
act your roleplay for the class
close your books
learn these words
tell me the time
Good! Excellent! Well done!

Unit surveys and teaching notes

First lesson
1 Administration and classroom organisation
2 Introduction to the book
3 Language work

1 Administration and classroom organisation

Registration
Try to deal with the class register, late enrolments, fees and distribution of books as rapidly as possible. The students will be waiting for the start of their first English lesson and it is important not to delay this too long.

Seating
A good seating arrangement is essential. For small groups (12–15 students) the best arrangement is to seat the students in groups of 4–6 around separate tables. A horse-shoe shape is also effective because it has the advantage of allowing the teacher to move around in front of the students, but it is more formal than the groups of tables, and less suitable for pair-changing and group activities. In very large classes, make sure the students are in pairs and can all see the blackboard or OHP easily and hear the tape recorder clearly.

Study equipment
All your students should have a pen or pencil, a reasonably-sized rough notepad or exercise book, a vocabulary book and ideally, a good bilingual dictionary. Students who are well organised with their study equipment are able to organise their learning better. It is important to encourage good study habits from the very beginning.

2 Introduction to the book

Let the students leaf through the book at random first. This will give them the feel of the book. In a class with a common first language, refer the students to the list of contents. Give a few examples of the sort of language they are going to cover in the first few weeks (e.g. names, numbers, nationalities, jobs, etc.) so they get the idea that the language to be learnt is expressed in terms of how it is used.
Many students will want to know where to find the grammar they are going to learn. Show them the unit-by-unit list of language form/focus in the end pages of the book and the grammar tables which occur at the end of each unit. Refer them also to the list of words and expressions to be learnt in each unit, a selection of basic grammatical systems and a list of irregular verbs with their past and participle forms also in the end pages of the book.

3 Language work

It is important that the students feel they have learnt some useful English even in the first lesson, so move on to the language work as swiftly as possible. Make sure that you have a cassette recorder, and cards or stiff paper for the students to write their names on.

1

Unit 1 Arrival

Presentation and practice		Set title	Language use	Examples
Dialogue:	Part 1			
	Set 1	Names	Introduce yourself Ask for and give names Confirm and correct information	*My name's Diana Trent.* *What's your name?* *Are you Paul Roberts? Yes, I am.* *Are you David Roberts?* *No, I'm not, I'm Paul Roberts.*
	Set 2	Greetings and titles	Greet people at different times of the day	*Good morning/afternoon/evening.*
Dialogue:	Part 2			
	Set 3	Numbers	Ask for and say room and telephone numbers	*What's your telephone number?* *It's 38994.*
Spoken transfer: Open dialogue Roleplay			Combined Combined	
Skills development: Listening		**Description** A conversation at a hotel reception desk: students listen and note down titles, names and numbers.		
Reading		A picture strip showing students arriving at Stansted Airport to join a Language School. Students read the captions containing the language practised in the sets.		
Writing		Students fill in a personal form and then write a note to a friend giving their address and telephone number.		
Oral exercises:	1		Introduce yourself	Good morning. *Good morning. My name's Vince Hall.*
	2		Confirm and correct information	Are you Paul Roberts? *Yes, I am.* Are you Diana Trent? *No, I'm not.*
	3		Correct information	Is your name John? *No, it isn't. It's Jack.*
	4		Give people's names	What's his name? *His name's Paul.* What's her name? *Her name's Diana.*
	5		Say numbers	My room number is 201. Oh good! I'm in 202.

Grammar focus

Present simple tense: verb *be* (singular) – positive,
negative and interrogative
Personal pronouns: *I, you, it*
Question word: *What?*
Possessive adjectives: *my, your, his, her*

Here's your + noun

Preposition: *in*
Conjunctions: *and, or*
Please + verb

Active vocabulary and expressions

hotel	key
name	Yes.	*What?*
(be)	No.	*Good morning (afternoon/evening.)*
Good morning.	Mr
Good afternoon.	Mrs
Good evening.	Miss
number	room	Thank you.
telephone	Numbers: 0–10
double	
receptionist	*Here's your key.*
Oh good!	
Thanks.	
address	in	Please
write	and	
phone	or	

Unit 1 Arrival

Students' Book pages 4, 5

NOTE

Suggestions on how to use the material are not always given in the order presented in the Students' Book, as in many cases work on the sets can usefully come before the presentation of the dialogue parts.

Set 1 Names

Active words and expressions:	name my your his her I you it not is are am Yes. No. What? Good morning (afternoon/ evening).

Exercise 1

Greet your class with *Good morning (afternoon/evening),* whichever is appropriate. Say it loudly and clearly. Ask them to repeat it several times in chorus. Establish at this stage a hand gesture which means *say that altogether* and use it whenever you want repetition. Remember that the fewer words you need to use at this stage the better. Your 'teacher language' should be restricted as far as possible to the language being presented, words of encouragement, and simple instructions. (See classroom language, page xiv).

Say: *My name's ...* (say your own name) and point to yourself. Say this a few times and write your name on the blackboard for the students to copy. Students repeat chorally: *My name's ... My name's ...* Point to individual students and get them to say their names, i.e. *My name's Miguel.*

Now point to a student and ask: *What's your name?* Say this several times. Ask the students to repeat it chorally. Use the back-chaining method: *... name? ... your name? .... What's your name?* Now say the whole exchange, varying your voice pitch to indicate change of speaker: *What's your name? My name's ...* (say your name). Work round the class in a chain S1–S2–S3 or in pairs. Students ask each other's names. After the exercise is complete, ask the students to write their names clearly in block capitals or neatly printed (demonstrate this on the blackboard), on a piece of card or stiff paper.

Exercise 2

Select a male student in the class (or draw one on the blackboard if you have an all-female class). Ask *What's his name?* Say this a few times. Then answer *His name's ...* (say the student's first name). Now select a female student (or draw one if necessary) and ask *What's her name?* Say this a few times and then answer *Her name's ...* (say the student's first name). Ask everyone to repeat after you: *What's his name? What's her name?* Point to different male and female students while you ask the questions. Now get them to repeat the answers chorally. In a new class, the practice can now take place as a form of a quiz. A student asks another person the question *What's his/her name?* (pointing to a member of the class) and the second student must try and remember the name. This is a good way of getting the students to get to know each other's names as well as practising basic language forms. Do not worry about the exercises in the Students' Book at this stage: these can be done for consolidation after presenting the dialogue. At this stage extra names will only confuse the students. Write the questions and answers on the blackboard next to the previous examples.

Exercise 3

Present the first exchange: *Are you ...* (your own name)? *Yes, I am,* giving the question and answer yourself, changing your voice to indicate change of speaker. Students repeat chorally. Spend some time over this to make sure they copy your intonation as closely as possible.

Work T–S asking each student his or her name: *Are you ...* etc.? Each student responds: *Yes, I am.* Students then work in pairs asking each other the question and answering it. Next practise the negative answer, making sure that the students elide *I + am* to form *I'm* when they say *No, I'm not.* Go round the class again at random, picking on different students and asking their identity, using the wrong name each time. Students practise in pairs afterwards. Write the sample questions and answers on the blackboard.

Exercise 4

Present and practise in the same way as Exercise 3. If the students find it difficult to think of 'wrong' names, collect in the name cards, shuffle and distribute them. In this way, the students can ask their partner if he/she is the name on the card. In most cases, they will have the wrong name.

They should put this card in front of them so that it is clearly visible to everyone including you. While they are doing this, write on the blackboard: *What's your name? My name's Miguel* so that the students have something to refer to.

In future, it will be assumed as general practice first to present and practise new language and then write sample language on the blackboard, not the other way round.

🔲 Dialogue: Part 1

Active words:	hotel	key

Direct the students towards the pictures that accompany the dialogue. Hold the page up and describe the picture like this: *This is a hotel.* Point to Diana Trent and say *Her name is Diana Trent* /dai'ænə trent/. Point to Paul Roberts and say *His name is Paul Roberts* /pɔːl 'rɒbəts/. Check with questions: *What's his name? What's her name?* If you have a key in your pocket or bag, hold it up to the students and say: *This is a key.* Students repeat the word. Play the tape of the dialogue and ask the students to follow it in their books. Play this part of the dialogue twice, pausing to explain any other new words or expressions, then pause it for choral and individual repetition. Ask three students to read it aloud in parts. Ask another three to act it out in front of the class.

Set 1 (continued)

The students can now do Set 1, Exercises 2, 3 and 4. For Exercise 2 students will need to practise saying the names before doing the exercise. Although this exercise only calls for the use of the first name the students will benefit in the following exercise if they can practise the full name of each person in this exercise. The first four names belong to characters who feature regularly in the book. Care should be taken, therefore, that the students can pronounce these names more or less correctly. The names of the people in the pictures are:
1. Vince Hall /vɪnts hɔːl/
2. Joanne Tessler /dʒəʊ'æn 'teslə/
3. Paul Roberts /pɔːl 'rɒbəts/
4. Diana Trent /dai'ænə trent/
5. Jack Feldman /dʒæk 'feldmən/
6. Sally Jones /'sæli dʒəʊnz/
Work T-S and S-T with the first two examples. Ask students to work in pairs with the rest of the questions and answers. Do Exercises 3 and 4 student to student in a chain. Give an example first. Those students who finish quickly can write the questions and answers to Exercise 4 in their exercise books.

Students' Book pages 6, 7

Set 2 Greetings and titles

Active words and expressions:	Good morning. Good afternoon. Good evening. Mr Mrs Miss

Exercise 1

Hold up the page in the book, point to each picture and say the greeting. Students repeat chorally. If you have a lot of space in the classroom, ask the students to get up, walk around and greet each other, choosing one of the three greetings listed in the book.

Point to each of the characters and say their names with their titles: *Mr, Mrs* or *Miss.* Students repeat.

Combine a greeting with a person, using the title first, e.g. *Good morning, Mr Hall./Good afternoon, Mrs Trent./Good evening, Miss Jones.* Students repeat after you. Then ask them to repeat the greetings, this time addressing the characters by their first names, e.g. *Good morning, Vince.*

NOTES

Ms /mɪz/: in English-speaking countries, the title *Ms* is often used to address women. This can mean either *Mrs* or *Miss.* It is used mostly in written language, especially on envelopes and letters

Exercise 2

Students look at the pictures and say which greeting is appropriate. They can answer first orally and follow this up in writing.

KEY

10.15	*Good morning.*	15.40	*Good afternoon.*
7.45	*Good morning.*	18.00	*Good evening.*
9.10	*Good morning.*	20.30	*Good evening.*

If the students usually call you by your first name, think of some other people in the school/college or at work whom they would address by their titles and surnames. Ask the students to roleplay greeting them at different parts of the day.

NOTE

You may like to teach at this stage *Good night.* as a leave-taking phrase (e.g. *Goodbye.*)

Exercise 3

Ask the students to choose to take the part of the six characters on page 5. In pairs, they introduce themselves to their partner, using their first and surnames. Their partners greet them using their title in return.

Students then greet each other in the same way using their own names.

🔲 Dialogue: Part 2

(For the presentation of dialogues, see Course specific procedures 1, page x.)

Active words and expressions:	number room Thank you.

Play the tape while the students follow the text. Play again without the students looking at the text. Pause for repetition.

Ask: *What's Paul's room number?* The students should be able to say *202*, even if they are not at all familiar with English numbers yet.

Ask the students to read and/or act out Parts 1 and 2 of the dialogue in groups of three.

Students' Book pages 8, 9

Set 3 Numbers

Active words:	telephone double oh one two three four five six seven eight nine ten

Go through the pictures and see if the students between them can recite the numbers 1 to 10. If you notice that the whole class is confidently chanting the numbers together, do a simple spot check on the numbers to see that they can remember them out of sequence. If only a few seem to know them, start by saying the numbers in sequence and getting them to repeat after you. Use different patterns for repetition so that practice does not become boring, e.g. *123-234-345-456-678-789-8910; 2-4-6-8-10; 1-3-5-7-9; 10-9-8-7-6-5-4-3-2-1.*

Now practise the pronunciation of 0 (oh) and the use of *double: 88 = double 8.* Simple adding exercises, e.g. *What's 3 and 2?* can check knowledge of numbers, too. Do not spend more time than is necessary on the practice work as most students are probably familiar with these early numbers. It is more important that they can recall the numbers in a practical situation, such as giving one's room number in a hotel or one's telephone number.

Exercise 1

Check round the class by asking questions at random: *What is Mrs Trent's room number? What is Mr Feldman's room number? What is Mr Hall's number?* and so on.

Exercise 2

Practise the questions with the students. See that they get the stress on *TELephone number* correctly. Say your own number, using *oh (0)* and *double...* if appropriate. Students ask each other in pairs and write down their partner's telephone number. Ask questions about the numbers on the pad, e.g. *What's the school's telephone number?* and so on. Do not ask students to make the questions. The words *school, doctor, taxi, bank* are for passive recognition at this stage.

Exercise 3

This reference exercise can be done in pairs. Try not to let the students worry about the additional language contained in the extract from the International Dialling Code Booklet. A quick check may be necessary to see if the students know which of the two countries the towns listed are in. They should not worry about the pronunciation of any of the place names in Australia and Austria.

KEY

Hans   = 010 43 222 23 44 03
Anna   = 010 43 5222 77 89 043
Bill   = 010 61 3 856 7845
Katina = 010 61 2 765 5322

🔊 Open dialogue

(For handling open dialogues, see Course specific procedures 3, page xi).

Active word and expression:	receptionist Here's your key.

Set the situation by reading the rubric. Ask a student to read the part of the receptionist. Give the answers yourself. Then change parts so that you establish that the reply to *Is your name Trent?* will change according to the person taking part in the dialogue. Divide the students into pairs and ask them to practise the dialogue, changing parts afterwards. Go round and listen. As a final check, play the tape and select one student to give the replies.

SSR

RECEPTIONIST:	Good morning.
YOU:	*Good morning.*
RECEPTIONIST:	Is your name Trent?
YOU:	*No, it isn't. It's...*
RECEPTIONIST:	Ah, yes. What's your room number?
YOU:	*401./It's 401./My room number is 401.*
RECEPTIONIST:	Thank you. Here's your key. Number 401.
YOU:	*Thank you.*

Roleplay

(For handling roleplay, see Course specific procedures 4, page xi.)

It is important that the student playing the part of the receptionist has a list of the guests. The students may use their real names here and the receptionist will have to address them by their titles, e.g. *Mr Rodriguez.* The receptionist must also give each guest a room number.

SSR

RECEPTIONIST:	*Good morning.*
GUEST 1:	*Good morning. My name's Miss Gonzalez.*
RECEPTIONIST:	*Gonzalez... Yes, your room number is 504. Here's your key.*
GUEST 1:	*Thank you.*
RECEPTIONIST:	*And what's your name?*
GUEST 2:	*Juan Rodriguez.*
RECEPTIONIST:	*Ah yes, Mr Rodriguez. Your room number is... etc.*

📼 Listening

(For handling listening texts, see Course specific procedures 5, page xi.)

Direct the students' attention towards the gaps in the hotel register, i.e. the missing information.

Ask questions like: *Is it Miss or Mrs Jones? Is her room number 301 or 504?* Ask them to listen and fill in the answers. Play the tape once or twice, stopping at the key points if necessary.

TAPESCRIPT

Some guests are arriving at the Tower Hotel. They talk to the receptionist. Fill in the missing information. It may be a title like Mr or Mrs, a surname like Hall, or a room number.

RECEPTIONIST:	Good morning. Welcome to the Tower Hotel.
GUEST 1:	Good morning. My name is Roberts.
RECEPTIONIST:	Roberts. Ah yes. Is it Mr C. Roberts?
GUEST 1:	That's right. Charles Roberts.
RECEPTIONIST:	Room number 503, Mr Roberts.
GUEST 1:	Thank you.
GUEST 2:	Good morning. My name's Jones. Miss Susan Jones.
RECEPTIONIST:	Good morning, Miss Jones. Let me see. Yes, your room number is 904.
GUEST 2:	904. That's the top floor.
RECEPTIONIST:	That's right.
GUEST 2:	Oh good!
RECEPTIONIST:	Good morning.
GUEST 3:	My name's John Churchill.
RECEPTIONIST:	Ah, yes. Mr J. Churchill. Your room number is 807.
GUEST 3:	Thank you. 807.
RECEPTIONIST:	Here's your key, Mr Churchill.
GUEST 3:	Thank you.

KEY

NAME	ROOM NUMBER
Mr Charles Roberts	503
Miss Susan Jones	*904*
Mr *J/John* Churchill	*807*

Students' Book pages 10, 11

Active expressions:	Oh good! Thanks.

Reading

(For handling reading texts, see Course specific procedures 6, page xi.)

Ask the students to read the picture strip and list the five questions asked by the man from the Tower Language

School who is meeting John Porter. These are: *Is your name John Porter? Are you John Porter?, John Porter?, What's your name?, Are you Mr Porter?*

With a class of students who all speak the same language, ask in the native language: *Who is meeting who? How many people does the man talk to before he finds John Porter?* The students can answer the questions in English. Students then act out the situation in class, substituting their own names.

(NOTE: The location for these pictures is Stansted Airport, about 35 miles from London. It is likely to become London's third airport after Heathrow and Gatwick. At the moment there is considerable controversy about enlarging it.)

Writing

(For handling writing tasks, see Course specific procedures 7, page xi.)

Exercise 1

Draw a similar form on the blackboard and show the students how to fill it in. This will get across the meaning of *first names* and *address*. Ask the students to fill in the form in class so that you can go round and check.

Exercise 2

Active words:	address write phone in and or Please

NOTES

W8: a postal district in West London. W = West
Dave: a short name for David

Read the note out loud to the students. Demonstrate by miming the meaning of *write* and *phone*. Ask some students what their addresses are: they can ask each other in pairs before they do the writing. The students can transfer the location to their own city if this is more relevant, e.g. *My address in Vienna is...* Students write the note in class and exchange their notes with each other for checking.

Homework

Choose from:
1. Set 1 Exercises 3 and 4, page 5. Write out the questions and answers.
2. Open dialogue, page 9. Write out the missing part.
3. Writing 2, page 10. Write the note.
4. Write out selected oral exercises, page 11.
5. Unit 1 Workbook exercises.

Refer the students to the list of words and expressions to be actively learnt in this unit. This is on page 124 at the back of their books. Encourage them after each unit to look carefully through the grammar boxes and the list of words before doing their homework.

📼 Oral exercises

(For handling oral exercises, see Course specific procedures 8, page xii.)

1. Introduce yourself

Good morning.
Good morning. My name's Vince Hall.

Now you do the same. Use the names of the people in this book.

Good morning.
Good morning. My name's Vince Hall.
Good morning.
Good morning. My name's Joanne Tessler.
Good morning.
Good morning. My name's Paul Roberts.
Good morning.
Good morning. My name's Diana Trent.
Good morning.
Good morning. My name's Sally Jones.
Good morning.
Good morning. My name's Jack Feldman.

2. Confirm and correct information

Are you Paul Roberts?
Yes, I am.
Are you Diana Trent?
No, I'm not.

Now you say 'Yes' or 'No' in the same way.

Are you Paul Roberts?
Yes, I am.
Are you Diana Trent?
No, I'm not.
Are you Jack Feldman?
No, I'm not.
Are you Sally Jones?
Yes, I am.
Are you John Gibbs?
Yes, I am.
Are you Sue Grant?
No, I'm not.

3. Correct information

Is your name John?
No, it isn't. It's Jack.

Now you go on and give the right name.

Is your name John?
No, it isn't. It's Jack.
Is your name Ann?
No, it isn't. It's Diana.
Is your name Paul?
No, it isn't. It's David.
Is your name Sally?
No, it isn't. It's Sue.
Is your name Charles?
No, it isn't. It's Tim.
Is your name Diana?
No, it isn't. It's Ann.

4. Give people's names

What's his name?
His name's Paul.
What's her name?
Her name's Diana.

Now you give the names of the people.

What's his name?
His name's Paul.
What's her name?
Her name's Diana.
What's his name?
His name's Tim.
What's her name?
Her name's Joanne.
What's his name?
His name's Vince.
What's her name?
Her name's Sue.

5. Say numbers

My room number is 201.
Oh good! I'm in 202.

Go on. Give the next room number.

My room number is 201.
Oh good! I'm in 202.
My room number is 407.
Oh good! I'm in 408.
My room number is 508.
Oh good! I'm in 509.
My room number is 102.
Oh good! I'm in 103.
My room number is 206.
Oh good! I'm in 207.
My room number is 605.
Oh good! I'm in 606.

Unit 2 Pleased to meet you

Presentation and practice		Set title	Language use	Examples
Dialogue:	Part 1			
	Set 1	Greetings and introductions	Greet people informally and formally Introduce people	*Hello. I'm Diana.* *How do you do.* *This is Paul.*
Dialogue:	Part 2			
	Set 2	Countries and nationalities	Say where you and people are from Ask where people are from Say what nationality you are Ask about people's nationality	*I'm from Brazil.* *She's from Japan.* *Where are you from?* *I'm American.* *Are you American?*
Dialogue:	Part 3			
	Set 3	Objects	Ask about and identify objects	*What's that (in English)?* *It's a key.*
Spoken transfer: Open dialogue Roleplay			Combined Combined	
Skills development: Listening		**Description** Short examples of different languages: students guess the nationality of each speaker.		
Reading		A paragraph in which a language school student describes her class, her friends and her teacher.		
Writing	1	Students copy and fill in a form with personal details.		
	2	Students write a paragraph about themselves and their class using the reading paragraph as a model.		
Oral exercises:	1		Meet people	Hello, I'm Jack. *Hello. Pleased to meet you, Jack.*
	2		Greet people formally	How do you do. My name's Vince Hall. *How do you do, Mr Hall.*
	3		Introduce people	*I'm Jack and this is Ruth.*
	4		Say where people are from	He's American. Where is she from? *She's from America, too.*
	5		Say where you and your friends are from	Are you French? *Yes, we're from Paris.*

Grammar focus	Active vocabulary and expressions
	come meet polite this
Demonstrative pronoun: *this*	Excuse me. How do you do. Hello. Pleased to meet you. Hi.
Present simple tense: verb *be* (singular and plural) – positive, negative and interrogative Verb *be* + nationality adjective Verb *be* + preposition: *from* + country Question word: *Where?* Pronouns: *he, she, we, you* (plural), *they* Definite article: *the*	America – American Britain – British (for other nationality words see page 129) country(ies) flag from nationality(ies) Where?
	taxi map that here over there
Demonstrative pronouns: *this, that* Indefinite articles: *a, an* Adverbs: *here, there*	book pen in English comb pencil diary purse dictionary ticket exercise book umbrella identity card wallet
	class friend Goodbye.

It's ⎫
He's ⎭ + adjective. *It is/isn't + very* + adjective
It's a/an + adjective + noun
It's a/an + very + adjective + noun
Adjectives: *big, small, good, new, nice*
Quantifier: *all*
	school big all
	student good but
	teacher new too
	                 nice very
	                 small

Unit 2 Pleased to meet you

Students' Book
pages 12, 13

Check homework from Unit 1.

🔊 Dialogue: Part 1

Active words:	come meet polite this

Ask the students to look at the pictures and the dialogue in their books. After playing it through once, ask them to read the questions after the dialogue and listen to it once again. Check the answers either T-S or S-S. Do not expect short form answers to the questions: a simple *Yes* or *No* is sufficient to check comprehension. Play the paused version for choral and individual repetition or save this part for the language laboratory if you have access to one. Ask the students to read the dialogue in groups of four.

Set 1 Greetings and introductions

Active words and expressions:	Excuse me. Hello. Hi. How do you do. Pleased to meet you.

Exercise 1

Act out the exchange in the language box, changing your voice and position to indicate change of speaker. Students repeat chorally by the back-chaining method.

Students work in threes, changing parts so that each person has a chance to make the introductions. Remind the students to substitute their own names.

NOTES

Shaking hands is less common in Britain than in other countries. People will usually shake hands when meeting for the first time in a formal setting, e.g. at work, but otherwise, and especially among young people, it is not common practice. Kissing is usually reserved for close friends and family and is not appropriate for a first meeting. (Back-slapping is an American rather than a British custom.) It is not always necessary to add *Pleased to meet you. Hello* and a smile is just as acceptable.

Exercise 2

Refer the students back to the dialogue. Joanne said *Hi* when she met Diana but Paul said *How do you do.*

NOTES

How do you do: the formal way of greeting people for the first time. It is more often used if you greet someone who is recognisably older, or superior in a professional situation. Some people are naturally

more formal than others and use it more often. Americans, in general, are more informal when greeting, hence Vince's surprise and amusement when Paul uses 'How do you do.' Vince says *That's neat! 'How do you do!'*

That's neat!: an American expression meaning *That's nice/clever/interesting/fun*, depending on the context.

The exercise practises using titles for formal introductions. Practise the model exchange with the students. Get them to elide the *do you* so that it sounds like /dju:/. Select two students from the class, tell one of them that he is, for example, 'Mr Hall' and practise the introduction in front of the class. Ask the students to work in groups of three introducing the characters in the book. Ask them to change parts each time so that they take turns in doing the introducing.

Exercise 3

Act out the model exchange changing your voice and position to indicate change of speaker. Or ask one student to read the part of Paul Roberts. Show that *Excuse me* is used for attracting attention. You can indicate this by walking up to the student (Paul Roberts) from behind, making him turn round when you say *Excuse me.* Practise the exchange with the whole class chorally and individually. Ask the students to act out the same situation in pairs using their own names. If possible, ask them to get up out of their seats and act the situation, as you have demonstrated.

Students' Book
pages 14, 15

🔊 Dialogue: Part 2

Play the tape and ask the students to follow the text in their books. If possible have a large map of the world (or one of Britain and one of the USA) with you for this lesson. You can point to Los Angeles and Manchester as they are mentioned in the dialogue. Point out to the students that when Vince says *We* he is referring to himself and Joanne; Diana uses *we* to refer to herself and Paul (although neither Joanne or Paul are visible in the picture).

Set 2 Countries and nationalities

Active words:	country(ies) flag nationality(ies) from Where? America American Britain British (plus own and neighbouring countries and nationalities as appropriate) he she you (*plural*) we they

NOTE

The countries and nationalities in this set have been chosen for their range of endings in adjectival form. No country has been selected or rejected on political grounds. A fuller list of the countries and nationalities of the world can be found at the back of this Teacher's Book, page 129. Students are not expected to remember all the countries and nationalities listed but it is reasonable that they should learn their own and three or four others, apart from those listed under the active words at the head of the set.

Practise the pronunciation of the countries before doing Exercise 1. Do not worry too much about the pronunciation of the names.

Exercise 1

Present the first example in the box. Ask the students to look at the people and find on the map the countries they come from. Say: *Hello, I'm Jorge. I'm from Brazil.* Students repeat chorally. Point to other single people and make similar introductions. Students repeat. Then present the couples. Use the second example in the box to introduce the personal pronoun *we*. Point to other couples and ask the students to repeat the introductions chorally. They now work in pairs or groups choosing a person or couple and introducing themselves.

Exercise 2

Present the three examples in the box together and introduce the other personal pronouns *he, she, they,* with reference to the people on the map. Students work in pairs again introducing the people in the 3rd person singular or plural. Make sure they make a distinction between *he* and *she*.

Exercise 3

Introduce the question form: *Where are you from?* Students repeat chorally and individually. Work T-S and S-T establishing that the students must say where they themselves come from. If the class has a common first language, only a short time need be spent on this.

Exercise 4

Practise the nationality adjectives, first chorally then individually. Ask the students to work in pairs and name the countries to which the flags belong. Point out the use of the definite article *the.* You may like to make a game of this. Ask them to cover the box of nationality words and have different groups competing to see who can identify all the flags first, asking and answering as in the book, e.g. *What's number 2? It's the British flag.*

Exercise 5

Students can now introduce themselves to their partners and say their nationality.

Exercise 6

Point to the people again and practise the example sentences from the box. Students continue introducing the other people by nationality.

Exercise 7

This exercise practises *yes/no* questions and short answers, with the verb *to be*. Ask the students to look at and read the examples in the box first. Ask questions which expect the answer *Yes* first so they practise alternating between *Yes, she is/Yes, he is* and *Yes, they are.* Then ask questions which expect the answer *No.* When you are sure that they know how to answer, ask them to work in pairs, asking and answering about the people in the exercise. If some students finish early, ask them to write the questions and answers in their books.

KEY
1. *Is Jorge Spanish?*
   No, he isn't. (He's Brazilian.)
2. *Are Robert and Ann British?*
   Yes, they are.
3. *Is Sabine Italian?*
   No, she isn't. (She's French.)
4. *Is Peter German?*
   Yes, he is.
5. *Is Yoshimi Japanese?*
   Yes, she is.
6. *Are Bruno and Sylvia Mexican?*
   No, they aren't. (They're Italian.)
7. *Is Habib Spanish?*
   No, he isn't. (He's Egyptian.)
8. *Is Carlos Brazilian?*
   No, he isn't. (He's Spanish.)
9. *Is Juan Spanish?*
   No, he isn't. (He's Mexican.)
10. *Is Oumon British?*
    No, she isn't. (She's Senegalese.)

Students' Book pages 16, 17

🔊 Dialogue: Part 3

Active words and expressions:	map taxi that here over there

Bring in a map of London (preferably a tourist map) if you can get hold of one and introduce the word to the students before playing the dialogue. Ask students to look at the centre of London and show them where Piccadilly Circus and the Tower of London are. Try to use the language of the dialogue when you speak: *Here's Piccadilly Circus. The Tower of London is over there...* Play the tape of the dialogue. Students look at the statements, and answer *It's true* or *It's false*. Show the photograph of Diana getting out of a typical London taxi on page 4. Play the tape again with the students repeating in the pauses. If time allows, ask them to read/act out the whole dialogue from the beginning.

Set 3 Objects

Active words and expressions:	book comb diary dictionary exercise book identity card pen pencil purse ticket umbrella wallet in English

Exercise 1

Learning will be more effective if you can bring into the classroom actual objects, i.e. a real diary, wallet and so on. It is then easier to practise the example exchange, and different objects can be passed around the students for identification. Start by identifying each object. Say: *This is a diary. Repeat after me 'a diary'. This is an identity card*, etc. Point out the use of the indefinite article *an* before a vowel.

Establish the difference between *What's that?* and *What's this?* Normally we ask *What's that?* when we point to something at a distance, or somebody else is holding the object. *What's this?* is used when we are referring to something we are holding or which is close enough to touch.

The naming of objects will probably be most useful to the students when they are searching for the English equivalent of familiar objects. The question: *What's this/that in English?* is going to be useful, therefore, and special practice in making this question is essential.

Exercise 2

Once you have introduced the names of the objects and the question forms, and done some T-S and S-T work with the objects, ask them to work through Exercise 2 in pairs, alternating question and answer each time.

Exercise 3

Don't worry if some students produce other articles from their pockets, e.g. a letter, a handkerchief, etc. Give them these new words if they want to learn them.

Exercise 4

Restrict the articles here to those previously introduced, i.e. don't point to any items of furniture or equipment.

To revise the vocabulary at a later stage, a version of Kim's game can be fun. Put all the objects on a tray, ask the students to look at and memorise them, then remove a few and show them again. They must write down the ones that you have taken away. You can do this several times until there are only a few objects left.

Open dialogue

Active words:	friend class Goodbye!

Introduce the words *friend* and *class* first.

Ask a good student to read the part of Diana. Supply the answers yourself. Ask the students to practise in pairs changing parts afterwards.

SSR

DIANA: Hello.
YOU: *Hello.*
DIANA: What's your name?
YOU: *Christina Stavros./My name's Christina./I'm Christina.*
DIANA: I'm Diana. And this is a friend, Paul.
PAUL: Hello.
YOU: *Hello./Hi!*
DIANA: We're British. We're from Manchester. Where are you from?
YOU: *I'm Greek. I'm from Athens.*
DIANA: Well, enjoy your English class. Goodbye!
YOU: *Goodbye.*

Students' Book pages 18, 19

Roleplay

If you have a mixed nationality class, it will not be necessary to use the invented names and nationalities here. The main object of the exercise is for the students to recognise the difference in formality between the two situations and to use suitable language for each situation. Give an example yourself of the difference, e.g.
Situation 1: *How do you do! My name's Miss Lewis. I'm from the United States. This is Mr and Mrs Watkins. They're from Britain.*

Situation 2: *Hello. My name's Josie. I'm from the United States. And this is Robert and Ann. They're from Britain.*

Whether using the invented names or the students' own names, ask them to write them and their countries and nationalities on a card or a piece of paper clearly visible to the person introducing.

Students perform in groups of five. Go round and monitor while they speak.

Listening

This listening quiz revises nationality words: the content of the short extracts of foreign languages is irrelevant. The students make intelligent guesses as to which language is being spoken.

KEY

1. *German* 2. *English* 3. *French* 4. *Japanese*
5. *Spanish*

Reading

Active words:	school student teacher
	big good new nice small
	all but too very

Introduce the new vocabulary before asking the students to read the text. Write each new word on the blackboard after it has been mentioned and repeated.

Say: *I'm a teacher. You're a student. You're a student, too.* Repeat pointing to different students. Then make an expansive gesture saying, *You're all students. You're all new students. You're all good students. You're all very good students.* (smiling broadly) *This class is big/small. It isn't very big/small. It's very nice.*

Ask the students to read the text and find the answer to these questions:
Where's Sylvana from?
Is Mr Lewis a student?

Check the answers after the first reading. Then ask the students to read the text once more, noting whether the statements beneath the text are true or false as they go along.

KEY

True. False. False. True. False. True. True.

Some teachers may like to use the reading text for pronunciation and stress practice. If so, read one sentence or sense group at a time, getting the students to repeat chorally after you. Proceed at a brisk pace otherwise this can easily turn into very unrhythmical and boring chanting.

Writing

1. Tell the students that for *Place of Birth* you put the town and country where you were born, e.g. Manchester, England.

Students copy and fill the form in for homework or in class.

2. Write the first few sentences on the blackboard to demonstrate to the students that you want them to keep to an identical text structure but simply substitute certain personal and factual information. This writing task consolidates structures and certain useful vocabulary items and also gives valuable practice in accurate copying.

Homework

Choose from:
1. Open dialogue, page 17. Write out the missing part.
2. Writing 1 and 2, page 18. Fill in the form; write about your class.
3. Unit 2 Workbook exercises.

⊙⊙ Oral exercises

(For procedures, see page xii.)

1. Meet people

Hello. I'm Jack.
Hello. Pleased to meet you, Jack.

Now you meet the people.

Hello. I'm Jack.
Hello. Pleased to meet you, Jack.
Hello. I'm Sue.
Hello. Pleased to meet you, Sue.
Hello. I'm Tim.
Hello. Pleased to meet you, Tim.
Hello. I'm Ann.
Hello. Pleased to meet you, Ann.

2. Greet people formally

Listen to a man meeting Vince for the first time.

How do you do. My name's Vince Hall.
How do you do, Mr Hall.

Now you greet all the people. Use their titles each time.

How do you do. My name's Vince Hall.
How do you do, Mr Hall.
How do you do. My name's Diana Trent.
How do you do, Mrs Trent.
How do you do. My name's Sally Jones.
How do you do, Miss Jones.
How do you do. My name's Paul Roberts.
How do you do, Mr Roberts.

3. Introduce people

Jack and Ruth
I'm Jack and this is Ruth.

You introduce people in the same way.

Jack and Ruth
I'm Jack and this is Ruth.
Robert and Ann
I'm Robert and this is Ann.
Lois and Frank
I'm Lois and this is Frank.
Bruno and Sylvia
I'm Bruno and this is Sylvia.
Diana and Paul
I'm Diana and this is Paul.
Joanne and Vince
I'm Joanne and this is Vince.

4. Say where people are from

He's American. Where is she from?
She's from America, too.

Go on. Say where the girl is from each time.

He's American. Where is she from?
She's from America, too.
He's British. Where is she from?
She's from Britain, too.
He's French. Where is she from?
She's from France, too.
He's Mexican. Where is she from?
She's from Mexico, too.
He's Italian. Where is she from?
She's from Italy, too.
He's Greek. Where is she from?
She's from Greece, too.

5. Say where you and your friends are from

Listen to these people saying where they are from.

Are you French?
Yes. We're from Paris.

Go on. Say where you and your friends are from. Name the city each time.

Are you French?
Yes. We're from Paris.
Are you Spanish?
Yes. We're from Madrid.
Are you American?
Yes. We're from New York.
Are you Japanese?
Yes. We're from Tokyo.
Are you Brazilian?
Yes. We're from Rio.
Are you Italian?
Yes. We're from Milan.

Unit 3 I like London

Presentation and practice	Set title	Language use	Examples
Dialogue: Part 1			
Set 1	Greeting friends	Greet friends informally	*Hello. How are you?*
Set 2	Likes and dislikes (1)	Ask and talk about likes and dislikes	*Do you like cats?* *Yes, I do.* *No, I don't.*
Dialogue: Part 2			
Set 3	Places: location (1)	Ask and say where people live	*Where do you live?* *I live in the south of England.*
Dialogue: Part 3			
Set 4	Jobs	Ask and say what people do	*What do you do?* *I'm a cameraman.*
Dialogue: Part 4			
Set 5	The alphabet	Ask people how to spell words Spell your name and address	*What's your surname?* *It's Baker.* *How do you spell that?* *B-A-K-E-R.*
Spoken transfer: Open dialogue Roleplay		Combined Combined	
Skills development: Listening	**Description** Students listen to part of an interview at a job agency and fill in information about the interviewee.		
Reading	Students read a paragraph in which Georgina describes her job, her sister and brother. The questions are grouped according to the topics within the paragraph.		
Writing	Students write a few sentences about themselves and a friend, or a brother or sister.		
Oral exercises: 1		Say what you like (Open exercise)	Do you like pop music? *Yes, I do./No, I don't.*
2		Ask about likes and dislikes	Ask if Diana likes classical music. *Does Diana like classical music?* Ask if Paul likes pop music. *Does Paul like pop music?*
3		Answer about likes and dislikes	Say what Diana likes or doesn't like. Does she like children? *Yes, she does.*
4		Ask for personal information	*What's Diana's surname?* It's Trent. *What's Diana's telephone number?* I don't know.
5		Say where places are	Where's Bristol? *It's in the south-west of England.*

Grammar focus	Active vocabulary and expressions
	coffee cup have Let's go out. OK.
Question word: *How? (How are you?)* *very* + adverbs: *well, fine*	How are you? I'm very well, thank you. I'm fine, thanks. Not too bad, thanks.
Present simple tense: verb *like* (singular) – interrogative, positive and negative with auxiliary: *do/does* Plural of nouns (regular and irregular) Conjunction: *but* *very* + adverb: *much*	animal(s) classical music like baby(ies) people very much cat(s), dog(s) pop music child(ren)
	centre coast

Present simple tense: verb *live* (singular and plural)
   – positive, negative and interrogative
Prepositions of place: *in, on*
Definite article *the*
	England north in
	place south of
	live east on
	            west

	film make work
Present simple tense: verbs *do, work, study* Genitive singular ending *'s*	company do I don't know. doctor study Really? housewife secretary
	both I don't understand. What does that mean?
Question word: *How? (How do you spell . . . ?)*	Letters of the alphabet *A–Z* first name surname spell
	food
	boy job called by brother man teach for flat sister married near girl town unemployed with house woman young

Unit 3 I like London

Students' Book pages 20, 21

Check homework from Unit 2.

Set 1 Greeting friends

Active expressions:	How are you? I'm fine, thanks. I'm very well, thank you. Not too bad, thanks.

Practise the exchanges separately, getting the students to imitate your intonation. Divide the class into two halves and ask one half to greet the other half. Change parts afterwards. Establish and practise the interchangeability of the three answers: *I'm fine/very well/not too bad, thanks.* The students may omit *I'm* if they like. Make sure they return the question to their partner: *And you?* Students greet their partner, another friend and you. This exchange should be revised naturally at the beginning of every class. This sort of greeting is used for people and friends you know but do not see every day.

🔲 Dialogue: Part 1

Active words and expressions:	coffee cup have Let's go out. OK.

Before playing the dialogue, present the words. Say: *I like coffee. I like coffee very much.* Ask a student: *Do you like coffee?* Expect the answer *Yes* or *No*. Get a student to ask you the question: *Do you like tea?* (or any other drink you don't like.) Answer: *No, I don't. I don't like tea very much.* Write question and answer forms on the blackboard. Ask the students to look at the true/false statements after the dialogue. Play the dialogue and check the statements. Play the dialogue again, stopping where necessary to explain difficult or new words. Ask students to read it together in pairs and if time, select one pair to read it in front of the whole class.

Set 2 Likes and dislikes (1)

Active words:	animal(s) baby(ies) cat(s) child(ren) classical music dog(s) people pop music like very much

Exercise 1

Use examples or pictures to explain the new vocabulary in the chart of likes and dislikes. Point out the plural formation of the items listed. Give an example of the question with the various types of answer, varying your facial expression to show the difference between *Yes, I do* and *Yes, very much,* and between the two negative answers. Students practise chorally. Students write down their own answers and then work in pairs, noting down *Yes* or *No* for their partner's answers.

Exercise 2

Present the statements in the box and revise the use of *and, but* and *or.* Give the students a minute or two to look at their own answers, and see if they can pair them off so as to make three different types of statement. Ask them to write down the statements in their exercise books afterwards. Go round and check their work.

Exercise 3

Present the 3rd person singular question and short answer forms, referring to Diana and Paul's answers in the chart. Practise the exchanges chorally and individually. Make sure the students do not add an 's' at the end of *like* in the question form. Work T-S with a few examples of Diana's answers, and similarly with some of Paul's answers. Students work in pairs asking and answering about the remaining answers.

Exercise 4

Present the sentences from the example box referring the students back to the chart. The students can write more sentences for homework.

Students' Book pages 22, 23

Set 3 Places: location (1)

(Note that this set comes before Dialogue: Part 2.)

Active words:	place live north south east west in of on England

Exercise 1

Refer the students to a map of Britain or their own country. Say: *I live in (London). Where do you live?* (pointing to a student). Elicit *I live in (London), too.* Practise the question and answer form with the whole class. If you live in a capital city, encourage the students to specify the area or suburb in which they live. Students ask and answer in pairs. Refer to the pictures of the compass and the compass points. Practise the pronunciation of *north, south, east* and *west* and combinations of these (e.g. *north-west, south-east*). Choose a town in another part of the country, or a suburb of the capital, point to the place on the map and say: *(Name of town) is in the north/south/east/west/north-east/* etc. *of (name of country or capital city.)* Practise the pronunciation and stress in the following phrases: *in the north of England; in the south of England; in the east of England; in the west of England.*

Now ask the students a few check questions; choose some places in their country and ask: *Where's...?* Students must answer using a point of the compass.

Leave Exercises 2 and 3 until after the dialogue.

🔘🔘 Dialogue: Part 2

Active words:	centre coast

Present the two words before playing the dialogue. Work through the dialogue in the normal way, checking the true/false statements after the first hearing. If you can, draw a sketch map of the United States, marking Los Angeles on the west coast. Refer them also to the photographs of Los Angeles and Manchester in their books.

Set 3 (continued)

Exercise 2

Read out the sample sentences from the box. Students tell the class where their partners live, using a compass point if relevant. Do not worry about the question form yet. Instead, elicit the answers by saying: *Tell me about (name of student).*

Exercise 3

Present the question form with *does* first. Students repeat chorally. Make sure they do not put an *s* at the end of *live* in the question form. Give prompts with the other names: *Robin, Kevin* and *Kate.* Now present the question form with the 3rd person plural: *Where do Lucy and Andrew live?* Practise chorally and get them to substitute the other couples' names in the question: *Sarah and Clive, John and Mary* (make up a few names of your own too). Students ask and answer about the people in pairs. If time, ask them to write out the questions and answers too.

KEY

Robin lives in the north-east (or north) of England.
Lucy and Andrew live in the south of England.
Kate lives in the east of England.
Kevin lives in the south-west of England.
Sarah and Clive live in the south-east of England.
John and Mary live in the north-west of England.

🔘🔘 Dialogue: Part 3

Active words:	film make work

Introduce the dialogue by pointing to yourself and saying: *I'm a teacher.* Point to a student and say *You're a student.* Point to another student and ask *What do you do?* Elicit *I'm a student too* or *I'm a* (and help the student

with the word for his/her occupation). Choose a well-known company which the students will know. Draw a picture on the blackboard of a building marked, e.g. *Fiat* and a person beside it. Say: *He/she's an engineer. He/she works for Fiat. Fiat is a big company. It makes cars. He/she works for a company called Fiat.*

Play the tape of the dialogue and work through it in the normal way. Check the true/false statements. Do not worry about practising the jobs mentioned in the dialogue. Indicate by acting, example or translation what each job is.

Set 4 Jobs

Active words and expressions:	company doctor housewife secretary do study I don't know. Really?

Exercise 1

Practise the question form *What do you do?* chorally. Establish the different ways of answering. Help the students with the names of their professions. Ask them to walk round the class asking as many people as possible what they do. Now present the question form for the 3rd person singular. Practise also substituting a proper name in place of *he* and *she.* If appropriate, ask a few students what some of their fellow members of the class do and see if they can answer. If they cannot remember or simply do not know, present the form *I don't know.*

Draw the students' attention also to the genitive *'s* in *He's Diana's assistant.* Give a few more examples of this genitive form on the blackboard, e.g. *My teacher's name is... Sally's address is... John's telephone number is...* Refer the students back to Unit 1 Set 3 Exercise 2, on page 9. Ask them to ask and answer *What's the bank's number?* etc.

Exercise 2

Students match the statements with the pictures of the people doing their jobs. Practise the pronunciation of the jobs.

Practise the example conversation chorally and in pairs. Work T-S and S-T with the first few examples. Ask the students to work in pairs for the whole exercise changing parts afterwards.

Exercise 3

Students write the first two or three in class and finish the rest for homework.

Exercise 4

Present the meaning of *brother* and *sister* by drawing a family tree. Ask them to use a dictionary if necessary when writing about their jobs.

21

Students' Book pages 24, 25

🔘 Dialogue: Part 4

Active words and expressions:	both I don't understand. What does that mean?

Present the dialogue in the normal way. Show the difference between *both* and *all*. Point to the students and say: *You're all students.* Then select two students of the same nationality and say: *You're both (French).* See if the students can produce other true sentences about themselves, using *all* and *both*.

Practise the two expressions chorally: *I don't understand* and *What does that mean?* These should become part of their classroom language: they should be encouraged to ask if they are not sure of a word or an instruction.

Focus their attention on the letter *S*. Say *This is an S*. Write one or two more letters on the blackboard and say: *This is a/J/This is an X.* Ask if anyone can spell their name, to give you an idea if they know any of the letters in English. In general, they will have difficulty over the vowels and certain of the consonants: G H J R W especially.

Set 5 The alphabet

Active words:	first name surname spell

Exercise 1

Present and practise the letters in the groups of sounds in the second box before practising them in alphabetical order (first box). Special spelling games can be used to give variety. (See Index 5, Selected further reading, page 130, for a book on games.)

Exercise 2

Refer the students back to the use of the abbreviations *S and S* in the dialogue. Write up *LA, USA* and *UK* on the board. Ask them to read the letters and say what they stand for *(Los Angeles, the United States of America, the United Kingdom)*. Ask them to look at the airline names in the illustration and match them with the names of the countries. They may work in pairs or individually, reading the airline names aloud as they match them.

KEY

KLM is from Holland; SAS is from Scandinavia; JAT is from Yugoslavia; TWA is from America; PIA is from Pakistan; JAL is from Japan

Ask the students to read out the whole answer so that they get practice in saying the letters and countries.

Ask different students to read out the different car registration plates illustrated. If appropriate, ask students for their own car registration numbers.

Exercise 3

Work S-T and spell your own surname and part of your address. Students work in pairs copying down the proper names as they are spelt out to them by their partner.

🔘 **Open dialogue**

Work S-T first to give an example, then T-S with one student. Finally ask the students to work in pairs, changing parts afterwards.

SSR

PAUL:	Hello! I'm Paul. Paul Roberts. What's your name?
YOU:	*(Jorge Suarez.) My name's (Jorge Suarez).*
PAUL:	How do you spell your surname?
YOU:	*(S-U-A-R-E-Z)*
PAUL:	What do you do?
YOU:	*I'm a student/engineer/computer programmer.*
PAUL:	Are you English?
YOU:	*No, I'm not. I'm (Brazilian).*
PAUL:	Well, I'm English. I'm from Manchester. That's in the north-west of England. Where are you from?
YOU:	*I'm from (São Paulo). That's in the (south of Brazil).*
PAUL:	And do you like your English classes?
YOU:	*Yes, I do. Very much./Yes, I do./Yes, I like them very much.*
PAUL:	Good! Well, goodbye for now!
YOU:	*Goodbye!*

Roleplay

Active word:	food

Ask the students to look at the information about Sandra and Jeremy. Ask check questions on each person:

Sandra Macey

What is Sandra's surname? How do you spell it?
What nationality is she?
Where does she live?
What does she do?
What music does she like?
What food does she like?

Ask similar questions about Jeremy Hutchins. Or ask the students to make up the questions about him.

Students now take the parts of Sandra and Jeremy. They work in pairs and find out about each other.

SSR

SANDRA:	*Hello! I'm Sandra Macey. What's your name?*
JEREMY:	*Jeremy. Jeremy Hutchins. Are you British?*
SANDRA:	*No, I'm not. I'm American.*

JEREMY: *Oh! Where are you from?*
SANDRA: *I'm from Boston. That's on the east coast. And where are you from?*
JEREMY: *From Brighton.*
SANDRA: *Brighton? Where's that?*
JEREMY: *It's on the south coast of England. What do you do?*
SANDRA: *I'm a nurse, a student nurse.*
JEREMY: *Really?*
SANDRA: *Yes, I like it. It's a nice job. And you? What do you do?*
JEREMY: *I'm an engineer.*
SANDRA: *Oh . . . Do you like this music?*
JEREMY: *No, I don't. I don't like pop music very much.*
SANDRA: *Really? I like pop music but I like classical music, too.*
JEREMY: *Yes, I like classical music very much. What sort of food do you like? Do you like Italian food?*
SANDRA: *Yes, but I like Chinese food too.*

If the students find the roleplay difficult, make a gapped version of the SSR either on an overhead transparency or on a stencil, and ask the students to complete the key information. If you do this on an OHP, you can erase more of the dialogue progressively until they have memorised it completely.

🎧 Listening

Direct the students' attention towards the rubric. Say: *Angela wants a job. She's at a job agency. Listen and find out what her surname is . . .*, etc. Explain that *occupation = job*. Play the tape pausing at key places for the students to write down the information. Play once more without stopping for the students to check their answers.

TAPESCRIPT

Angela is looking for a job. She's at a job agency. The secretary takes down information. Look at the form in your books and fill in the missing information. Listen.

MAN: Good morning. Can I help you?
ANGELA: Good morning. Yes, er . . . I want a job!
MAN: Yes, I see. Er . . . I'd better have some details first.
(*gets out a form*) . . . first your name please, surname first.
ANGELA: Barnet.
MAN: Is that IT or ET?
ANGELA: ET. B-A-R-N-E-T.
MAN: Thank you. And now your first names.
ANGELA: Angela Mary.
MAN: (*writing*) Right. And what's your address?
ANGELA: It's 2, Denbigh Road. That's D-E-N-B-I-G-H.
MAN: I-G-H? Not 'Y'?
ANGELA: That's right I-G-H. 2, Denbigh Road, London W7.
MAN: Fine. And your phone number at home?
ANGELA: It's 578 2115.
MAN: 578 2115. Good. Now, let's see. What do you do?

ANGELA: I don't have a job. I'm unemployed. But I was a secretary before I married.
MAN: A secretary? Right. Now, let's have a look . . .

KEY

SURNAME: *BARNET*	M̶R̶/MRS/M̶I̶S̶S̶
FIRST NAMES: *Angela Mary*	
ADDRESS: *2, Denbigh Road, London W7.*	
PRESENT OR PREVIOUS OCCUPATION: *Secretary*	
TELEPHONE NUMBER: *578 2115*	

Students' Book pages 26, 27

Reading

Active words:	boy brother flat girl house job man sister town woman teach married unemployed young called by for near with

Draw a family tree on the blackboard:

BLACKBOARD

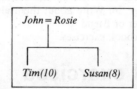

Say: John is a *man*. Tim is a *boy*. Rosie is a *woman*. Susan is a *girl*. Tim is Susan's *brother*. Susan is Tim's *sister*. John and Rosie are *married*. Rosie is a teacher. She likes her job. They live in Enfield. That's a *town near* London.

Write up the new words on the blackboard as you mention them. Give the plurals of the nouns too. Ask the students to repeat them chorally. Ask them to read the text and find the answers to these two questions:
What does Georgina do?
Where does her sister work?
Use the photograph to explain the meaning of *dentist, dental nurse,* (i.e. a dentist's assistant). Explain *unemployed = doesn't have a job.*

Ask the students to read the text again and find the answers to the questions printed beneath the text, as they read. Notice that questions are divided into groups to help the students read the text. The students can ask and answer these questions in pairs afterwards.

KEY

Georgie.
Near York, in the north-east of England.
No, she doesn't.
She's a dental nurse.
No, she doesn't. Not very much.
A man.
Yes, she does.
Rosie.
Yes, she is.
She's a teacher.
In a big school in the north of London.
Yes, she does. Very much.
No, she doesn't. She lives near London, in a town called Enfield.
She lives in a house.
He doesn't have a job. He's unemployed.
His name is Andrew.

Writing

Students use the text and the organisation of the questions about Georgina as a model for their own writing. They should follow the structure of the text, i.e. the order in which the information is presented.

Ask them to start this in class and perhaps make notes first so that they can ask you if they need any help with new words.

Homework

Choose from:
1. Set 2 Exercise 4, page 21.
2. Set 4 Exercises 3 and 4, page 23.
3. Open dialogue, page 25. Write out the missing part.
4. Roleplay, page 25. Write out the conversation.
5. Writing, page 26. Write about themselves and their sister, brother or friend.
6. Unit 3 Workbook exercises.

⊙⊙ Oral exercises

(For procedures, see page xii.)

1. Say what you like (Open exercise)

Listen to Diana and Paul saying what they like.

Do you like pop music?
Yes, I do./No, I don't.

Now you say what you like.

Do you like pop music?
. . . .
Do you like classical music?
. . . .
Do you like cats?
. . . .
Do you like your job?
. . . .
Do you like English classes?
. . . .
Do you like your home town?
. . . .

2. Ask about likes and dislikes

Ask if Diana likes classical music.
Does Diana like classical music?
Yes, she does.
Ask if Paul likes pop music.
Does Paul like pop music?
Yes, he does.

Look at the chart of people's likes and dislikes.
Ask questions about the people.

Ask if Diana likes classical music.
Does Diana like classical music?
Yes, she does.
Ask if Paul likes pop music.
Does Paul like pop music?
Yes, he does.
Ask if Paul likes children.
Does Paul like children?
Yes, he does.
Ask if Diana likes babies.
Does Diana like babies?
Yes, she does.
Ask if Diana likes dogs.
Does Diana like dogs?
No, she doesn't.
Ask if Paul likes cats.
Does Paul like cats?
No, he doesn't.

3. Answer about likes and dislikes

Say what Diana likes or doesn't like.
Does she like children?
Yes, she does.

You take Paul's part. Say what Diana likes or doesn't like.

Does she like children?
Yes, she does.
Does she like pop music?
No, she doesn't.
Does she like classical music?
Yes, she does.
Does she like cats?
Yes, she does.
Does she like babies?
Yes, she does.
Does she like dogs?
No, she doesn't.

4. Ask for personal information

Listen to these questions.

What's Diana's surname?
It's Trent.
What's Diana's telephone number?
I don't know.

Now you ask the questions.

What's Diana's surname?
It's Trent.
What's Diana's telephone number?
I don't know.

What's Paul's surname.
It's Roberts.
What's Joanne's address?
I don't know.
What's Mr Hall's first name?
It's Vince.
What's Joanne's telephone number?
I don't know but she's nice. She's really nice.
Mmm. Is she?

5. Say where places are

Where's Bristol?
It's in the south-west of England.

Now you tell Joanne where places are.

Where's Bristol?
It's in the south-west of England.
Where's Manchester?
It's in the north-west of England.
Where's Norwich?
It's in the east of England.
Where's Dover?
It's in the south-east of England.
Where's Brighton?
It's in the south of England.
Where's Newcastle?
It's in the north of England.
Where's Los Angeles, Joanne?
It's on the west coast of America.

Unit 4 Coffee or tea?

Presentation and practice	Set title	Language use	Examples
Dialogue: Part 1			
Set 1	Food, drink and money	Ask what people want Say what you want Ask and say how much things cost Order things	*Do you want coffee or tea?* *I want a cheese sandwich.* *How much is a cup of coffee?* *That's 25 pence, please.* *Can I have two coffees, please?*
Dialogue: Part 2			
Set 2	Likes and dislikes (2)	Ask and talk about likes and dislikes Agree or disagree with people's likes and dislikes	*Do you like reading?* *Yes, I do./No, I don't.* *I like reading.* *Yes, so do I./Really? I don't.* *I don't like writing letters.* *No, nor do I./Really? I do.* *I like Brooke Shields.* *Yes, I like her too.*
Set 3	Skills and sports	Ask and talk about ability	*Can you ski?* *Yes, I can. Can you?* *No, I can't.*
Dialogue: Part 3			
Set 4	Age	Ask and say how old people and places are Apologise Accept apologies	*How old is it/he/she?* *It's about 300 years old.* *He's 10 (years old).* *Sorry.* *That's all right.*
Spoken transfer: Open dialogue Roleplay		Combined Choose and order food and drink	
Skills development: Listening	**Description** An interview for a home help: a Swedish girl talks about her likes, dislikes, interests and skills		
Reading	An advertisement for a penfriend and a letter of reply from a German teenager from which students extract information in chart form.		
Writing	Students use the organisation of the chart to write a letter of reply to the penfriend.		
Oral exercises: 1		Ask what people like	Ask if Paul likes sightseeing. *Does Paul like sightseeing?*
2		Agree with people	I like cooking. *Yes, so do I.* I don't like writing letters. *No, nor do I.*
3		Disagree with people	I love going to the theatre. *Really? I don't.* I don't like going to discos very much. *Really? I do.*
4		Talk about activities and skills (Open exercise)	Do you like sightseeing? *(Yes, I do./No, I don't.)* Can you ski? *(Yes I can./No, I can't.)*
5		Order food and drink	Tea for me, please. *OK. Can I have two teas, please?*
6		Ask the price	Ask how much the egg sandwich is. *How much is that egg sandwich?* Ask how much the biscuits are. *How much are those biscuits?*

Grammar focus	Active vocabulary and expressions
	black white just *There you are.*
Present simple tense: verb *want a piece/cup/glass of/ a packet of...* Question word: *How much?* Demonstrative adjectives: *this, that, these, those* Modal verb: *can* (request)	biscuit glass piece want *How much?* box milk pound can (request) Numbers cake orange sandwich 10–1,000,000 cheese packet tea *these* chocolate pence water *those*
	lots of sightseeing sugar *It's great fun.*
Gerund (*-ing* form) after verbs *like, hate, love* Inversion with auxiliary verb: *do (So do I./Nor do I.)* Question word: *Who? (Who's that?)* Object pronouns: *him, her,* etc.	café hate watch *Who?* cinema love at all *So do I.* concert read home (at home) *Nor do I.* disco see party sightsee round television sit to theatre walk
Modal verb: *can* (ability) – positive, negative and interrogative	can (ability) play swim cook ride type drive speak
Question word: *How old?*	cathedral *How old?* *See you later.* late *years old* *Sorry.* about *That's all right.*
	drink record
	language smoke a little *Dear...,* sports soon

27

Unit 4 Coffee or tea?

Students' Book pages 28, 29

Check the homework from Unit 3.

Set 1 Food, drink and money

(Note that this set comes before Dialogue: Part 1.)

Active words and expressions:	biscuit box cake cheese chocolate glass milk orange packet pence piece pound sandwich tea water can (request) want these those How much? Numbers 10–1,000,000

If possible bring into the class actual objects or pictures on flash cards to demonstrate the meaning of the new lexical items. Not all the food and drink words are expected to be learnt. Practise the pronunciation of all the items on the menu once you are sure the students know their meaning. Practise only the food and drink items at this stage, not the prices, e.g. Say after me: *a cheese sandwich... a cheese and tomato sandwich... an egg sandwich... a beef sandwich... a packet of biscuits... a piece of chocolate cake... a cup of tea... a glass of milk...*, and so on.

NOTES

cakes and biscuits: in Britain cake has a soft texture whereas biscuits are hard. Cakes are either small and individual, or large and cut into portions or pieces. A very large cake decorated with cream, is called a *gateau* (a French word)

sandwiches: these are usually closed, with the filling, e.g. cheese and tomato, between two slices of bread. Scandinavian-style 'open sandwiches' are often served in Britain, as are American style 'triple decker' sandwiches

please: *please* is used after a request for something or for people to do something, e.g. *Coffee, please./Can I have some coffee, please?/Can you give me some of that cake, please? Do you want some? Yes, please.*

thank you: this is used when you have received something or when saying *No*, e.g. *No, thank you.* Saying *please* and *thank you* is an important part of British culture and foreign speakers of English can often cause offence by omitting to say them

Exercise 1

Practise the example exchange chorally and in pairs. Make sure the students' voices go up on *coffee* and down on *tea*, and that when saying *Coffee, please* they sound pleasant and interested (i.e. spoken with a high fall followed by a short rise) and not flat and impolite. Ask the students to work through the menu offering and choosing alternately.

Exercise 2

Present the example sentence and ask each student *What do you want?* Ask one student to note down what the others want. At the end he/she can list the total, e.g. *12 cups of coffee, two glasses of coke, a...*, etc.

(There is no *please* here, as this is not a request, only a statement of what the students want.)

Exercise 3

Present and teach the numbers listed on page 28 in the same way as in Unit 1. Practise with different combinations of numbers, adding and subtracting games and so on, until you are sure that the students can confidently say any number. Make sure that the stress falls on *-een* of the numbers 13 to 19 so that they do not confuse them with *30, 40*, etc. where the stress falls on the first syllable. Numbers and spelling are things that should be revised at regular intervals.

Present the two units of money: *pound* and *pence* and show how the symbols £ and *p* are written. Refer the students to the pictures of the different English coins and notes. Get them to say the amounts, printed at the top right-hand side of SB, page 29, after you. If you have some real English money to pass round, this would be an ideal occasion to do so. Write a few prices on the board and ask students to say them.

Ask the students to read and then write down the prices in the book.

KEY

£150.00 = *one hundred and fifty pounds*
£1.99 = *one pound ninety-nine (pence)*
£29.95 = *twenty-nine pounds ninety-five (pence)*
34p = *thirty-four (pence)*
£11.75 = *eleven pounds seventy-five (pence)*
£6.50 = *six pounds fifty (pence)*

Exercise 4

Ask the students to look at the menu again. Ask the questions and answer them yourself: *How much is a cup of coffee/cheese sandwich?* Students practise the question form then ask each other the prices of the items listed in the exercise.

Exercise 5

Demonstrate with pens and books the difference between *this/that* and *these/those*. Practise first with *this/these*. Get the students to make questions while you hold up certain articles, e.g. *How much is this/these?* do the same for *that/those* pointing to articles from a distance and getting the students to make the questions. Students work through the exercise in pairs, answering with the price of the items.

Exercise 6

Practise the exchange chorally. Concentrate first on the request *Can I have...?* Select different pairs of students to perform in front of the class and check their pronunciation and fluency.

Notice that when ordering drinks, it is common to omit the word *cup*.
a cup of coffee = a coffee; two cups of coffee = two coffees

KEY

1. *Yes, that's £1.75 (one pound seventy-five (pence)), please.*
2. *Yes, that's 40 pence, please.*
3. *Yes, that's 30 pence, please.*
4. *Yes, that's £2.85 (two pounds eighty-five (pence)), please.*
5. *Yes, that's £1.05 (one pound five (pence)), please.*

🔘 Dialogue: Part 1

Active words and expressions:	black white just There you are.

NOTES

black coffee: black coffee is coffee without milk or cream; white coffee is coffee with milk or cream. Tea, however, is either 'with' or 'without milk' (not 'black' or 'white')

Work through the dialogue. Students say which of the four statements are true and which are false. Ask the students to act out the situation in threes.

Students' Book pages 30, 31

🔘 Dialogue: Part 2

Active words and expressions:	sugar sightsee lots of It's great fun.

Play the tape of the dialogue and ask the students to read it in pairs. Some teachers may like to use the dialogue as a basis for substitution work, with the students supplying their own ideas.

Set 2 Likes and dislikes (2)

Active words and expressions:	café cinema concert disco letter party television theatre hate love read see sightsee sit walk watch at all home (at home) round to Who? So do I. Nor do I. me you him her it us you them

Exercise 1

Bring pictures from magazines, draw on the blackboard or mime in order to explain the meaning of the different activity words in the chart on the left of page 30. As you present each activity, write the base form of the verb on the blackboard beside the *-ing* form:

BLACKBOARD

e.g. *read ... reading*
write ... writing
sit ... sitting

This will be the first time the students have met many of these key words. Show the relationship between the base and the *-ing* form in terms of spelling. (The general rule is to double the final consonant (only) when the preceding vowel is *stressed* and spelt with a *single letter*. Words ending in *'e'* drop the *e*.) Students repeat each phrase chorally.

Say to a student: Ask me *Do you like reading?* Work S-T like this with one or two examples from the chart to show the range of answers possible. Show by the expression on your face the meaning of *love* and *hate*. Point out that *it* refers to the activity.

Ask the students to repeat the different types of answer chorally. Students copy the chart in their exercise books. They first note down their own answers (a tick or a cross will do) and then work in pairs noting down their partner's answers.

Exercise 2

Present both halves of the exchange in the box yourself or ask one student to tell you one or two things he/she likes doing. Agree or disagree. Then ask the students to name something he/she doesn't like doing. Agree or disagree. Practise the answers chorally. Practise both types of agreement first, then both types of disagreement. Make sure the stress falls in the right place, i.e. on *so* or *nor* and on *I*.

Refer back to the chart and ask the students to work in a chain like this: s1 chooses one thing to say from the chart, e.g. *I don't like writing letters.* s2: *Really? I do.* (to s3) *I like reading.* s3: *Yes, so do I.* and so on round the class. Students can then circulate and see how many people they can find who like the same things.

Exercise 3

Read out the examples. Students make similar statements about their own and their partner's likes and dislikes. Ask a few students to express these orally, then ask everyone to write down one or two similar statements. These can be completed for homework.

Exercise 4

Write on the blackboard or show pictures of a nationally or internationally famous female star, male star and a popular group, known to the students. Present the object pronouns *her, him* and *them* like this: point to the woman and say *I like her,* or *I don't like her. Do you?* Then point to the man and say *I like/don't like him. Do you?* and to the group *I like/don't like them. Do you?* Elicit their opinions each time. Write the paradigm on the blackboard beside that of the personal pronouns to show their correspondence. Include the object pronouns *you* and *me* and *us* and give one or two examples of their use.

BLACKBOARD

I	*– me*	*we*	*– us*
you	*– you*	*you*	*– you*
he	*– him*	*they*	*– them*
she	*– her*		
it	*– it*		

Ask the students to look at the pictures of the stars.

NOTES

Brooke Shields: an American film star who became world famous in the film *The Blue Lagoon*

Olivia Newton-John: an Australian singer and actress famous for her role in the film *Grease* and for her records. She lives in Los Angeles

John McEnroe: an American tennis champion

The Muppets: TV and film puppets which include Miss Piggy, Kermit the Frog and Fozzie the Bear

Practise the first exchange (John McEnroe) and the last exchange (Brooke Shields) with the students repeating after you chorally. Make sure their voices go up on the word *Really?* and that *all* carries the main stress. Ask the students to look at the other example exchanges and then ask their partners about each of the pictures. They then choose some current personalities for extra practice.

Set 3 Skills and sports

Active words:	can (ability) cook drive play ride speak swim type

Exercise 1

Students practise the example exchanges chorally and in pairs. Identify the sports in the pictures and practise their pronunciation. Ask the students to make a list of the sports in a column in their exercise books. They ask everyone in the class (if it is not too large – otherwise divide the class into groups) if they can or cannot do or play the sports listed. They should collect the ticks and crosses against each sport, add up the totals and express the results in writing.

Present any new vocabulary before going on to the next part of the exercise.

Exercise 2

Read the questions out to the class. The students listen to each question and note down *Yes* or *No* each time. They now ask their partners the same questions. Ask individuals to report back on a few of the questions, e.g. *I can drive but I can't ride a horse. I can't type or play chess.*

Students' Book pages 32, 33

Dialogue: Part 3

Active words and expressions:	cathedral late about years old How old? See you later. Sorry. That's all right.

NOTES

St Paul's Cathedral: a famous landmark in London and a very popular tourist attraction. The cathedral was designed by Sir Christopher Wren (1675–1711). The Prince and Princess of Wales were married in St Paul's Cathedral in July 1981. The cathedral is situated in the heart of the City of London. Many of the streets in the City are narrow and flanked by tall, impressive buildings. The City is the commercial centre of London, c.f. Wall Street in New York

So long!: American English for *Goodbye!* (colloquial use)

Work through the dialogue and check the true/false statements. Practise especially the phrases: *Sorry* and *See you later.*

Set 4 Age

Refer the students back to the dialogue. Ask the students: *How old is St Paul's Cathedral?* Write both question and answer on the blackboard. Ask other questions about the age of buildings and objects, e.g. *How old is this building/school/college?*
        your car/bicycle/flat /house?
It's about . . . years old.

Present and practise the other questions and answers with *he* and *she* from the examples in the box. Point out that you can omit *years old* when referring to people's ages but not when referring to the age of a building or object.

With a class of young people you can also practise *How old are you? I'm* ... but use your discretion here as adults can be sensitive about age.

Refer the students to the photographs and ask them to ask and answer about the ages in pairs.

KEY (from left to right)

He's five.
She's ... (work out date from 1964)
He's seven and she's ten.
It's ... (work out date from 1981) *years old.*
They're (the twins) *four.*
It's ... (work out date from 1982) *years old.*

📼 Open dialogue

Active words:	drink record

SSR

PAUL:	Hello.
YOU:	*Hello./Hi.*
PAUL:	Let's have a drink. Do you want coffee or coke?
YOU:	*Coffee/Coke, please.*
PAUL:	Do you want a biscuit or a piece of cake with it?
YOU:	*No, thanks./Yes, please.*
PAUL:	OK. Listen! That's a new record by Haircut 100. Do you like it?
YOU:	*Yes, I do./Yes, I love it./No, I don't, not very much./No, I hate it.*
PAUL:	What sort of music do you like?
YOU:	*I like pop music/classical music/jazz/rock/folk (etc.)*
PAUL:	So do I. What do you like doing in your spare time?
YOU:	*I like ... ing.*
PAUL:	Really? I like going to see friends and driving my car. Can you drive?
YOU:	*Yes, I can./No, I can't.*
PAUL:	Let's play a record. What do you want?
YOU:	*I want the new record by ... (name of a band)*
PAUL:	Great! I love that record, too.

Roleplay

It can be more amusing to work out your own menu with the class contributing items. They may already know other words like hamburger, ice cream, cream cake, etc. Ask them to give prices, too. Write the menu on the blackboard so that everyone can see it clearly. Remind them of useful language like: *How much is/are* ...? *Can I have* ..., *please? Do you want* ...? *That's* ... *pence, please.*

You could make part of the classroom look a bit like a coffee bar counter so that the students can act the situation more naturally and attempt the exercise without looking at their books.

Students' Book pages 34, 35

📼 Listening

Explain the context first. This is an interview between the mother of the family and a Swedish girl, Karin Hallberg. Go through each question first, by transferring the question to the students. Ask individual students at random: *Do you like children? Do you like cooking?* Demonstrate or explain any new words as they come up. Ask the students to listen to the interview and tick in the *Yes* or *No* column as they hear Karin's answers. Play the tape twice and check the answers.

TAPESCRIPT

A Swedish girl called Karin Hallberg has applied for a job as a home help for a family in London. Listen to her talking to the mother of the family and answer the questions below.

MRS X:	Oh, hello.
KARIN:	Hello.
MRS X:	Come in and have a cup of tea.
KARIN:	Thank you.
MRS X:	The children aren't here. They're at school.
KARIN:	Oh yes. How old are they?
MRS X:	William's seven and Amanda's five. Do you like children?
KARIN:	Yes, I do. Very much. I had a job in a kindergarten before I came here.
MRS X:	Oh good. Well, you speak very good English!
KARIN:	Well, in Sweden we start English when we're eight.
MRS X:	Eight! Goodness. Well, tell me a little about yourself, Karin ... er ... cigarette?
KARIN:	No, thank you. I don't smoke.
MRS X:	Good for you. Tell me, what do you like doing in your spare time?
KARIN:	I like reading, listening to music ...
MRS X:	Oh yes. What sort of music do you like?
KARIN:	All sorts. I like some pop music and, of course, classical music.
MRS X:	That's good. We like classical music, too. What about sports ... tennis, swimming ...?
KARIN:	Yes, I like swimming but I like dancing best.
MRS X:	Dancing? At discos you mean?
KARIN:	No, no. I do jazz dance.
MRS X:	Jazz dance. How lovely! Well, you can do all sorts of things in London. Can you drive, by the way?
KARIN:	Yes, I can.
MRS X:	Good. You need a car here. More tea?
KARIN:	No, thanks.
MRS X:	Well, you know about the job ...
KARIN:	Yes, but there's just one thing ... er ... I'm afraid I can't cook very well ...
MRS X:	You can't cook? Never mind, you'll soon learn. And my husband does most of the cooking in this house ... When can you start by the way?

31

KARIN: Well, er . . . next week if you like.

MRS X: Fine! We'd like to have you very much. I'm sure you'll be happy here.

KEY

Does she like children?	*Yes*
Can she cook?	*No*
Does she speak English?	*Yes*
Can she drive?	*Yes*
Does she smoke?	*No*
Does she like pop music?	*Yes*
classical music?	*Yes*
reading?	*Yes*
Other interests?	*Yes (swimming, jazz dance)*
Does she get the job?	*Yes*

Reading

Active words:	language sports smoke a little soon Dear . . .,

WANTED PENFRIENDS

Ask the students to read the advertisement silently.
Questions:
Who is it from? (Jean Ploton.)
Is he English? (No, he isn't. He's French.)
How old is he? (He's fifteen.)
What does he like? (He likes sports, films and pop music.)

LETTER FROM GISELA HANZ

NOTES

P.S. (post script): something you have forgotten to write in the main body of the letter

Ask the students to read the letter silently.
Questions:
Who is it from?
Is that a boy or a girl's name?
Is she French?
What does she do?
Where does she study?
What does she like doing in her spare time?
What doesn't she like doing?
What language does she speak?
What does she like doing in the summer?
Does she smoke?
Ask the students to fill in the form underneath the letter.
Go round and check the answers.

Writing

Students use Gisela's letter as a model for their own. For extra preparation students can work in pairs asking each other the relevant information contained in the chart. Ask them to start writing the letter in class and complete it for homework.

Homework

Choose from:
1. Set 2 Exercise 3, page 30. Students write sentences about Paul.
2. Open dialogue, page 25. Write out the missing part.
3. Writing, page 34.
4. Unit 4 Workbook exercises.

🔘 Oral exercises

(For procedures, see page xii.)

1. Ask what people like

Ask if Paul likes sightseeing.
Does Paul like sightseeing?
Yes, he does.

Now you ask what people like.

Ask if Paul likes sightseeing.
Does Paul like sightseeing?
Yes, he does.
Ask if Diana likes skiing.
Does Diana like skiing?
I'm not sure. I think she does.
Ask if Joanne likes cooking.
Does Joanne like cooking?
No, she doesn't.
Ask if Vince likes windsurfing.
Does Vince like windsurfing?
No, he doesn't. He can't windsurf.
Ask if Paul likes writing letters.
Does Paul like writing letters?
No, he doesn't.
Ask if Diana likes playing tennis.
Does Diana like playing tennis?
Yes, she does. She loves it.

2. Agree with people

Listen to these people agreeing.

I like cooking.
Yes, so do I.
I don't like writing letters.
No, nor do I.

Now you agree.

I like cooking.
Yes, so do I.
I don't like writing letters.
No, nor do I.
I hate sightseeing.
Yes, so do I.
I don't like watching television.
No, nor do I.
I love windsurfing.
Yes, so do I.
I don't like shopping.
No, nor do I.

3. Disagree with people

Listen to these people disagreeing.

I love going to the theatre.
Really? I don't.
I don't like going to discos very much.
Really? I do.

Now you disagree with people in the same way.

I love going to the theatre.
Really? I don't.
I don't like going to discos very much.
Really? I do.
I don't like shopping.
Really? I do.
I love going to concerts.
Really? I don't.
I like watching TV, too.
Really? I don't.
I don't like going to parties at all!
Really? I do.

4. Talk about activities and skills (Open exercise)

·Listen to Diana, Paul and Joanne.

Do you like sightseeing?
Yes, I do./No, I don't.
Can you ski?
Yes, I can./No, I can't.

Now you answer about the things you like doing and the things you can do.

Do you like sightseeing?
. . . .
Can you ski?
. . . .
Can you windsurf?
. . . .
Do you like going to discos?
. . . .
Do you like writing letters?
. . . .
Can you drive?
. . . .

5. Order food and drink

Paul and Joanne are in a café.

PAUL: Tea for me, please.
JOANNE: *OK. Can I have two teas, please?*

Now you order food and drink.

Tea for me, please.
OK. Can I have two teas, please?
Coffee for me, please.
OK. Can I have two coffees, please?
Coke for me, please.
OK. Can I have two cokes, please?
A cheese sandwich for me, please.
OK. Can I have two cheese sandwiches, please?
A piece of chocolate cake for me, please.
OK. Can I have two pieces of chocolate cake, please?
A glass of mineral water for me, please.
OK. Can I have two glasses of mineral water, please?

JOANNE: This a real nice place, Paul. What's it called?
PAUL: The City Café. It's nice, isn't it? And the coffee's good, too.

6. Ask the price

Tim is in a sandwich bar at lunchtime.

TIM: *How much is that egg sandwich?*
GIRL: It's 30 pence.
TIM: *How much are those biscuits?*
GIRL: They're 15 pence a packet.

Now you ask the price of things.

Ask how much the egg sandwich is.
How much is that egg sandwich?
It's 30 pence.
Ask how much the biscuits are.
How much are those biscuits?
They're 15 pence a packet.
Ask how much the cheese and tomato sandwiches are.
How much are those cheese and tomato sandwiches?
They're 40 pence.
Ask how much the piece of chocolate cake is.
How much is that piece of chocolate cake?
It's 45 pence.
Ask how much the cheese sandwich is.
How much is that cheese sandwich?
It's 30 pence.
Ask how much the chocolate biscuits are.
How much are those chocolate biscuits?
They're 15 pence.
All the prices are on the menu, dear! You can read, can't you?

Unit 5 Consolidation

Skills	Description	Language uses/topics/activities
Speaking	Roleplay: 'The People Game' Charts present information about people from eight different countries. Students choose to be one of the people and ask questions to find someone who shares the same interests.	Greet people; introduce yourself; ask and say what nationality you are; what language you speak; what your job is and what your interests are
Listening	1. An interview with one of the characters from 'The People Game'. Students guess which person is speaking.	Combined as above
	2. Two interviews: students make notes under headings to extract information.	Age, home and interests
	3. A conversation in which a travel agent talks to American visitors to Britain about a visit to Stratford-upon-Avon (Shakespeare's birthplace). Students number the pieces of information in the order each is given.	Names, telephone numbers and price
	4. A conversation in which two guests book in at a hotel and then have a meal in the hotel restaurant. Students answer binary choice questions.	Booking a hotel room; likes and dislikes; paying a bill
Reading	A picture strip story about a family taking a summer holiday in Cornwall. Students answer true/false questions and complete sentences to summarise the story.	
Reading for Information (authentic)	Mixed authentic realia consisting of: 1. a business card, an editorial staff list from the front of a magazine; 2. entries from a telephone directory; 3. advertisement for a leisure club; 4. advertisements for a hotel and The Royal Shakespeare Restaurants in Stratford-upon-Avon; theatre tickets, programme note and part of a cast list; a map and an advertisement for a Tourist Office.	Names; jobs; numbers; postal districts; nationalities; prices; sports and activities
Roleplay	Students use a menu to order food and drink.	Choosing and ordering from a menu: food, drink and prices
Reading and writing	Students read a model paragraph and then use notes they have made in chart form to write paragraphs describing different people, their homes, their interests and their holidays.	
Language focus	1. Vocabulary: Sort the words	Sorting into word groups: people; jobs; drinks; compass points; entertainments
	2. Vocabulary: Complete the words	Word completion: students complete each word from an initial letter
	3. Word order: Put the words in the right order	Students rearrange words in the correct order to form good sentences
	4. Conversation: Complete the conversation	Students complete the missing words in a conversation
	5. Grammar: Which is correct?	Multiple choice: 10 mixed grammatical points

Students' Book pages 36, 37

Check homework from Unit 4.

The unit is divided into four sections: the first section, The People Game, encourages the students to converse, using key functions and structures from the early units. The second section on pages 38 and 39 gives extra practice in listening, reading and writing. In the listening section, the students have the opportunity of hearing authentic unscripted interviews with two people (Heather and Giles) talking about themselves and their tastes. The third section, Reading for information, on pages 40 and 41, contains a collection of authentic realia which not only extends the students' awareness of certain cultural aspects of Britain, but also gives them an opportunity to apply their native reading skills, combined with their knowledge of English, to search for specific information. The skills section is completed on page 42 with a reading and writing exercise.

The fourth and final section, Language focus, on page 43, tests lexical and grammatical knowledge.

Roleplay: The People Game

The personal information notes contain a lot of new vocabulary to enrich the profile of each character. This is for passive recognition and time need not be spent on initial presentation of all the new words. The students will be able to work out the meaning of some of them themselves, or they can consult each other, or use a dictionary. Help them only if they ask you.

INSTRUCTIONS

Ask students to prepare their roles by thinking about themselves like this: *My name is Dean Hudson. I'm American. I'm a sports writer,* and so on, so that they prepare the verbs which need to be used in conversation. Then ask each person to make a list of the questions they will have to ask to find out the same information about each other. If you like, you can do this with the whole class and write the questions on the blackboard.

When you think the students are sufficiently prepared, follow the instructions in the Students' Book and get them to mix with each other and find a friend. This is more successfully done if the students can walk around as if they were at a party. Encourage them to talk to everyone in their group before they make a decision. There are several possible matches of people although some are perhaps more obviously suited than others. The point of the activity is to build up information about other people.

Suggested pairs of friends

The obvious matches are as suggested on the page, i.e. Dean and Magdalena; Terri and Paloma; Della and Angelo; Pierre and Irma.

However students may choose other partners who share other things in common, e.g. both Magdalena and Pierre like America and American culture.

Using the same headings as in the 'personality notes', the students can now make a chart of their own, and interview someone in the class. At this stage it is important to pair the students differently from their normal classroom arrangement so that there is new information for them to find out. The answers to their questions should be written in note form.

Paragraph writing about the characters comes later (see page 42).

Students' Book pages 38, 39

Listening

See if the students can complete the answers or the activities as far as possible without preparation and without pausing the tape as you play.

1. TAPESCRIPT

Listen to a conversation between three people. One of them is a character from The People Game. Who is it?

HARRY: Hello.

TERRI: Hi.

HARRY: Come on in.

TERRI: Thanks.

HARRY: This is my wife, Marion.

TERRI: Hi.

MARION: Hello. Are you an American?

TERRI: No, I'm Canadian. I'm just here in Britain for a holiday. I live in Quebec.

MARION: Oh, do you? How funny! My sister lives in Quebec. She's married to an engineer.

HARRY: Just a minute. I'll turn the television off. Or do you like football?

TERRI: No, I hate watching football.

HARRY: Do you like any sports?

TERRI: Well, I like swimming very much. I share a flat at home with two girls and we often go swimming together. There's a fabulous pool near our flat.

HARRY: Really?

MARION: I like swimming, too.

TERRI: Mmm, Something smells good. What is it?

HARRY: It's roast beef – English style!

MARION: Harry loves cooking. Do you?

TERRI: Yes, I love it. I like cooking Chinese food.

MARION: Is this your first visit to Britain?

TERRI: No, it isn't. I was here in . . .

KEY

Terri Lichère

2. TAPESCRIPT

Listen to these people talking. Write the missing information about them in the chart in your book.

Could you tell me how old you are, please?

I'm twenty-five.

Would you like to tell me what you do, please?

I work in a bank in London in the International Department.

And where do you live?

I live in South London.

And what sort of accommodation have you got there?

I've got a rather nice little flat which I bought recently.

What sort of things do you like doing in your spare time?

Well, I'm interested in quite a lot of things. I like reading. I often go out with my friends to the cinema, to see a film, to a restaurant ... erm, I've just taken up photography as a hobby and I sometimes go to evening classes. I do yoga.

Do you play any sports?

I go swimming sometimes, but I'm not very fond of sports like hockey or tennis.

Where do you live?

I live in a rented flat in Harlow.

And what do you do for a living?

I'm a graphic designer.

What sort of things do you like doing in your spare time?

Well, I'm quite involved in a local church, and I'm also interested in all sorts of outdoor activities like camping and hill walking, and I do a bit of swimming as well.

Do you like any other sorts of sport?

I quite like badminton as well.

And what about cultural interests ... music?

Yes, I like, I like music and ... er, I like some modern dance as well. I quite often go to performances in London.

Could you tell me how old you are, please?

I'm twenty-three.

KEY

HEATHER
Age: 25
Home: in a flat in South London
Special interests: reading, going to the cinema, restaurants, photography, going to evening classes, yoga, swimming

GILES
Age: 23
Home: in a rented flat in Harlow
Special interests: involved in the church, camping, hill walking, swimming, badminton, music, modern dance

3. TAPESCRIPT

(NOTE: The students will need to know the meaning of play and restaurant to complete the activity.)

Listen to the travel agent talking to two Americans about a visit to Stratford. Look at the pieces of information in your book. Number them in the order in which the travel agent mentions them.

TRAVEL AGENT: Mr Corder?
MR CORDER: Yes?
TRAVEL AGENT: I have the details here for your trip to Stratford.
MR CORDER: Right.
TRAVEL AGENT: The name of the hotel is The Arden.
MR CORDER: The Arden Hotel. Right. And you got tickets for a show?
TRAVEL AGENT: Yes. I've got two tickets for you and your wife to see A Midsummer Night's Dream. (Oh.) That's a good play. You'll like it.
MR CORDER: That's good.
TRAVEL AGENT: And the tickets cost £12.00 each.
MR CORDER: Fine. And can we have dinner at the Hotel Arden?
TRAVEL AGENT: Yes, but I've booked a table for you at the restaurant in the theatre – at the Royal Shakespeare Restaurant at 6.30. (How wonderful!)
MR CORDER: And if I need to contact you before Saturday, how do I find you?
TRAVEL AGENT: My telephone number is 727 8665.
MR CORDER: 7-2-7 8 double six 5. Right.
TRAVEL AGENT: And I hope you both enjoy the trip.
MR CORDER: We will. And thank you very much for your help. (Thank you.)
TRAVEL AGENT: You're welcome.

KEY

The name of the play: 2
The name of the hotel: 1
The travel agent's telephone number: 5
The name of the restaurant: 4
The price of the theatre tickets: 3

4. TAPESCRIPT

Listen to these people talking. Look at the questions in your books and tick the right answers.

RECEPTIONIST: Good morning, sir. Good morning, madam.
MAN: Good morning.
WOMAN: Hello.
RECEPTIONIST: You have a room booked?
WOMAN: No, we'd like to book two rooms, please.
RECEPTIONIST: Two single rooms?
MAN: Yes, that's right.
RECEPTIONIST: Fine. There are two adjoining rooms on the top floor.
MAN: That sounds fine.
RECEPTIONIST: What is your name, please?
MAN: Brooks. Mr Brooks and Miss Barrett.
RECEPTIONIST: Right. Can you just sign here, please. And here are your keys.
WOMAN: Thank you. Oh, is there a restaurant in the hotel?

36

RECEPTIONIST: Yes, it's over there. It's called the Picnic Basket.

MAN: Good.

WOMAN: Mmm. This chicken is delicious.

MAN: Yes, it *is* good. The wine's a bit sweet though.

WOMAN: Yes, I don't like it very much either.

MAN: Never mind.

MAN: Let's pay. How much is it?

WOMAN: Fourteen pounds exactly. Let me pay it this time.

MAN: OK. Thanks. . . .

KEY

Mr Brooks and Miss Barrett are in a hotel.
They are booking rooms.
Yes. (They like the food in the restaurant.)
No. (They don't like the wine very much.)
The meal is £14 altogether.

Reading: A summer holiday in St Ives

Ask the students to look at each picture as you read each text aloud. Then ask them to read it through silently. Encourage them to ask you the meaning of any new words if they cannot guess them from the context. Students answer the true/false questions after reading the text and then complete the sentences.

KEY

1. False. False. True. False. True.
2. *The people in the hotel don't like the children because they play in the restaurant; they talk in the TV room; and the baby cries at night.*
   The Clark family don't like their holiday in Cornwall because they don't like the food; the water is cold; and it rains every day.

Students' Book pages 40, 41

Reading for information

The realia consists of:
(page 40)
1. a business card of a Public Relations Manager, Jill Faulds
   a list of the editorial staff of a magazine *(Woman)*
2. a list of telephone numbers of some embassies, legations and consulates in London
3. an advertisement for a social club
   (page 41)
4. an advertisement for the Royal Shakespeare Restaurants
   information about the cast of the play, *A Midsummer Night's Dream*

a programme note about a play
a small ad. for a tourist office in Stratford
two ticket stubs
an advertisement for a hotel
a stylised road map
a portrait of William Shakespeare

Divide the students into groups and ask them to read and search for the information. Check the answers in cross-groups. (See General teaching procedures on group work, page viii.)

KEY

1. The Tower Hotel

The Public Relations Manager is Jill Faulds.

Woman

The Editor in Chief of Woman magazine is a woman.
George Cannon is an Assistant Editor.
Betty Hale is a/the Managing Editor.

2. Embassies, Legations and Consulates

The telephone number of the French Embassy is:
299 9411.
The telephone number of the German Embassy is:
202 3844.
The telephone number of the Chinese Embassy is:
991 1730.
The telephone number of the Greek Embassy is:
727 0653.
The Soviet Embassy is in West London (W8).
The German Embassy is in North-West London (NW9).
The Chinese Embassy is in West London (W13).

3. London Linkup

music: *you can go to concerts, folk clubs, jazz clubs*

meeting people: *you can go to parties, discos, pub evenings and wine bars/you can meet people who are interested in cooking or astrology*

the arts: *you can go to films, concerts and ballets*

outdoor sports: *you can play football, go waterskiing and go horse riding*

indoor games: *you can play bridge and chess*

4. Stratford-upon-Avon

The telephone number of the Arden Hotel is:
0789 294949.
The telephone number of the Royal Shakespeare Theatre is 0789 292271.
The telephone number of the tourist office in Stratford is: 0789 294466.
There are nine in the main cast of 'A Midsummer Night's Dream'.
The seat numbers are Q4 and Q5.
The tickets are £8.50 each.

Students' Book
pages 42, 43

KEY

5. International Buffet Menu

2 black coffees	60p	3 cheese sandwiches	£1.56
2 coffees with cream	64p	2 jam doughnuts	52p
1 tea	20p	1 fresh cream gateau	55p
1 Coca-cola	30p		
		Total	£4.37

Students can write up their orders in the form of a bill at the end of the roleplay.

Reading and writing

SSR

Dean Hudson is American. He is married to Lynne, a history teacher, and lives in a house in Denver, Colorado. He has three boys, aged five, eight and eleven. He is a sports writer. In his spare time he likes cooking and listening to classical music, but he doesn't like washing up very much. He likes going to London and to Central America for his holidays.

Della Freeman is British. She is not married. She lives with her married sister in South London. She is a student at a college of engineering. In her spare time she likes meeting people from other countries and writing letters, but she doesn't like watching TV. She likes going to Italy for her holidays.

Language focus

KEY

1. Sort the words

coffee	man	cinema	doctor	south
milk	girl	theatre	secretary	east
tea	boy	disco	student	west
water	woman	concert	teacher	north

2. Complete the words

1. Good *afternoon*.
2. *Pleased to meet* you.
3. *Where* do you live?
4. My *address* is 23, Tiverton Road, Southall.
5. My *telephone number* is 574 3355.
6. Do you live in the *centre* of the town?
7. I live on the *west coast* of America.
8. I don't have a *job*. I'm *unemployed*.
9. Can I have two *coffees*, please?
10. Do you want an egg *sandwich*, or a *cheese sandwich*?

3. Put the words in the right order

1. *Pleased to meet you.*
2. *I like Americans very much.*

3. *Can I have two coffees, please?*
4. *What do you like doing in your spare time?*
5. *He lives in the north of Scotland.*
6. *Do you want coffee or tea?*
7. *Is your name David Roberts?*
8. *How much are these cheese sandwiches?*
9. *I love windsurfing in the summer.*
10. *She is married with three children.*

4. Complete the conversation

SANDRA:	Hello, Jim.
JIM:	Oh, *hello Sandra*. How *are you*?
SANDRA:	*Very well,* thanks, and *you*?
JIM:	Oh, I'm *fine thank you*. How's Martin?
SANDRA:	He's OK. He's at home with the children.
JIM:	*How old are* the children now?
SANDRA:	Damian's seven and Lucy's four.
JIM:	Really! And what do *you do* now? Are you still a teacher?
SANDRA:	Yes, *I am*. And *do* you still like your job at Shell?
JIM:	No, I *don't like it* very much.
SANDRA:	Oh! I'm sorry. You must talk to Martin. He *doesn't* like his job much either. Well, I must go now.
JIM:	Yes, I must too. Look after yourself, and come and see us sometime.

5. Which is correct?

1. *b)* 2. *b)* 3. *c)* 4. *c)* 5. *a)* 6. *a)* 7. *c)* 8. *b)* 9. *a)* 10. *c)*

Homework

Choose from:
1. Language focus exercises 1, 2, 3, 4, 5 as time allows.
2. Unit 5 Workbook exercises.

Unit 6 Getting around

Presentation and practice		Set title	Language use	Examples
Dialogue:	Part 1			
	Set 1	Past events	Ask and talk about past events	*Were you at the conference this morning? Yes, I was./No, I wasn't. Where were you yesterday? I was at a meeting. How was the conference? It was interesting.*
	Set 2	Shops and requirements	Say what you want to buy and get	*I want to buy a film. I want to get some shoes. I want to go to a chemist's.*
Dialogue:	Part 2			
	Set 3	Places: location (2)	Ask about places and shops Ask where you can buy/get things Say where places and shops are Say where you can buy/get things Give simple directions	*Is there a bank near here? Where can I buy some stamps?* *There's one opposite the post office. At the post office/chemist's.* *Turn left at the wine bar and it's on your right.*
Dialogue:	Part 3			
	Set 4	Clock times	Ask and tell the time	*What's the time?/What time is it? It's four o'clock. It's ten past four.*
	Set 5	Fixed times	Ask and talk about fixed times	*What time does the train leave? It leaves at five thirty.*
Spoken transfer: Open dialogue Roleplay			Combined Ask and talk about flight times	
Skills development: Listening		**Description** A telephone conversation making arrangements for an evening visit to the cinema. Students note the arrangements and the name of the film.		
Reading		Diana writes to her husband, James, from the conference. She mentions her flight, the hotel, the conference and some of the things she has done.		
Writing		Students use a model paragraph about opening and closing times of shops and banks in Britain to write about their own country.		
Oral exercises:	1		Check people's movements	Were you at the conference this morning? *At the conference? No, I wasn't.*
	2		Say where places and shops are	Excuse me, but is there a bank near here? *Bank? Yes, there's one over there.*
	3		Ask about places and shops	Ask for a bank. *Is there a bank near here?* Yes, next to the newsagent's.
	4		Give exact locations	Is the bank opposite the newsagent's. *No, it's next to the newsagent's.*
	5		Give fixed times	Does the bus leave at five to, or five past, four? *It leaves at five past.*
	6		Ask about fixed times	Ask when the bus leaves. *Excuse me, but what time does the bus leave?*

Grammar focus	Active vocabulary and expressions			
	conference	*meeting*	*together*	
Past simple tense: verb *be* (singular and plural) – positive, negative and interrogative Past time adverbials: *yesterday, this morning,* etc. Preposition of place: *at* *It was* + adjective	*programme* *tourist*	*early* *fun* *interesting* *at* (+ place)	*How?* *must*	*this morning* *last night* *last week* *yesterday*
Want to + verbs *buy, get, go to* Countable and uncountable nouns with *a, an, some* Genitive ending *'s* with shops	*bank* *cassette* *money*	*newspaper* *postcard* *post office*	*shoe* *shop* *soap*	*stamp* *get* *toothpaste* *buy*
	stranger	*ask* *turn*	*left* *right*	*How funny!* *Thank you very much.*
There is (There's...) Is there...? Prepositions of place: *near, next to, opposite, on* Modal verb: *can* (possibility) Indefinite pronoun: *one* Imperative (infinitive without *to*): verb *turn* Adverbs: *left, right*	*bar* *camera* *flower* *video* *wine*	*next to* *opposite*		
	hurry	*now*		
Clock times: full, half, quarter hours + five minute intervals Prepositions of time: *to, past*	*clock* *o'clock*	*half* *quarter*	*past* *to*	*What time?*
Present simple tense: verbs *open, close, leave, arrive, start finish* – positive and interrogative Time adverbials: *in the morning/afternoon,* etc. Preposition of time: *at* Question words: *When?/What time?*	*bus* *football match* *plane* *train*	*arrive* *close* *finish*	*leave* *open* *start*	*When?* *at* (+ time) *in* (+ parts of the day)
	car *parcel* *flight*	*rent* *send* *book*(v)	*today* *after* *before*	*Bye.* *See you soon.*
	street			
	ice cream *restaurant*	*busy* *lovely*	*again* *quite*	
Quantifiers: *some, many, most* Prepositions of time: *after, before, until*	*some* *many* *most*	*until*		

Unit 6 Getting around

Students' Book pages 44, 45

Check homework from Unit 5.

Without referring to the book, introduce the past simple tense of the verb *to be* with a diary entry on the blackboard/OHP (this can be prepared in advance).

Fill in relevant details for yourself, for example, like this:

BLACKBOARD

	(Yesterday's date)	(Today's date)
Morning	Teachers' meeting	8-9 Library Class
Afternoon	Class	
Evening	Cinema with Sylvia	

Point to the different sections and say (for example):
This morning. I was in the library this morning.
Yesterday morning. I was at a meeting yesterday morning.
Yesterday afternoon. I was in class yesterday afternoon.
Yesterday evening. I was at the cinema yesterday evening with Sylvia.
Last night. I was at the cinema last night with Sylvia.

(Point out that *yesterday evening* and *last night* refer to the same time.)

Write the following substitution questions on the blackboard/OHP.

Where were you	*this morning?*
	yesterday morning?
	yesterday afternoon?
	yesterday evening/last night?

Ask individual students to ask you questions. Reply according to your 'diary'. Note the pronunciation of the weak form of *was*/wəz/ in positive sentences.

🎧 Dialogue: Part 1

Active words:	conference meeting together

Set 1 Past time

Active words and expressions:	programme tourist early fun interesting must this morning last night last week yesterday at (+place) How?

Exercise 1

Refer students to the pictures on page 45. Say where the people were, like this:
Diana was at a meeting this morning. She wasn't at the conference.
Vince was at the conference this morning. He wasn't at a meeting.
Joanne and Paul were in town this morning. They weren't at the conference.
The Japanese tourists were at the Japanese Embassy. They weren't (in town/Stratford)

Write these sentences on the blackboard. Then ask students to look at the grammar box at the beginning of Set 1. Practise all the questions and answers chorally. Students can now ask and answer about Diana, Vince and the other people.

Exercise 2

Practise the model exchange chorally. Students work in pairs: first they roleplay the different people in order to use the *Where were you...? I/we was/were...* exchange, and then they go on as shown in the example sentences to practise the 3rd person singular and plural forms.

Exercise 3

Present the words *interesting* and *fun* (see page vii for notes on the presentation of new vocabulary). Then work chorally T-S once or twice before students ask and answer in pairs about the various events.

Exercise 4

Ask individual students to ask you the questions S-T. Then choose one or two to ask questions to other students across the class. Then in pairs, students work through all the questions in turn. Ask students to write down sentences about themselves and their partners. Go round the class monitoring their work and helping with any vocabulary they need, e.g. *sports centre, stadium, at my friend's house,* etc. Do a final cross-check by asking random students to answer the questions T-S.

Students' Book pages 46, 47

Set 2 Shops and requirements

Active words:	bank cassette money newspaper postcard post office shoe shop soap stamp toothpaste buy get

Exercise 1

Establish the concept of countable and uncountable nouns by referring to things on your desk that you can count, e.g. *a pen, a book, a pencil, a newspaper*. Then refer to the illustrations and point out the relationship between *a* and *some* with *a stamp, some stamps, a postcard, some postcards, a cassette, some cassettes*. Indicate all the uncountable nouns in the illustrations with *some*, e.g. *some toothpaste, some soap, some money*. Then practise the model sentences in the language box chorally and individually. Go through the matching work with the whole class, asking students at random to provide sentences. They then work S-S choosing the items they want to get or buy. Check by asking one or two students to tell you what their partner wants.

Students write down what they and their partners want to buy.

Exercise 2

NOTES

a chemist's: the genitive apostrophe 's' *('s)* means *belongs to*. A *chemist's* (shop) means, literally, the shop of a chemist. This is sometimes called the possessive case, c.f. *Paul is Diana's assistant.* ◄
Most chemist's in Britain sell film and develop photographs as well as selling personal toilet items. They also sell pharmaceutical products over the counter and in most cases on a doctor's prescription.

a newsagent's: newsagent's in Britain sell sweets, cigarettes and stationery as well as newspapers and magazines. If you wish, newsagent's will deliver newspapers and magazines to your home. This is usually done by teenage boys and girls who are paid to deliver newspapers

Refer to the pictures of the shops and ask students to work in pairs matching the name of each shop with the picture of it.

For the second part of this exercise, ask three or four students to tell you where they want to go to buy/get the items listed in Exercise 1. Then ask students to write six sentences. Monitor the work as they write, helping where necessary.

KEY

(toothpaste)   *I want to go to a chemist's.*
(film)   *I want to go to a chemist's.*
(chocolates)   *I want to go to a newsagent's.*
(shoes)   *I want to go to a shoe shop.*
(cassette)   *I want to go to a record shop.*
(book about
  Britain)   *I want to go to a bookshop.*
(map)   *I want to go to a bookshop/a newsagent's.*
(money)   *I want to go to a bank.*
(postcard)   *I want to go to a newsagent's/bookshop.*
(newspaper)   *I want to go to a newsagent's.*
(soap)   *I want to go to a chemist's.*

Exercise 3

This can be done orally in class as indicated and then set as written homework.

KEY

Paul wants to go to a chemist's (to buy some toothpaste), to a newsagent's or a bookshop (to buy some postcards) and to a post office (to get/buy some stamps).

Diana wants to go to a bank (to get some money), to a bookshop or a newsagent's (to buy a map) and to a shoe shop (to buy some shoes).

NOTES

stamps: in Britain you can buy stamps only in post offices. However, many small newsagent's have part of their shops set aside as a post office which is operated according to post office opening and closing times. Hotels sometimes have stamps for sale but you cannot rely on this. When in Britain it's useful to remember that you cannot buy stamps at the same time as you buy your postcards

Set 3 Places: location (2)

(Note that this set comes before Dialogue: Part 2.)

Active words:	bar camera flower video wine next to opposite

Before playing the dialogue, work through the set exercises, 1–3. These establish ways of talking about locations with the prepositional phrase *next to* and the prepositions *opposite* and *near*. Refer students to the diagrammatic map showing the location of different places in a shopping centre.

Exercise 1

Students work in pairs identifying the shops as instructed.

Exercise 2

Establish the meaning of *opposite* and *next to* by using the students' seating arrangement in the classroom. Practise the model exchange chorally and then ask students to ask and answer about the various shops. Tell them to alternate their questions and answers. When they have finished, check by asking individual students random questions.

Exercise 3

Handle this exchange in the same way as in Exercise 2.

Ask students to write sentences to describe the location of four or five shops using *opposite* and *next to*.   43

Dialogue: Part 2

Active words and expressions:	stranger ask turn left right How funny! Thank you very much.

Set 3 (continued)
Exercise 4

Practise the model exchanges chorally. Do one example, (e.g. the newspaper) working S-T, then students work as directed asking and answering about the remaining items.

KEY

(a newspaper)	At the newsagent's. Turn right at the shoe shop and it's on your right.
(a cassette)	At the record shop. Turn right at the shoe shop and it's on your left next to the video shop.
(a book about London)	At the book shop. Turn left at the flower shop and it's on your right.
(a cup of tea and a sandwich)	At the café. Turn left at the flower shop and it's on your left.

Exercise 5

Students should spend a few minutes preparing this before starting the exercise. Choose three or four pairs of students to perform their conversation for the rest of the class.

Ask all the students to write out the conversations for homework.

SSR

S1: *Excuse me, is there a record shop near here?*
S2: *Yes, there's one next to the video shop.*
S1: *Thanks. Oh, and where can I get some stamps?*
S2: *At the post office. It's over there on the left, opposite the chemist's.*
S1: *Thank you very much.*
S2: *You're welcome.*

If there is a local shopping centre or city centre which all the students are familiar with and which can be shown as a sketch map, ask them, either in class or for homework, to draw a sketch map and to mark different shops. They can then roleplay giving real (simple) directions to visitors or write one or two short conversations with tourists/visitors.

Students' Book pages 48, 49

Set 4 Clock times

Active words and expressions:	clock o'clock half quarter past to What time?

Handle the teaching of clock times as a separate section and use it as preparation for the short Dialogue: Part 3.

The best aid to teach clock times is a large cardboard or plastic model clock with movable hands to show different clock times. These are usually available from any good suppliers of educational equipment to schools. If you cannot buy or borrow one, then it is worthwhile making one from card as it will be useful at other times.

Exercise 1
NOTE
a.m./p.m.
(ante meridian/
post meridian) Latin terms for *before noon* and *after noon* used on timetables using the 12 hour clock. They are not generally used in conversation. Although the 24 hour clock is used officially, spoken English seems to prefer using the 12 hour clock times.

Practise chorally the two ways of asking the time which are given in the box. Explain that they mean exactly the same and can be used interchangeably. Ask students to work S-T so that you can provide a model for saying all the different clock times. This page presenting clock times has been designed so that students can use it as a reference. The concept of clock times is essential here as preparation for the important language work involving fixed times and the use of the present simple tense in Set 5.

KEY
It's ten past five.
It's half past six. (six thirty)
It's ten to seven.
It's five past twelve.
It's quarter to five. (four forty-five)
It's five to ten.
It's quarter past seven. (seven fifteen)

Exercise 2

Work S-T to establish the stress on *to* and *past*. Then students work with the clock faces in pairs.

KEY
Is it six o'clock? No, it's half past.
Is it seven o'clock? No, it's ten to.
Is it twelve o'clock? No, it's five past.
Is it four o'clock? No, it's quarter to.
Is it ten o'clock? No, it's five to.
Is it seven o'clock? No, it's quarter past.

Dialogue: Part 3

Active words:	hurry now

Use this short dialogue exchange as an introduction to Set 5. Note the pronunciation difference between /ɪz/ in *closes* and /s/ in *starts*.

Set 5 Fixed times

Active words:	bus football match plane train arrive close finish leave open start at (+time) in (+parts of the day) When?

Exercise 1

Choose a student and conduct the following conversation with him/her.
T: *What's the time now?*
S: *It's...*
T: *Oh! I want to get some money. Is there a bank near here?*
S: *Yes, there's one...*
T: *Is it open now?*

(if 'Yes')	(if 'No')
S: *Yes, it is.*	S: *No, it isn't.*
T: *What time does it close?*	T: *What time does it open?*
S: *At...*	S: *At...*
T: *Thank you.*	T: *Thank you.*

BLACKBOARD

Write a sentence relating to your local area, like this:
The (name) bank on (name of street) opens at (time) a.m. and closes àt (time) p.m.

Ask the students to look at the sentence and then use the timetables to make similar statements about the different items and fixed times. Prompt the statements by saying: *Tell me about the film/bus,* etc.

Exercise 2

(NOTE: *When* cannot be used to ask the time; you must use *What time is it?* However, *When?* and *What time?* are interchangeable when asking about fixed times as here.)

Introduce the sentence *What time does the ... open/close/start/finish/arrive?* and practise chorally and individually, substituting *when* for *what time* occasionally to show their interchangeability here. Then ask the students to ask and answer the questions in pairs. Students write the sentences in class.

Exercise 3

Students write the note for the film in class and write notes for the other two for homework.

Extra practice

Collect a sample of newspaper advertisements for local concerts, pop/rock concerts, films and sports events for students to use in communicative tasks. (For notes on communicative tasks see General teaching procedures 10, page ix.) They can use the language in the following ways:
1. Suggest something to see/go to. *(Let's see...; I want to see...)*

2. Ask where it is. *(Where is...? name of event.)*
3. Say where it is. *(It's at... name of place.)*
4. Ask for the starting time. *(What time does it start?)*
5. Suggest a suitable time and place to meet. *(Let's meet at +time at +place.)*

They can roleplay the conversations in pairs and write a similar one for homework.

🔲 Open dialogue

Active words:	car parcel rent send today after Bye! See you soon.

SSR

VINCE:	Hi, there! How are you?
YOU:	*Very well, thank you, How are you?*
VINCE:	Fine, thanks. What time is it?
YOU:	*It's (twenty-past eleven).*
VINCE:	Is it? I want to send a parcel to the States. Is there a post office near here?
YOU:	*Yes, there's one in... opposite... next to...*
VINCE:	And where can I rent a car?
YOU:	*You can rent one at Avis.*
VINCE:	OK. What time does your class finish today?
YOU:	*It finishes at (twelve o'clock).*
VINCE:	What do you want to do after your class?
YOU:	*I want to get some... go... play...*
VINCE:	OK. See you soon. Bye!

Students' Book pages 50, 51

Roleplay

Active words:	flight book (v) before

SSR

For the flight to Edinburgh

STUDENT:	*Good morning. I want to go to Edinburgh. Is there a flight in the morning?*
TRAVEL AGENT:	*Yes, there is.*
STUDENT:	*Oh good. What time does it leave?*
TRAVEL AGENT:	*It leaves at 8.40/ twenty to nine.*
STUDENT:	*I see. And what time does it arrive?*
TRAVEL AGENT:	*It arrives in Edinburgh at 9.25/ twenty-five past nine.*
STUDENT:	*That's fine. (I want to be in Edinburgh before 10 o'clock.) Can you book me on that flight, please.*
TRAVEL AGENT:	*Yes (of course). The flight number is BE916.*
STUDENT:	*Thank you.*
TRAVEL AGENT:	*You're welcome.*

🔊 Listening

Active word:	street

TAPESCRIPT

Listen to this telephone conversation between Paul and a friend, Dave. As you listen, note down the answers to the questions in your books.

DAVE: 574 2457. Hello?

PAUL: Oh, hi, Dave. It's Paul here. Paul Roberts from Manchester.

DAVE: Oh hello! Are you in London?

PAUL: Yes, I'm here for a conference. Listen, are you doing anything tonight?

DAVE: No, nothing. Shall we meet? Go to a film or something?

PAUL: Yes, I want to go and see *New York, New York*.

DAVE: What's that?

PAUL: It's a musical.

DAVE: OK. What time is it on?

PAUL: Let's see . . . *(rustles newspaper)* the programme starts at 7.45 but the main film starts at 8.40.

DAVE: 8.40. OK. Well, let's meet at half past eight. Where is it on?

PAUL: It's on at the Odeon in Kensington High Street. Shall we meet outside?

DAVE: Fine. Do you want to eat afterwards? Because we can go to Pizzaland. It's right next to the cinema.

PAUL: OK. That sounds great. So I'll see you at 8.30 outside the Odeon in Kensington High Street.

DAVE: Right. See you then. Cheers!

PAUL: Bye!

KEY

New York, New York
7.45
8.40
the Odeon
Kensington High Street

Reading

Active words:	ice cream restaurant busy
	lovely again quite

A very good class can use this letter as a basis to roleplay a telephone conversation between Diana and James. Working together in pairs, students make the questions for which the relevant information is provided in the letter.

SSR

DIANA: *Hello, James.*

JAMES: *Hello, Diana. How are you?*

DIANA: *I'm fine. How are you and Delia?*

JAMES: *We're both very well. We miss you very much.*

DIANA: *Yes, and I miss you.*

JAMES: *How was the flight to London?*

DIANA: *Oh, it was fine.*

JAMES: *And what's the hotel like?*

DIANA: *Comfortable.*

JAMES: *And what about the conference?*

DIANA: *It's quite interesting, but I am very busy.*

JAMES: *Oh really?*

DIANA: *Yes, yesterday I was at a meeting with some Americans. The girl from CBS was very interesting. I want to meet her again. And I want to meet a director at the BBC. He wants to see our film.*

JAMES: *Oh good. Is there a good restaurant in the hotel?*

DIANA: *Well, there's a good one next to the hotel. You can get lovely ice cream there! Well, I must hurry. I want to get some money.*

JAMES: *See you soon. Bye!*

DIANA: *Lots of love to you and Delia. Bye!*

Writing

Active words:	some many most until

Students read the model paragraph before writing about their own country. This writing can be done as homework

Homework

Choose from:
1. Set 2 Exercise 3, page 46.
2. Set 3 Exercise 5, page 47.
3. Set 5 Exercise 3, page 49.
4. Writing, page 50.
5. Unit 6 Workbook exercises.

🔊 Oral exercises

1. Check people's movements

Were you at the conference this morning?
At the conference? No, I wasn't.
Were they at the hotel last night?
At the hotel? No, they weren't.

Now you go on in the same way.

Were you at the conference this morning?
At the conference? No, I wasn't.
Were they at the hotel last night.
At the hotel? No, they weren't.
Were they at the embassy yesterday?
At the embassy? No, they weren't.
Were you in town last night?
In town? No, I wasn't.
Was she with you this morning?
With me? No, she wasn't.
Were they at the meeting last week?
At the meeting? No, they weren't.

2. Say where places and shops are

Listen to this tourist.

Excuse me, but is there a bank near here?
Bank? Yes. There's one over there.

Now you are in town. You say where places and shops are.

Excuse me, but is there a bank near here?
Bank? Yes. There's one over there.
Excuse me, but is there a post office near here?
Post office? Yes. There's one over there.
Excuse me, but is there a restaurant near here?
Restaurant? Yes. There's one over there.
Excuse me, but is there a flower shop near here?
Flower shop? Yes. There's one over there.
Excuse me, but is there a book shop near here?
Book shop? Yes. There's one over there.
Excuse me, but is there a video shop near here?
Video shop? Yes. There's one over there.
Excuse me, is there a travel agent's near here?

3. Ask about places and shops

Listen to this conversation in a street.

Is there a bank near here?
Yes, next to the newsagent's.

Now you ask for places and shops.

Ask for a bank.
Is there a bank near here?
Yes, next to the newsagent's.
Ask for a shoe shop.
Is there a shoe shop near here?
Yes, next to the wine bar.
Ask for a book shop.
Is there a book shop near here?
Yes, next to the pizza bar.
Ask for a record shop.
Is there a record shop near here?
Yes, next to the video shop.
Ask for a café.
Is there a café near here?
Yes, next to the flower shop.
Ask for a cinema.
Is there a cinema near here?
Yes, next to the flower shop.

4. Give exact locations

Is the bank opposite the newsagent's?
No. It's next to the newsagent's.
Is the pizza bar next to the travel agent's?
No. It's opposite the travel agent's.

Now you give the exact locations.

Is the bank opposite the newsagent's?
No. It's next to the newsagent's.
Is the pizza bar next to the travel agent's?
No. It's opposite the travel agent's.
Is the cinema opposite the flower shop?
No. It's next to the flower shop.
Is the post office next to the chemist's?
No. It's opposite the chemist's.

Is the record shop opposite the video shop?
No. It's next to the video shop.
Is the flower shop next to the pizza bar?
No. It's opposite the pizza bar.
Oh, yes, so it is. I can see it now.
But hurry! The shops all close at 6.

5. Give fixed times

Does the bus leave at five to, or five past, four?
It leaves at five past.
Does the train arrive at ten past, or ten to, three?
It arrives at ten to.

Now you go on in the same way. Give the fixed times.

Does the bus leave at five to, or five past, four?
It leaves at five past.
Does the train arrive at ten past, or ten to, three?
It arrives at ten to.
Does the film start at twenty past, or half past, seven?
It starts at half past.
Does the match finish at five o'clock, or quarter to?
It finishes at quarter to.
Does the bank open at nine o'clock, or half past?
It opens at half past.
Does the shop close at half past five, or six?
It closes at six.

6. Ask about fixed times

Listen to this stranger in town.

Excuse me, but what time does the bus leave?
At half past ten.

Now you are the stranger. Ask about fixed times in the same way.

Ask when the bus leaves.
Excuse me, but what time does the bus leave?
At half past ten.
Ask when the Newcastle train arrives.
Excuse me, but what time does the Newcastle train arrive?
At five o'clock.
Ask when the main film starts.
Excuse me, but what time does the main film start?
At half past two.
Ask when the post office closes.
Excuse me, but what time does the post office close?
At half past five.
Ask when the match finishes.
Excuse me, but what time does the match finish?
At four o'clock.
Ask when the bank opens.
Excuse me, but what time does the bank open?
At half past nine.

Unit 7 Sunday in the park

Presentation and practice	Set title	Language use	Examples
Dialogue: Part 1			
Set 1	Present activities	Ask and talk about present activities	*What's he doing?* *He's doing yoga.* *What are they doing?* *They're sailing model boats.*
Dialogue: Part 2			
Set 2	Routines	Ask and talk about routines	*My wife goes jogging every morning.* *What time does she get up?*
Dialogue: Part 3			
Set 3	The family	Ask and talk about the family	*Have you got any children?* *I've got two sons and a daughter.*
Set 4	The weather	Ask and talk about the weather	*What's the weather like?* *It's quite hot.* *Isn't it a lovely day!*
Spoken transfer: Open dialogue		Combined	
Skills development: Listening	**Description** In monologues, a taxi driver and a police-woman talk about their daily routines. Students note down details of the routines in chart form.		
Reading	Photographs with captions: a Mexican family describe how they spend their Sunday.		
Writing	Students use guided paragraphs to write a composition about how they spend a typical Sunday–answers to groups of questions provide the information and the organisation.		
Oral exercises: 1		Explain present activities	What are you doing? Are you working? *No, I'm not working now.*
2		Talk about people's exercise routines	Is Michael jogging? *No, he isn't. He doesn't jog every day.*
3		Talk about people's routines	Vince starts work at 8. *No, he doesn't. He starts work at 8.30.*
4		Talk about your family (Open exercise)	I've got three sisters. What about you? *(I haven't got any sisters.)*
5		Talk about the weather	What's the weather like in Mexico now? *It's very hot.*

Grammar focus	Active vocabulary and expressions			
	boat exercises look at day park across			
Present continuous tense (singular and plural) – positive, negative and interrogative	*floor* *lie (down)* *a lot* *hour* *listen to* *song* *paint* *other(s)* *story* *stand up* *table* *think*			
	at the weekend *even*			
Present simple tense: verbs of daily routine Time adverbials: *every + day/morning*, etc., *at the weekend* Gerund (*-ing* form) after verb *go* Prepositions of time: *after, before, on* Zero article, e.g. go to *work/school/church*	*beer* *get up* *at work* *Monday* *breakfast* *go home* *every(day)* *Tuesday* *canteen* *go to bed* *on (+ days* *Wednesday* *church* *talk to* *of the week)* *Thursday* *lunch* *visit* *Friday* *pub* *Saturday* *supper* *Sunday*			
	look after *already* *outside* *only*			
Have got – positive, negative and interrogative *Any* in interrogative and negative sentences Possessive adjectives: *our, their*	*college* *father* *parent* *have got* *daughter* *husband* *son* *our* *family* *mother* *wife* *their*			
It's quite/very + adjective Exclamations with *Isn't it . . .!*	*rain* *cold* *awful* *snow* *hot* *beautiful* *weather* *warm* *terrible*			
	beach *along*			
	bicycle *city* *catch (bus)* *under* *bread* *fruit* *sleep* *then* *butter* *photograph*			

Unit 7 Sunday in the park

Students' Book pages 52, 53

Check homework from Unit 6.

🔘 Dialogue: Part 1

Active words:	boat day exercises park look at across

NOTES

the Park:	Hyde Park is a large, lozenge-shaped park in the centre of London, which provides an enjoyable recreational area for the city. Diana and Vince are at the Kensington end of Hyde Park which includes the Round Pond (see below)
work-out:	e.g. exercises
yoga:	a Hindu system of exercises
model boats:	the Round Pond, a small, circular lake at the Kensington end of Hyde Park is a favourite spot for people to sail model boats. Some of these boats are very ingeniously made and are a great attraction
Hey, that's neat!:	an American term of approval, c.f. *That's marvellous!/great!*

Set 1 Present activities

Active words:	floor hour song story table lie (down) listen to paint (v) stand up think a lot other(s)

Establish the idea that the present continuous tense is used to express *activities that are taking place at the present time*, (i.e. *Now*), by looking round the classroom and asking questions like:
What's Bruno doing? (He's looking out of the window.)
Where's Mario sitting? (He's sitting next to Paula.)
What's Isabel doing? (She's writing.)

Exercise 1

Refer to the picture on page 52. Point to the man and practise chorally the exchange: *What's he doing? He's doing yoga/exercises.*

Then point to the people near the lake and practise: *What are they doing? They're sailing model boats./ They're sitting down./They're watching the boy.*

Ask questions about all the pictures for students to answer chorally or individually. Students then ask and answer about the pictures in pairs.

Exercise 2

Refer to the picture of the children in the Free Activity Hour. Build up the relevant verbs on the blackboard. (For teaching vocabulary, see General teaching procedures page vii.)

BLACKBOARD

do	play	stand up
lie	read	watch
listen to	sit	write
paint		

Ask the students to copy the verbs in their notebooks in a column. Read the text aloud, while the students look at the picture. Point to various children and ask the whole class, *What's this boy doing? (He's reading). What are these girls doing? They're painting.* Ask the students to work in pairs, each choosing a different child to ask about.

Refer students to their list of verbs and ask them to write a similar list of the verbs in the *-ing* form. Note the spelling of *sitting, lying, writing.* (See spelling rules in the teacher's notes for Unit 4 Set 2.)

Exercise 3

Write a table of short form answers on the blackboard, like this:

BLACKBOARD

Yes,	she he	is.	No,	she he	isn't.
Yes,	they	are.	No,	they	aren't.

Refer back to the picture of the children and tell the students that you want them to ask and answer in the same way about the children's activities.

Ask the students to look at the main picture of the activities in the park. Ask questions:

Are Diana and Vince in the picture?	*No, they aren't.*
Are the boy and girl sitting?	*No, they aren't.*
Are they carrying boats?	*Yes, they are.*
Is the boy running?	*No, he isn't.*
Who else can you see in the picture? What are they doing?	

Students' Book pages 54, 55

🔘 Dialogue: Part 2

Active words and expressions:	at the weekend even

50

Set 2 Routines

Active words and expressions:	beer breakfast canteen church lunch pub supper get up go home go to bed talk to visit at work every (day) on (+days of the week) Monday Tuesday Wednesday Thursday Friday Saturday Sunday

BLACKBOARD

On the blackboard/OHP transparency prepare a chart showing your own daily routine, like this:

```
My daily routine
6.30  I get up.
7.15  I have breakfast.
7.45  I go to work/college/class.
8.30  I start work./I leave home./I arrive at school. etc.
1.30  I go home.
2.00  I have lunch.
```

The times will obviously vary according to people's different work schedules.

Ask students to make a similar chart about their own daily routines. Then ask individual students questions from the following table.

BLACKBOARD

What time When	do you	get up? have breakfast? leave home? start school/work? go home? have supper? go to bed?

Students then ask and answer in pairs about each other's routines. If necessary, introduce *usually* (which will be taken up in Unit 8 Set 1).

Exercise 1

Students work in pairs matching the right caption with the right picture.

Students write linked sentences in a paragraph. Check their work orally by asking random questions about the different times in Kelly Hall's daily routine.

SSR

A day in the life of Mrs Kelly Hall
Kelly Hall gets up at six o'clock in the morning and goes jogging at half past six. She has breakfast with the family at half past seven and goes to work at quarter past eight. She finishes work at half past four and goes home. She

makes supper for the children at half past six. After supper she studies.

Exercise 2

Students work S-S asking and answering the questions printed in the book.

Exercise 3

Refer back to the chart you have made on the blackboard/OHP showing the question form after *What time/When?* with the present simple tense. Now add the 3rd person singular:

BLACKBOARD

What time When	do does	you Vince Diana he she	get up?

Work T-S1, S2, S3, etc. asking questions about Vince. Students give answers from the information in the chart. Ask students to work in pairs asking alternately about the four people. Students write about Vince and one other person in class and about their own routine for homework.

SSR

Vince gets up at seven o'clock (7.00 a.m.) and starts work at half past eight (8.30 a.m.). He has lunch in a restaurant. He finishes work at seven o'clock (7.00 p.m.). After supper he reads the newspaper and watches TV. He goes to bed at eleven o'clock (11.00 p.m.).

Exercise 4

Say the days of the week and ask students to repeat them chorally. Their pronunciation is:
/ˈmʌndi/, /ˈtjuːzdi/, /ˈwenzdi/, /ˈθɜːzdi/, /ˈfraɪdi/, /ˈsætədi/, /ˈsʌndi/.

Practise them with a short quiz, like this: *What's the day before Friday? What's the day after Monday?* Write up the following substitution table:

BLACKBOARD

What	do you does he/ she	do on	Monday Tuesday Wednesday Thursday Friday Saturday Sunday	morning? afternoon? evening?

You take the part of Diana and Vince. Students ask questions and you answer according to the sentences printed in the book, e.g. *What do you do on Tuesday evening? On Tuesday evening I go to French class.*

Tell students to copy the diary layout into their notebooks and fill it in according to the sentences about Diana and Vince, e.g. *Tuesday p.m. – go to French class.*

Then work T-S1, S2, S3, etc. asking about the two people, e.g. *What does Diana do on Tuesday evening? (She goes to a French class.)* If necessary, introduce the word *nothing*.

Exercise 5

Ask students to prepare a similar diary for themselves. They ask and answer in pairs about the special things they do during the week. Ask several to tell the rest of the class what they do. (You may need to help with special words and phrases.)

Students' Book pages 56, 57

🔘 **Dialogue: Part 3**

Active words:	look after already only outside

NOTES

kids: colloquial for children
High School: c.f. upper secondary school
UCLA: University of California and Los Angeles in Los Angeles
pub: short for public house. A place which sells alcoholic drink and food. Pubs in Britain are only open for certain periods of the day. These times can vary, but they are usually 10.30 a.m. – 2.30 or 3.00 p.m. and from 5.30 p.m. – to 10.30 or 11.00 p.m. These are called 'licensing hours'.

Set 3 The family

Active words:	college daughter family father husband mother parent son wife have got our their

Exercise 1

Read the sentences in the language box then refer students to the family tree showing the relationships within Vince's family. Read the sentences which describe the relationships and ask students to repeat the words in italics chorally and individually. Draw attention to the two possessive adjectives *our* and *their*. Ask individual students to tell you about Paul's family in the same way. Students write full sentences about Paul's family.

Exercise 2

Refer students to the first and last sentences in the box at the beginning of the set. Practise chorally and individually. Then ask one of them to ask you (in the role of Kelly) if you have got any children. Point out the use of *any* with plural nouns in questions and negative questions. Students work in pairs taking different roles as instructed in the sentences.

KEY

Kelly: *Yes, I've/we've got three children/kids.*
Brad: *Yes, I've got one/a sister and one/a brother.*
Frank: *Yes, I've got three children.*
Carrie: *I've got two brothers but I haven't got any sisters.*
Paul: *I've got two sisters but I haven't got any brothers.*

Exercise 3

Ask students to make their own family trees similar to those shown in Exercise 1. Then ask them to use their trees to talk about their families. Ask random questions to one or two students.

Students write about their families either at home or in class.

Set 4 The weather

Active words:	rain snow weather awful beautiful terrible cold hot warm

Exercise 1

Practise the sentences in the box and establish the meaning of the words to describe the weather. Ask one student to ask you about Picture 1 and give the answer, *It's very warm/quite warm/very nice/beautiful/a lovely day.* Ask the students to work in pairs, alternating the question and answer.

Ask students to write captions describing the weather for each picture.

KEY

1. *It's very warm./It's very nice./It's quite warm/hot.*
2. *It's very hot.*
3. *It's raining.*
4. *It's snowing. It's very cold.*

Exercise 2

Practise the models in the box chorally to establish the falling intonation on the last word, e.g. *Isn't it a lovely day? Isn't it warm?* Then practise once or twice with individual students before setting them to work in pairs.

Ask students to make comments about the weather today and yesterday with questions, *What's the weather like today? What was the weather like yesterday/last week?*

🔘 Open dialogue

Active words:	beach along

NOTES

It is?: British English would tend to invert and say *Is it?*

Is that so?: American English for *Really?*

SSR

KELLY: Hi! It's really hot here. What's your weather like?

YOU: *It's quite/very cold, etc. It's beautiful/awful, etc.*

KELLY: It is? And where are you now? What are you doing?

YOU: *I'm in Class ... at ... school/college and I'm learning English.*

KELLY: Really? What's your routine like now? Do you get up early every day?

YOU: *Yes, I do./No, I don't. I get up at ...*

KELLY: Is that so? What time do you go to bed?

YOU: *I go to bed at ...*

KELLY: I like walking along the beach at Santa Monica on Sundays. What do you like doing?

YOU: *I like ... ing and ... ing.*

KELLY: Well, enjoy your lesson. Bye!

YOU: *Bye!/Goodbye.*

Students' Book pages 58, 59

🔘 Listening

Use the verbs in the chart to revise questions like, *What time do you get up? What time do you start school/work?* etc. This will guide students towards the information they have to listen for and fill in. Ask them to copy the chart into their notebooks. Remind them to leave plenty of space for each piece of information.

TAPESCRIPT

Listen to Terry and Veronica talking about their daily routines. Fill in the missing information.

I'm a taxi driver. I work at London Airport out at Heathrow. I always work the early morning shift. I usually get up very early, at 5 o'clock. It's OK in the summer, but it's awful in the winter when the weather's cold. I start work at 5.45. Lunch? Well, I have a very early lunch at 11.30. You get very hungry driving a taxi. I finish work at 3 p.m. Then I go home. My wife works too. She works in a supermarket. I get home first so I make the supper. We both work hard and so we don't go out much. After supper we watch TV.

On Friday nights we go dancing. No, not disco or anything like that. Real dancing! Ballroom dancing. It's really good. On Sunday we play golf.

I'm a policewoman. I work in Central London around the Covent Garden area. At the moment I work on the night shift. It's tiring. I don't work every week on nights. On the night shift I get up about 5 in the evening. I read the paper, have something to eat, tidy up a bit in the flat and then go to work. I start at 8. Have my 'lunch' in the police canteen at 3 a.m. That's when you're sleeping! I finish my shift at 7.30. Well, my supper is your breakfast. And after supper I go straight to bed. It's difficult to sleep in the daytime. You try it!

On Friday night, if I'm not working, I relax and go out with my boyfriend. On Saturday night it's usually very busy because of the football fans. On Sunday I work—unfortunately.

KEY

	TERRY a taxi driver	VERONICA a policewoman
get up	*5 a.m.*	*5 p.m.*
start work	*5.45 a.m.*	*8 p.m.*
lunch	*11.30 a.m.*	*3 a.m.*
finish work	*3 p.m.*	*7.30 a.m.*
after supper	*watch TV*	*go to bed*
Friday night	*go ballroom dancing*	*relax, go out with boyfriend*
Sunday	*play golf*	*work*

Ask if anyone knows a taxi driver or a police officer. If so, ask them to tell the class about their daily routines.

Reading

Active words:	bicycle bread butter city fruit photograph catch (bus) sleep under then

NOTES

Chapultepec Park /tʃ ə'pʊltəpek/ a large public park in the centre of Mexico City. The pictures show some of the many activities people can do there

Ask students the following questions about the pictures:
Who are in the pictures?
How old do you think the children are?
What are they doing?
What's the weather like?
What time of day do you think it is?
Where can you go boating/riding near here?

Students read the text in pairs and correct the statements which follow. Students can write correct sentences for homework. Tell them to write full sentences (see Key of written version below).

KEY

Oral version	Written version
1. *No, they don't. They get up early.*	1. *They don't get up late. They get up early.*
2. *No, they don't. They have a small breakfast.*	2. *They don't have a big breakfast on Sunday. They only have coffee and bread and butter.*
3. *No, they don't. They go to church.*	3. *They don't go straight to the park. They go to church.*
4. *No, it isn't. The park is in the centre.*	4. *The park isn't outside the city. It is in the centre.*
5. *No, they don't. They have lunch under the trees.*	5. *The family don't have lunch on the lake. They have lunch under the trees.*
6. *No, they don't. They play with their kites. The father sleeps after lunch.*	6. *The children don't sleep in the afternoon. They play with their kites.*
7. *No, she doesn't. She likes riding in a little goat cart.*	7. *Baby Bianca doesn't like riding a bicycle. She likes riding in a little goat cart.*
8. *No, they don't. They have fruit or ice cream at five o'clock in the park.*	8. *They don't have fruit and ice cream for supper. They have fruit or ice cream at five o'clock.*
9. *No, they don't. They go to bed early on Sunday.*	9. *They don't go to bed late on Sunday night. They usually go to bed early.*

(Note that the reading text will be used to practise past time in Unit 13 page 106.)

Writing

Ask the students to ask and answer the questions in pairs before they start writing.

Ask them to make notes about their own answers and group them according to the paragraph organisation suggested in the SB. Ask them to write the complete paragraphs as homework. They can start this in class.

Homework

Choose from:
1 Set 2 Exercise 3, page 55.
2 Set 3 Exercise 3, page 56.
3 Reading: Correct these statements, page 58.
4 Writing, page 58.
54 5 Unit 7 Workbook exercises.

▣ Oral exercises

1. Explain present activities

Listen to these two people talking on the telephone.

What are you doing? Are you working?
No, I'm not working now.

Now you go on and explain what you are doing.

What are you doing? Are you working?
No, I'm not working now.
What are you doing? Are you reading?
No, I'm not reading now.
What are you doing? Are you studying?
No, I'm not studying now.
What are you doing? Are you listening to the radio?
No, I'm not listening to the radio now.
What are you doing? Are you watching television?
No, I'm not watching television now.
What are you doing? Are you playing with the children?
No, I'm not playing with the children now.
Good. Well, let's have a nice long talk ...

2. Talk about people's exercise routines

Listen to these people. They are sitting in the garden.

Is Michael jogging?
No, he isn't. He doesn't jog every day.

Now you talk about people's exercise routines.

Is Michael jogging?
No, he isn't. He doesn't jog every day.
Is Sandra playing tennis?
No, she isn't. She doesn't play tennis every day.
Is Keith playing football?
No, he isn't. He doesn't play football every day.
Is Anna doing yoga?
No, she isn't. She doesn't do yoga every day.
Is Helen swimming?
No, she isn't. She doesn't swim every day.
Is Martin running round the park?
No, he isn't. He doesn't run round the park every day.
Really? Does he run round the park at night?

3. Talk about people's routines

Look at the chart on page 55. Listen to this example.

Vince starts work at 8.
No, he doesn't. He starts work at 8.30.

Now you give the correct information from the chart.

Vince starts work at 8.
No, he doesn't. He starts work at 8.30.
Diana has lunch in a restaurant.
No, she doesn't. She has lunch in the canteen or at home.
Joanne goes to bed at 10.
No, she doesn't. She goes to bed at 11 or 12.
Paul gets up at 6 o'clock.
No, he doesn't. He gets up at 8 o'clock.
Vince reads the newspaper at breakfast.
No, he doesn't. He reads the newspaper after supper.
Joanne watches TV after supper.
No, she doesn't. She goes to see some friends.

4. Talk about your family (Open exercise)

I've got three sisters. What about you?
I haven't got any sisters.

Now you talk about your family. And pets – if you've got any.

I've got three sisters. What about you?
. . . .
I've got two brothers. What about you?
. . . .
I've got five children. What about you?
. . . .
I've got a sister and a brother. What about you?
. . . .
I've got a cat. What about you?
. . . .
I've got a dog. What about you?
. . . .

5. Talk about the weather

What's the weather like in Mexico now?
It's very hot.

Now you talk about the weather in the same way.

What's the weather like in Mexico now?
It's very hot.
What's the weather like in London now?
It's raining.
What's the weather like in Madrid now?
It's quite nice.
What's the weather like in New York now?
It's very warm.
What's the weather like in Oslo now?
It's quite cold.
What's the weather like in Paris now?
It's lovely.
Really? Let's go there then. I love Paris. *(sings)*

Unit 8 At the Kennedy's

Presentation and practice	Set title	Language use	Examples
Dialogue: Part 1			
Set 1	Journeys	Ask and say how people get to work Ask and say how far away places are Ask and say how long journeys take Ask and say how often you do things	*How do you get to work?* *I go by bus.* *How far is it to work?* *It's about 8 kilometres.* *How long does it take?* *It takes about twenty minutes.* *Do you ever cycle to work?* *Yes, often.* *How often do you go out?* *About twice/three times a week.*
Dialogue: Part 2			
Set 2	Food and drink	Offer, accept or refuse food and drink Ask about, state and make a choice of food and drink	*Would you like some salad?* *Yes, please./No, thank you.* *What is there? There's salad.* *What sort of salad would you like?* *I'd like a green salad, please.*
Spoken transfer: Open dialogue Roleplay		Choose and order food Choose and order food and drink	
Dialogue: Part 3			
Set 3	House and home	Ask and talk about the rooms of a house Ask and talk about colours	*How many floors are there?* *Where's the study? It's in the basement.* *There's a big kitchen on the ground floor.* *What colour is the bathroom?* *It's green.*
Skills development: Reading	**Description** A letter from a British student spending a study year in Paris. He writes to a college friend back home.		
Writing	Students write a letter to a friend describing the hotel where they are staying in London. They answer questions linked to the organisation of the paragraphs, and use the Tower Hotel as the source of information.		
Listening	A local inhabitant of Brighton talks about the Brighton Pavilion. Students note down the rooms she mentions.		
Oral exercises: 1		Ask about rooms	You want to find the bathroom. *Is this the bathroom?*
2		Talk about journeys	How far is it to work, Doug? *It's about 3 miles. It takes me twenty minutes.*
3		Answer about your routine (Open exercise)	Are you ever late for work? *(Yes, sometimes.)* Do you ever take a taxi? *(No, never.)*
4		Answer about your life (Open exercise)	How often do you get up before seven? *(About once a week.)*
5		Offer a choice of food and drink	I'd like some salad. *Would you like some green salad or some tomato salad?*

56

Grammar focus	Active vocabulary and expressions		
	lazy	*lucky*	*far*
Present simple tense: verbs *take, go, get* Question words: *How? (How far? How long? How often?)* Adverbs of frequency *By* + means of transport *Every* + *day, week, month* *(About) once/twice a month* Question: *Do you/Are you ever . . .?*	*journey* *minute* *month* *underground* *year* *get (to work)* *take (a taxi)* *take (+ time)* *travel*	*abroad* *always* *ever* *never* *often* *on holiday* *once* *sometimes* *three times* *twice* *usually*	*How far?* *How long?* *How often?*
Modal verb: *would (What sort of . . . would you like?)* *I'd like . . .* Question word: *What sort?* *Would you like* + zero article/*a/an/some* + noun?	*fish* *meat* *sort* *vegetable*	*eat* *look*	*each*
			Cheers! *Happy birthday!* *What about you?*
	hungry *thirsty*		
	next		
Question words: *How many? (How many . . . are there?)* *There is/isn't/are/aren't . . .* Pronouns: *one, another* Question word: *What colour?*	*bathroom* *bedroom* *door* *floor* (= *storey*) *garden* *ground (floor)*	*hall* *kitchen* *sitting room* *stairs* *study* *toilet*	*blue* *brown* *green* *red* *yellow*	*first* *second* *top (floor)* *altogether* *another*
	country (opp. *town*) *river* *window*		*cheap* *different* *easy*

Unit 8 At the Kennedy's

Students' Book pages 60, 61

Check homework from Unit 7.

🔘 Dialogue: Part 1

> **Active words:**   lazy lucky far

NOTES

Doug and Liz: Douglas (pronounced /ˈdʌɡləs/) Kennedy is a director for BBC television. He also buys suitable films from independent film producers (e.g. Focus Film and Video). Diana hopes that she will be able to sell one of her films to the BBC for showing on one of their channels—BBC 1 and BBC 2. ITV and Channel 4 are the two commercial TV channels in Britain

Kensington: an attractive commercial and residential area of West London

Set 1 Journeys

> **Active words and expressions:**   journey minute month underground year get (to work) take (a taxi) take (+ *time*) travel abroad always ever never often on holiday once sometimes three times twice usually How far? How long? How often?

Exercise 1

Practise the sentences in the box and establish the meaning of *underground*.

Ask one of the students to ask you the question: *How do you get to work?* and write the answer on the board. Do the same with the other two questions in the box. Then work with one student T-S with you taking the part of Doug.

Ask students to work in pairs with the chart (starting with Doug) taking alternate roles so that they practise both questions and answers.

Exercise 2

Read out the example sentences yourself and ask students to repeat. Choose individual students to talk about the other three people.

As instructed, students write sentences about the other three people either in class or at home.

Exercise 3

Students ask and answer in pairs. They write sentences about each other's journey to work as in the example in Exercise 2.

Exercise 4

Establish the meaning of the different adverbs of frequency: *always, usually, often, sometimes, never,* giving different examples of your own routine. Relate your sentences to the diagrams in the SB. Point out the position of the adverb *before* the main verb, but *after* the verb *to be* (and other auxiliaries not presented here).

EXAMPLES

I always get up at .../have a cup of ... for breakfast, etc.
I usually leave home at .../travel by ...
I often go for a run before breakfast./I am often late, etc.
I sometimes drive my car/take a taxi to school/work, etc.
I never watch TV before nine o'clock.

Note that *ever* occurs in questions which imply infrequency.

Ask students to write similar sentences using each of the adverbs illustrated diagrammatically. Allow plenty of time for this. Help with new words and phrases. Collect two examples of each adverb from individual students by asking, *Tell me something you always do, Tancredi.* The student replies in the 1st person and you write the sentence in the 3rd person on the blackboard. Ask students to look at the information about Doug in the chart. Read the exchanges that concern Doug aloud and ask students to practise the short answers chorally, e.g. *Yes, usually.* Students work in pairs asking and answering; they change parts. Check by asking students real questions at random, like this:

Enrico, are you ever late for class?
Marta, do you ever play tennis?

Following the model, students write sentences about each of the characters and themselves either in class or for homework.

Exercise 5

Explain *month* and *year*. Present and practise the questions and answers in the box chorally. Ask individual students to ask you the questions underneath the box one by one. Students work freely in pairs noting down their partner's answers. Check two or three at the end, and ask them to work out sentences about themselves and/or their partners for homework.

Students' Book pages 62, 63

Set 2 Food and drink

🔘 Dialogue: Part 2

Active words:	fish meat sort vegetable
	eat look each

NOTES:

the menu:	this is an American style menu
salads for your first course:	it is the custom in America for restaurants to have a *salad bar* offering a wide choice of salads. These are offered as the first part (course) of a meal. The salad bar is usually self-service, the remaining courses are served. Here, the whole meal is self-service. The food is served from a buffet and customers can eat as much as they like.
dressings:	American restaurants and self-service cafeterias always offer a choice of dressing to accompany salads. Either the waiter/waitress will offer you the choice or you help yourself. Many restaurants in Britain now copy this American style. French and Italian dressings are made of a mixture of olive oil, vinegar and herbs. Blue cheese dressing is a mixture of blue cheese and mayonnaise. (Blue cheese has a strong, salty taste.)

Go through the menu using the illustrations to establish the meaning of each item of food. Monolingual classes can translate these or find an appropriate equivalent.

Work through the first conversational exchange T-S, asking *Would you like a salad?* etc. Then ask the students to ask and answer a few times. Do the same with the second conversational exchange before setting the students to work in pairs.

Note that in British restaurants, salads are usually served as individual portions. You ask for a *green salad* or a *tomato salad,* etc. In people's homes, salads are served in large bowls so you say *Would you like some salad?* or *Would you like salad?*

🔘 Open dialogue

Active words and expressions:	Cheers! Happy birthday!
	What about you?

NOTES

What about you?:	in this context means *What would you like to eat and drink?*
Cheers!:	this is a salutation offered to companions before you drink

The setting is a birthday celebration, and (in order to practise) students should accept the offers of food. Their chance for refusing comes in the freer roleplay.

SSR

FRIEND:	Would you like a salad for your first course?
YOU:	*Yes, please.*
FRIEND:	What sort would you like?
YOU:	*What is there?*
FRIEND:	There's green salad, tomato salad, red bean salad and potato salad.
YOU:	*I'd like ... and ... salad, please.*
FRIEND:	Would you like some dressing with it?
YOU:	*No, thank you./Yes, please, I'd like some (Blue Cheese dressing).*
FRIEND:	What about the second course? What would you like?
YOU:	*I'd like ...*
FRIEND:	Would you like roast or boiled potatoes with it?
YOU:	*I'd like .... potatoes, please.*
FRIEND:	And what sort of vegetables would you like?
YOU:	*I'd like some beans and peas.*
FRIEND:	Fine. And to drink?
YOU:	*What is there?*
FRIEND:	There's red or white wine, beer, lager, coke or mineral water.
YOU:	*I'd like ....*
FRIEND:	Mmm. That chicken was delicious. I think I'd like a dessert now. What is there?
YOU:	*There's vanilla or chocolate ice cream, fresh fruit salad and apple pie.*
FRIEND:	I'd like apple pie. What about you?
YOU:	*I think I'd like ...*
FRIEND:	Well, cheers! And happy birthday!

Roleplay

Active words:	hungry thirsty

Divide the class into groups of four. If class numbers are not divisible in this way, make smaller groups and ask students to combine parts where necessary. Establish that everyone understands what *to have a good meal, to be on a diet, vegetarian, hungry* and *thirsty* mean. Ask students in each group to choose the parts they want to be.

Refer them to the menu and ask them to order a meal. Ask them to do this two or three times, changing their roles each time. They have to choose food and drink according to the roles they have chosen.

Ask one group to perform their roleplay for the class.

Students' Book pages 64, 65

Set 3 House and home

🔊 **Dialogue: Part 3**

Active words:	bathroom bedroom door floor (=storey) garden ground (floor) hall kitchen sitting room stairs study toilet blue brown green red yellow first next second top (floor) altogether another

As students listen to the dialogue, they refer to the plan of the Kennedy's house.

NOTES

ground floor: in Britain the ground floor is the floor at the ground level. The next floor is the first floor and so on. Rooms beneath the ground floor are called the basement. The Kennedy's have a small study beneath ground level in the basement. (Note the two meanings of *floor,* i.e. the surface of a room and the storey of a house)

study: Liz and Doug are both professional people and have a room each which they use as a sort of office

patio: a small, paved area outside the house

Exercise 1

Practise the exchange in the box chorally and then ask the students to work in pairs.

KEY

There are three bedrooms, two studies, two bathrooms, and two toilets (W.C.'s). There are eight rooms apart from the hall, the bathrooms and toilets.

Exercise 2

Practise the exchanges S-T and T-S first, then ask students to work in pairs.

GAME

Hide and Seek in the house.
One person chooses to 'hide' in a certain room of the house. Others find out the room by asking *yes/no* questions like: *Are you in the bathroom on the second floor? Are you in the study in the basement?* This can be played in pairs, groups or with the whole class.

Exercise 3

Establish the colour words by using the colour spectrum in the illustration. Use classroom objects, furnishings and students' clothes to ask and answer questions about

colour before setting the students to work in pairs talking about rooms in the Kennedy's house. Ask random check questions to monitor students' performance. For extra work on colours, use the flags in Unit 2, page 15.

Exercise 4

This can be done in class or for homework. Students follow the model sentence and the instructions.

Writing

This can be started in class and finished for homework.

Students' Book pages 66, 67

Reading

Active words:	country (opp. town) river window cheap different easy

NOTES

all the best: an informal salutation to close a letter

Students can work in pairs reading and answering the multiple choice comprehension questions. These can be done orally *after* students have worked through them, e.g. *Where is Gavin studying? (In Paris.) Is he living in the country? (No, he isn't.) Is he living in the centre of Paris? (Yes, he is.)*

KEY

1. *b*) 2. *c*) 3. *a*) 4. *a*) 5. *b*) 6. *a*)
Discuss the options with the students if necessary.

Writing

NOTES

West End: the West End of London, where the main shops, cinemas and theatres are centred

Go through the questions orally with the whole class, asking individual students to answer the questions. Ask them to work on their own and make notes to the questions. Tell them to refer back through the earlier units to find their information. The finished writing task can be done as homework.

🔊 **Listening**

Introduce and explain the following words: *banquet, salon (=sitting room)* and *octagonal.*

TAPESCRIPT

What did you think of the Brighton Pavilion?

Well, I thought it was very, very beautiful and interesting, too, as well. The views from the windows were quite impressive because it's quite close to the sea, and the rooms at the back of the building overlook a rather beautiful park and you can see the stable, the Indian-style stable, from the windows.

Which room impressed you most?

I think it was the banqueting hall. Erm ... In the centre of the banqueting hall there is a beautiful chandelier that's suspended from the ceiling in the ... either the jaws or the claws of a large red and green and yellow dragon. So that was extremely impressive. The kitchen, too, was interesting. There were the original pots and pans – still in their place and you saw a spit working. Erm ... I think, too, that ... er, the salon was interesting. A beautiful, rather pretty room in fact, where the family were able to withdraw and be private and alone and away from the rest of the court.

What about the king's bedroom?

Ah yes. That was rather dark and sombre and I didn't particularly like that room or his suite of rooms. They probably reflected his age because by the time they were designed he was well into his fifties, sixties and I suspect that's why they were rather stately.

Was there any other room that you particularly liked?

Yes, I liked the octagonal room where – which was used for receptions and for meeting his court, and also the music room which was extremely beautiful, but unfortunately it's been damaged by fire ... er, in about 1975.

KEY

banqueting hall; kitchen; salon; king's bedroom; octagonal room; music room

Homework

Choose from:
1. Set 1 Exercises 2, 3 and 5, page 61.
2. Set 3 Exercise 4, page 65.
3. Writing, page 66.
4. Unit 8 Workbook exercises.

⊙⊙ Oral exercises

1. Ask about rooms

You are in a friend's house or flat. You want to find the bathroom.
Is this the bathroom?
No, the bathroom's over there.

Now you ask about the rooms.

Ask about the bathroom.
Is this the bathroom?
No, the bathroom's over there.
Ask about the toilet.
Is this the toilet?
Yes, that's right.
Ask about the kitchen.
Is this the kitchen?
Yes, it is.

Ask about the bedroom.
Is this the bedroom?
No, it's the next one.
Ask about the dining room.
Is this the dining room?
No, it's next to the sitting room.
Ask about the sitting room.
Is this the sitting room?
That's right. Come and join the others.

2. Talk about journeys

Diana is talking to Doug.

How far is it to work, Doug?
It's about 3 miles. It takes me twenty minutes.

Now you answer in the same way about the journeys.

How far is it to work, Doug?
It's about 3 miles. It takes me twenty minutes.
How far is it to work, Liz?
It's about 2 miles. It takes me 25 minutes.
How far is it to work, Paul?
It's about 5 miles. It takes me 10 minutes.
How far is it to work, Diana?
It's about a mile. It takes me 15 minutes.
How far is it to work, Vince?
It's about 10 miles. It takes me 45 minutes.
How far is it to work, Joanne?
It's about half a mile. It takes me 5 minutes.
And what about you? How far is it from where you live?
. . . .
And how long does it take you?
. . . .

3. Answer about your routine (Open exercise)

Are you ever late for work?
Yes, sometimes.
Do you ever take a taxi?
No, never.

Now you answer about your routine.

Are you ever late for work or school?
. . . .
Do you ever take a taxi?
. . . .
Do you ever walk to work or school?
. . . .
Do you ever work at weekends?
. . . .
Do you ever go home for lunch?
. . . .
Do you ever travel in your job?
. . . .

4. Answer about your life (Open exercise)

How often do you get up before seven?
About once a week.

Now you answer Tim's questions about your life.

How often do you get up before seven?
. . . .

61

How often do you go to bed after midnight?

. . . .

How often do you watch TV?

. . . .

How often do you go to a concert?

. . . .

How often do you buy a new record?

. . . .

5. Offer a choice of food and drink

Diana and Paul are having lunch at the Kennedy's.

DOUG: Now Diana, what about you? What would you like?
DIANA: I'd like some salad.
DOUG: *Would you like some green salad or some tomato salad?*
DIANA: Some green salad, please.

Now you offer food and drink to your guests in the same way.

I'd like some salad.
Would you like some green salad or some tomato salad?
Some green salad, please.
I'd like some dressing
Would you like some French or Italian dressing?
French dressing, please.
I'd like some meat.
Would you like some beef or chicken?
I'd like some beef, please.
I'd like some vegetables.
Would you like some beans or peas?
I'd like some beans, please.
I'd like some wine.
Would you like some white or red wine?
I'd like some white wine, please.

DOUG: Here you are.
PAUL: Thank you.
DOUG: Well, everybody, Enjoy your meal.

Unit 9 An evening out

Presentation and practice		Set title	Language use	Examples
Dialogue:	Part 1			
	Set 1	Telephoning	Talk on the telephone	*Is that Judy?* *Yes, speaking.* *It's Diana Trent here.* *Can I speak to Judy, please?* *I'm afraid she's out.* *Can I take a message?*
Dialogue:	Part 2			
	Set 2	Months and dates	Ask and talk about months, seasons and dates	*My birthday is on January 6th.* *Which months are hot in your country?*
Dialogue:	Part 3			
	Set 3	Invitations	Make an arrangement Invite people to do things Accept invitations	*Are you free on Saturday?* *No, I'm afraid I'm not.* *Would you like to go out?* *Yes, I'd love to.*
	Set 4	Suggestions	Ask for and make suggestions	*Shall we go to the cinema?* *OK. Which film shall we see?* *Let's see . . .* *They say it's very good.*
Dialogue:	Part 4			
	Set 5	Opinions	Ask for and give opinions Ask for and give reasons	*Did you enjoy the concert?* *Yes, I did./No, I didn't.* *Why not? It was too slow.*
Spoken transfer: Open dialogue Roleplay			Combined: invitations, dates, suggestions and times Combined: as above	
Skills development: Reading		**Description** An extract from a magazine article in which a teenager describes her own town, the lack of facilities there and what she feels about it.		
Listening		A telephone conversation about a fancy dress party. Students complete the missing information on an invitation card.		
Writing		Using a theatre advertisement, students complete a letter of invitation as a model for a similar one which they can send to a friend.		
Oral exercises:	1 2 3 4 5		Say who you are on the telephone Talk about arrangements Make suggestions (1) Make suggestions (2) Ask and talk about availability	2314. Hello. Sally speaking. *Oh, hello, Sally. It's Di here.* Are you free on the 9th? *No, not on the 9th, I'm afraid.* What shall we do? *Shall we go to the theatre?* Yes, let's. What shall we give Paul for his birthday? *Let's give him a T-shirt.* Is there anything to drink? *I'm afraid there isn't anything.* *There's nothing to drink at all.*

Grammar focus	Active vocabulary and expressions		
	Speaking.	*How nice!*	
Modal verb: *can* (possibility) *I'm afraid*+clause *I'll*+verb	assistant library message	back (I'll phone back) *I'm afraid*	
	See you then.		
Prepositions of time: *on*+dates, *in*+months and seasons	spring summer autumn winter	date end station term	months of the year Ordinal numbers: *1st–31st*
	drink	know (something)	expensive on (It's on at…)
Modal verb: *would* (*Would you like to* + verb?)	card club	dance	free (opp. busy)
Let's (*Let us*) + verb Modal verb: *shall* (I/we) – interrogative *Give* + 2 objects (Give somebody something) Question word: *Which?*	bag perfume sweater T-shirt watch	give say suggest	Let's (+ verb) Which?
	fresh air enjoy need slow tired Why? Why not?		
Past simple tense: verbs *like, enjoy* – positive, negative and interrogative Question word: *Why?* *Too* + adjective	meal	fast long (time) loud	sad too (+ adjective)
nothing, anything, something *nothing to* + verb; *nothing* + adjective *not … either* *because* + clause	factory happen look forward to tell	boring exciting	anything own nothing not … either something because

65

Unit 9 An evening out

Students' Book
pages 68, 69

Check homework from Unit 8.

🔲 **Dialogue: Part 1**

Active expressions:	Speaking. How nice!

Set 1 Telephoning

Active words and expressions:	assistant library message back (I'll phone back) I'm afraid

Exercise 1

Point out the differences between the two situations: informal and formal, e.g. the use of the first and short names in the informal situation and the use of the titles and the full names in the formal situation.

Find out from one or two students what their short names are. Give yours if you have one.

Practise these exchanges chorally, with you taking the part of Diana and John Watson respectively.

Students work through the remaining telephone conversations in pairs. Ask them to alternate Judy's role. Ask one or two pairs to perform their conversations for the rest of the class.

Exercise 2

Practise the whole exchange chorally. Then set students to work. Choose different pairs to act their conversations.

🔲 **Dialogue: Part 2**

Active expression:	See you then.

NOTES

Bob: Judy's husband
Leicester Square: a square in the centre of London's West End; an area where there are many theatres, cinemas, restaurants, discos and nightclubs

Set 2 Months and dates

Active words and expressions:	date end station term spring summer autumn winter in (+ months and seasons) on (+ dates) Ordinal numbers 1st–31st.

Exercise 1

Refer students to the box and practise the pronunciation of the months. Refer them also to the photographs showing the four seasons of the year in Britain.

Explain that in Britain (with its temperate climate) spring officially starts on March 21st, summer on June 21st, autumn on September 23rd and winter on December 21st. Ask the questions to individual students.

Exercise 2

Tell the class when your birthday is, e.g. *My birthday is in March*. Write the sentence on the blackboard and underline the preposition *in*. Ask one or two students the same question and write the answers on the blackboard.

The ordinal numbers are presented in a box for student reference. They need care with pronunciation especially the /θ/ sound in fifth, eighteenth, etc. Ask the students to recite all the numbers chorally, then ask one or two students to say individual numbers (write the figures on the blackboard and point to them).

Ask and answer one or two questions orally with the whole class. Then ask students to work in pairs and to write full sentences as answers to each question.

Students' Book
pages 70, 71

🔲 **Dialogue: Part 3**

Active words and expressions:	drink know (something) expensive on (It's on at . . .)

NOTES

Mozart, Brahms /ˈməʊtzɑːt, brɑːmz/:	composers of classical music: Mozart (1756–91) was Austrian, Brahms (1833–97) was German
the Festival Hall:	a concert hall, part of the South Bank cultural centre in London which includes the National Theatre, the National Film Theatre, The Hayward Gallery. The (Royal) Festival Hall is named because it was built as part of the Festival of Britain in 1951

Set 3 Invitations

Active words:	card club dance free (*opp.* busy)

Exercise 1

Practise the exchange chorally. Present the activities. Ask the students to work in pairs inviting each other to do things. They change parts so that everyone takes the initiating role.

Exercise 2

Refer students to the dates in the box. Ask them to copy them into their notebooks in a list. They block out any four nights of the week (they do not need to write in what they are doing) leaving three nights free. Ask one student to practise the model exchange with you. Each student then has to try to find someone to go to a pop concert with on one of the nights they have free. If a pop concert is inappropriate to your teaching situation, choose some event relevant to the lives of the students

Ask one or two pairs to perform the model exchange for the rest of the group. Ask them to do this without the support of the book.

Set 4 Suggestions

Active words and expressions:	bag perfume sweater T-shirt watch give say suggest Let's (+ verb) Which?

Exercise 1

Practise the model exchange and write the sentence, *Let's give her some roses.* on the blackboard. Then write the sentence, *Let's give Diana a record.* Point out the position of the pronoun *her* as the indirect object immediately after the main verb.

Identify the presents. Practise T-S with the students suggesting a present for Paul. Ask them to practise suggesting presents for Vince and Joanne. If there is a suitable occasion, e.g. a birthday, a wedding which applies to your group, conduct a conversation around this real situation.

Exercise 2

The advertisements are taken from newspapers and magazines. The small advertisements contain certain stylistic features such as sentences without verbs, e.g. *A good mid-week venue with party night Tues and Thurs.* (This is a good place to go to in the middle of the week, especially as there are 'party' nights on Tuesdays and Thursdays), abbreviations, e.g. *M/ship* (Membership) and *Sat mats* (Saturday matinees–afternoon performances).

NOTES

Disco advertisements

W1:	a London post code–West One
M/ship:	membership. You have to be a member to go to these clubs
tube:	underground
Dress smart:	You must wear smart clothes.
pool (room):	a game (like billiards) played on a large table with coloured balls and cues
venue/ˈvenuː/	a place where events are held
membs:	members, c.f. M/ship
w/ends:	weekends
Dress casual but smart:	i.e. men don't need to wear a jacket or a tie

Theatre advertisements

Greenwich BR(S):	the railway station (British Rail) at Greenwich which is part of the Southern Region (S) rail network
SE10:	a post code: South East 10
public school:	in fact a private fee-paying school (not a state school where education is free)

These advertisements can be replaced by local ones.

Ask students to choose a film, a play and a disco.

Refer students to the language box, and practise the questions and the statements chorally. Notice the two ways of making suggestions, *Shall we go to the cinema* and *Let's see . . .* Conduct an exchange about the cinema with one of the students, to show them how to extract similar exchanges from the substitution table in the box. Students make the conversations, changing parts and using the printed advertisements. Ask two or three pairs to perform their conversations for the class.

Students' Book pages 72, 73

🔲 Dialogue: Part 4

Active words and expressions:	fresh air enjoy need slow tired Why? Why not?

Set 5 Opinions

Active words:	meal fast long(time) loud sad too (+ adjective)

This set introduces the past simple tense with regular verbs. *Did* is used in questions, short form answers and negative statements. Students use the tense here to ask for and give opinions about events that have passed.

Exercise 1

Practise the exchanges in the box chorally. Point out the contrast in the last sentence with *but*. Work S-T with a similar exchange about the meal, e.g.
Did you enjoy the meal?
Yes, I did. Did you?
It was all right. I liked the chicken but I didn't like the dessert very much.
Students talk about the concert, the holiday, and the film in the same way. Note the pronunciation of Diane Keaton/ˌdaɪæn ˈkiːtən/, Warren Beatty/ˌwɒrən ˈbiːti/

Exercise 2

This exercise introduces the negative short form answer with reasons linked to an opinion and a new range of   67 adjectives: *slow, long, cold, sad, loud, fast*. Establish the meaning of these words and the qualifier *too*. Practise the model exchange chorally. Ask students to work in pairs with the items listed. Finish the exercise by asking random questions about events that you know to be within the students' shared experience.

🔘 Open dialogue

Students refer to the advertisements printed in the book on page 71 or to their own from a recent local newspaper.

SSR

PAUL: Hello. Isn't it a beautiful evening?
YOU: *Yes, it is.*
PAUL: Would you like to do something?
YOU: *Yes, I'd love to.*
PAUL: OK. What's the date today?
YOU: *It's . . . .*
PAUL: Right. Let's look in the paper and see what's on. What shall we do?
YOU: *Let's go to/see . . . .They say it's very good.*
PAUL: OK. Shall I meet you at your house?
YOU: *Fine.*
PAUL: What's the address?
YOU: *It's . . . .*
PAUL: What time shall I come?
YOU: *At eight o'clock./What about eight oclock?/Is eight o'clock all right?*
PAUL: Fine! I'll see you then. Bye!
YOU: *Bye!*

Roleplay

The roleplay will be made more effective if students use their own printed realia as input.

SSR

S1: *Hello. Is that (name)?*
S2: *Yes, speaking.*
S1: *It's (short name) here./(Full name)*
S2: *Oh, hello (name). How are you?*
S1: *Fine, thanks. And you?*
S2: *Oh, very well.*
S1: *Are you free on (date)?*
S2: *Yes, I am. Why?*
S1: *Well, would you like to (activity)?*
S2: *Yes, I'd love to. Thank you/Thanks very much.*
S1: *Shall we/Let's meet at (time).*
S2: *Fine. Where shall we meet?*
S1: *Let's meet at (place).*
S2: *OK.*
S1: *Where shall we go after (activity)?*
S2: *Let's go to . . . .*
S1: *Fine! See you on (day) at (time) at (place).*
S2: *Bye!*

Students perform the roleplay in class. For extra practice and revision, ask them to write out the conversation for homework.

Students' Book pages 74, 75

Reading

Active words and expressions:	factory happen look forward to tell boring exciting anything nothing something own not . . . either because

NOTES

Scawsby: a small town near Doncaster, a large town in Yorkshire. Yorkshire is a county in the north-east of England (see map)

KEY

1. *Where does Sharon live?*
2. *Does she like Scawsby?*
3. *Why doesn't she like/does she hate Scawsby?*
4. *How far is it from Scawsby to Doncaster?*
5. *How long does it take to get from Scawsby to Doncaster by bus?*
6. *Where does Sharon want to live?*
7. *Why does she want to live there/in London?*
8. *When did Sharon finish school?*
9. *When does she start her new job?*
10. *Where is the job?*
11. *Is she looking forward to it?*
12. *What does she want to do on her seventeenth birthday?*

🔘 Listening

TAPESCRIPT

Liz Kennedy has received an invitation to a party. She thinks her friend Mary has also got an invitation. She telephones Mary to ask her. Listen to them talking and complete the details of the invitation in your book.

LIZ: Mary, it's Liz here.
MARY: Oh, hello Liz. How are you?
LIZ: Fine, thanks. Did you get your invitation this morning?
MARY: No. The post hasn't come yet. Who's the invitation from?
LIZ: From Adam and Diana.
MARY: Adam and Diana Black?
LIZ: That's right.
MARY: Oh, that's nice. What is it? Drinks?
LIZ: No, it's a Fancy Dress party.
MARY: Fancy Dress? Oh no, I hate Fancy Dress parties, I never have anything to wear.
LIZ: Well, I'm going as Minnie Mouse and Doug is going as Mickey Mouse.
MARY: Great! When is it anyway?
LIZ: It's on Saturday.
MARY: Saturday? This Saturday? That's tomorrow!
LIZ: No, no. Next Saturday. Saturday, May 15th.
MARY: May 15th . . . yes, I think that's free. What time does it start?

LIZ: Nine o'clock.
MARY: Nine! That's quite late. Is it at their house?
LIZ: No, it isn't. It's ... wait for it ... it's at the Hilton!
MARY: The Hilton? At the Hilton Hotel?
LIZ: Yes, they say hundreds are coming.
MARY: Well, it sounds fabulous. Ah, here's the post now ...
(opens letter) Yes, here it is.
LIZ: See you at the party, Mary! Bye!

KEY

Adam and Diana Black
would like you to come to a
Fancy Dress Party
on *Saturday, May 15th* at *9 p.m.*
at *the Hilton Hotel*, London W1

Writing

NOTES

Paul Daniels: Paul Daniels, a magician, is a popular TV personality and stage performer

Students complete the letter for homework. Ask them to select a date in the near future that suits them. Point out that after *for* and *on,* more than one word will be needed.

KEY

Dear Malcolm,
I've got two tickets for Paul Daniels in 'It's Magic' at the Prince of Wales theatre (on Friday, May 24th.) Are you free that evening? Would you like to come with me? They say it's very good. Please write or telephone and tell me if you can come.
Yours,
Dave.

Students write a similar letter to one of their friends inviting them to do something one evening next week.

Homework

Choose from:
1. Open dialogue, page 73. Write out the missing part.
2. Roleplay, page 73. Write the telephone conversation.
3. Reading activity, page 74.
4. Writing, page 74.
5. Unit 9 Workbook exercises.

🔊 Oral exercises

1. Say who you are on the telephone

2314. Hello. Sally speaking.

Oh, hello, Sally. It's Di here.

Now you answer the phone each time and say who you are.

2314. Hello. Sally speaking.
Oh, hello, Sally. It's ... here.

3406. Hello. Denis speaking.
Oh, hello, Denis. It's ... here.
4413. Hello. Robert speaking.
Oh, hello, Robert. It's ... here.
1216. Hello. Delia speaking.
Oh, hello, Delia. It's ... here.
9378. Hello. Ann speaking.
Oh, hello, Ann. It's ... here.
6514. Hello. John speaking.
Oh, hello, John. It's ... here.
Who? Who is that speaking?
. . . .
I'm sorry. You've got the wrong number! Bye!

2. Talk about arrangements

Are you free on the 9th?
No, not on the 9th, I'm afraid.

You go on. Say you are not free each time.

Are you free on the 9th?
No, not on the 9th, I'm afraid.
Are you free on the 1st?
No, not on the 1st, I'm afraid.
Are you free on the 3rd?
No, not on the 3rd, I'm afraid.
Are you free on the 5th?
No, not on the 5th, I'm afraid.
Are you free on the 2nd?
No, not on the 2nd, I'm afraid.
Are you free on the 28th?
No, not on the 28th, I'm afraid.
Well, Sally, when are you free this month?
I'm not free at all, really. I'm working very hard at the moment.

3. Make suggestions (1)

What shall we do?
Shall we go to the theatre?
Yes, let's.

Now you make suggestions.

What shall we do?
Shall we go to the theatre?
Yes, let's.
What shall we do?
Shall we go to the cinema?
Yes, let's.
What shall we do?
Shall we go to a concert?
Yes, let's.
What shall we do?
Shall we go to a disco?
Yes, let's.
What shall we do?
Shall we go to a restaurant?
Yes, let's.
What shall we do?
Shall we watch TV?
Yes, let's. What's on?
It's *Dallas.*

4. Make suggestions (2)

Listen to Diana talking to a friend about Paul's birthday present.

What shall we give Paul for his birthday?
Let's give him a T-shirt.

Now you make suggestions for presents for different people in the same way.

What shall we give Paul for his birthday?
Let's give him a T-shirt.
What shall we give Diana for her birthday?
Let's give her a pen.
What shall we give my mother for her birthday?
Let's give her some flowers.
What shall we give my brother for his birthday?
Let's give him a book about cars.
What shall we give the children for their birthday?
Let's give them a Walt Disney video cassette
What shall we give my parents for their birthday?
Let's give them some theatre tickets.

5. Ask and talk about availability

Is there anything to drink?
I'm afraid there isn't anything. There's nothing to drink at all.

Now you answer your friend in the same way.

Is there anything to drink?
I'm afraid there isn't anything. There's nothing to drink at all.
Is there anything to eat?
I'm afraid there isn't anything. There's nothing to eat at all.
Is there anything to read?
I'm afraid there isn't anything. There's nothing to read at all.
Is there anything to watch on television?
I'm afraid there isn't anything. There's nothing to watch at all.
Is there anything to listen to on the radio?
I'm afraid there isn't anything. There's nothing to listen to at all.
Well, is there anything to do in the town?
Yes. We can go for a walk and look at the shops.

Unit 10 Consolidation

Skills	Description	Language use/topics/activities
Speaking	Roleplay: finding the way round Chichester, a town on the south coast of England, asking about shops, facilities and entertainment.	Location of shops and places; fixed times; journeys and transport; prices
Listening and writing	1. A woman is directed from the bus station in Chichester to a shop. Students follow the route and name the shop.	Directions and location
	2. Four children talk about their favourite subjects at school. Students list their interests and write about some children *they* know.	Likes and dislikes; activities and pastimes
	3. Karen, a seven-year-old, talks about the other members of her family. Students fill in Karen's family tree and write about a family they know.	Family relationships and ages
	4. Puzzle it out! Students listen to seven short scenes. They must guess the place where the scene is being enacted in each case, and write the word in a word puzzle space in order to complete another word.	
Reading	'A Day in the life of Peter Maxwell': this is an extract from a magazine article. It is an interview with an unemployed young man in which he tells how he spends his day. Students write questions and roleplay the interview about how Peter spends his day.	Daily routine
Reading for information	A presentation of a variety of printed authentic realia consisting of: cinema advertisements, an advertisement for a cruise on the River Thames, a 'House for Sale' advertisement and a letter. Students extract information to answer questions, plan a day out and complete the letter.	Fixed times; travel and journeys; rooms of the house
Language focus	1. Grammar: Which is correct?	A series of multiple choice items to highlight some of the grammatical forms presented in the previous units
	2. Grammar: Fill in the verbs	The correct form of the verb in brackets must be filled in
	3. Conversation: Complete the conversation	Students complete a conversation in a restaurant
	4. Reading and writing: Put sentences in the right order and write the paragraph	A series of sentences describing a person's day are presented out of sequence. Students rearrange the sentences in correct chrono-logical order, after which they write the paragraph out in full. This is the model on which to base a similar paragraph about someone they know well
	5. Vocabulary: Word puzzle	Word search: students find words hidden in a puzzle and sort them into four categories. These are: colours; rooms of the house; shops or buildings; family relations

Unit 10 Consolidation

Students' Book pages 76, 77

Check homework from Unit 9.

Chichester

Active words:	garage greengrocer grocer hairdresser's library

NOTES

Chichester:	a cathedral town on the south coast of England in the county of Sussex. It is in between Brighton and Portsmouth
The Cross:	a monument in the shape of a cross where the four streets meet
W.H. Smith's and Boots	two well-known chains of stores. W.H. Smith's is basically a stationer's and Boots is a chemist's, although both stores now sell a range of other articles
The Ship/ The Sussex Arms:	the names of public drinking houses or 'pubs' in Britain can be quite varied: nautical terms, names of royalty, animals, names of the county it is in (as here, the Sussex Arms)
Banks:	the names of the four biggest banks in Britain are Barclay's, Lloyd's, National Westminster, and the Midland
Dep./Arr.:	Departs/Arrives
Parties:	coach parties
Bistro:	a small, fairly simple restaurant in the French style
last orders:	the latest you can order a meal, i.e. enter the restaurant
fully licensed:	having official permission to sell alcoholic drinks
ring road:	a road that goes round the edge of a large town or city so that traffic need not pass through the centre

Make the students familiar with all the separate pieces of printed information by using the following steps:

(i) Identify each piece of information by asking students to point to
— the diagram of the centre of Chichester.
— the Tourist Information list of opening and closing times of banks, public houses and a department store.
— the bus timetable
— information about a place of interest—Goodwood House, a Duke's palace
— the seating plan from a theatre booking form and the diary of a week's theatrical events.
— the advertisement for a restaurant (bistro)

(ii) Guide students through the information by asking questions about:

the diagram
What are the names of the four main streets in Chichester?
Where is the theatre, the railway station and the bus station?
Is the cathedral near East Street or West Street?
What's the name of the cinema and where is it?
Where is the Tourist Information Office? etc.

the Tourist Information about opening and closing times
When do the banks open and close?
When do the pubs close after lunch and open again in the evening?
Where is the Sussex Arms?
What's the name of the department store? Where is it?
What time does it close on Mondays?

the bus timetable
When does the first bus leave Chichester to go to Waterbeach?
When does the last bus leave Waterbeach?

information about Goodwood House
How many days a week is Goodwood House open in May?
How many in August?
What time is it open?
Can you have lunch at Goodwood House?

theatre information
How many performances of 'A Midsummer Night's Dream' are there on Thursday, May 6?
How much are the tickets immediately opposite the stage?
What time does the ballet start every evening?

the restaurant advertisement
What's the name of the restaurant?
Where is it?
What's its telephone number?
When are the last orders for dinner?
When you go up South Street is the restaurant on the right or on the left?

Exercise 1

Students now work in pairs. One person looks at the information, the other looks at the task. (For notes on communicative tasks see page ix.)

Give students plenty of time to work out and practise their conversations. Ask two or three pairs to perform theirs for the rest of the group.

SSR

TIO = Tourist Information Officer   v = Visitor

TIO:	*Good morning. Can I help you?*
V:	*Yes, please. I'd like some information about Chichester. Is there anything interesting to see outside Chichester?*
TIO:	*Yes, there's Goodwood House (the home of the Dukes of Richmond).*
V:	*Really? Is it open on Mondays?*
TIO:	*Yes, it is.*
V:	*What time does it open and close?*
TIO:	*It opens at 2 p.m. and closes at 5 p.m.*
V:	*Oh good. How do I get there?*
TIO:	*By bus. There's a bus from Chichester to Waterbeach, near Goodwood House.*

V: *How often do the buses leave Chichester?*

TIO: *After 10 a.m., they leave Chichester every two hours. The last bus leaves at ten past six in the evening.*

V: *I see, and how long does the journey take?*

TIO: *It only takes 15 minutes.*

V: *Well, is there a bus at about 2 o'clock?*

TIO: *Yes, there's one at ten past two.*

V: *Good. Is there anything interesting on at the Festival Theatre?*

TIO: *Well, this week there's a ballet. It's a new production of 'A Midsummer Night's Dream.'*

V: *Oh good. What time does it start?*

TIO: *7.30.*

V: *And how much are the tickets?*

TIO: *£8.00, £6.00, £4.00, £3.00 and £2.00.*

V: *Can I have two £4 tickets please?*

TIO: *Yes, of course. Two £4 tickets for the evening performance.*

V: *And is there a good restaurant in Chichester?*

TIO: *Yes, there is. There's Jason's Bistro.*

V: *Where is it?*

TIO: *In South Street.*

V: *Is it open on Mondays?*

TIO: *Yes, it is.*

V: *What time does it close?*

TIO: *Well, the last orders are at 11.30.*

V: *That's OK. We want to eat after the theatre. And I'd like to go shopping this morning. Is there a department store here?*

TIO: *Yes, there is. Morant's/mə'ræntz/.*

V: *Where is it?*

TIO: *Near the centre, in West Street next to the Town Hall.*

V: *Is it open on Mondays?*

TIO: *Yes, it is, but it closes today at 1 p.m. Monday is early closing day.*

V: *I see. And where can I buy some stamps and a newspaper?*

TIO: *You can buy stamps at the post office. There's one in West Street. It's next to the hotel./It's next to Morant's, the department store./It's between the department store and the hotel. You can buy a newspaper at W.H. Smith's opposite this office or there's a newsagent's on the left in East Street.*

V: *Also I want to buy some new shoes and a film for my camera.*

TIO: *There's a shoe shop in the centre near the Cross, in fact there are two. There's a chemist's, Boots, on the right in East Street.*

V: *Thank you for all the information.*

TIO: *You're welcome.*

The above is a guide to a very good student performance. Average students can ask and answer the guided questions as indicated. Stronger students will want to use the questions as a starting point for freer conversation. Encourage this.

As you monitor the pair conversations, note any difficulties and refer students back to the relevant sections in Unit 6 where the presentation and practise of this work was covered in detail.

For the last part of this activity, ask students to change partners, and roleplay a telephone conversation. Ask them first to make a note of things they want to do before they telephone.

If appropriate, use your own area to roleplay similar conversations to that in the Tourist Office in Chichester. Choose fairly obvious and well-known features of your area to ask and answer questions about. As a preparation for this, ask students to prepare a collage of information extracts – if possible in English. This can be used in the transfer work concerning your area.

Exercise 2   GAME: Where am I?

This is the same as the game in Unit 8 Set 3.

Another game to play here is a version of the 'Shopping game' in which each person has to add to a list in alphabetical order, and repeat each item as the game proceeds, e.g.

PLAYER 1: *I want to buy some apples.*

PLAYER 2: *I want to buy some apples and some butter.*

Here, students have to choose a place or a shop and say the thing they want to buy or get (but not in alphabetical order). They have to remember what the person before them said and add that to the list. If they can't remember any items or shops, they drop out from the game. The person who lasts the longest is the winner, e.g.

PLAYER 1: *I want to go to the shoe shop and get some shoes.*

PLAYER 2: *I want to go to the shoe shop and get some shoes, and to the chemist's and get some toothpaste. etc.*

Players are not allowed to make notes during the game.

Students' Book pages 78, 79

🔘 Listening

1. TAPESCRIPT

Look at the plan of Chichester. A woman is at the bus station and asks for directions to a certain shop. Listen to the directions and follow them. Find out where the woman wants to go.

MAN: Walk up this street – this is South Street – and turn right at the Cross into East Street. Walk up East Street. Go past the National Westminster bank on your left, then past a sports shop, and a supermarket and there's a camera shop just past the supermarket on your left. You can't miss it.

WOMAN: So, up this street, right at the Cross and it's on my left after the supermarket.

MAN: That's it.

WOMAN: Thank you so much.

MAN: You're welcome.

KEY

camera shop

2. TAPESCRIPT

Listen to these children talking. Note down what things they like doing at school. Choose from the subjects in your book.

Would you like to tell me your name?

Paul Miller.

And how old are you, Paul?

I'm ten.

And what sort of things do you like doing at school?

I like maths, P.E. and sometimes I like art work and I like English.

What do you like in English?

Dictation.

What are your favourite games?

Football, rounders ... er, that's about all.

Would you like to tell me your name, please?

Amanda.

And how old are you?

Seven.

Do you like school?

Yes.

And what do you like doing?

I like doing maths, singing and dancing.

Any sports? Do you like doing gym?

I like doing handstands and cartwheels.

And what don't you like about school?

Writing stories and things like that.

Would you like to tell me your name?

My name is Alexander Luke Simpson.

Do you like school, Alexander?

Yes.

What do you like doing most?

Well, I like writing, mathematics, spellings, gym, outside gym.

What about painting?

Yes, I do like painting, drawing, writing.

Do you like music?

Yes, a little bit.

Would you like to tell me your name, please?

My name is Laura.

And how old are you?

I am seven.

Do you like school?

Yes, very much.

And what do you like doing?

Well, most of the time I like doing our projects and last time we did, we traced a map of Wales from 'Our World', the map and the book we have.

And what else do you like doing?

Well, I like my points of the compass, ... erm, computation and ... and painting pictures and most of the time doing tap.

What about singing?

Well, I don't enjoy that so much, but I like it a little bit.

What other things don't you like?

Well, I don't like ... erm, well I don't like doing so much hard work that I can't do, but I learn a lot.

What's the hard work that you don't like? What are those subjects called?

Well ... sometimes when ... when we do group reading there's very hard words because most of them are not easy books, because I am in *The Iron Man* group and it's a hard book.

KEY

Paul: *mathematics*
Amanda: *mathematics; singing; dancing*
Alexander: *writing; mathematics; spelling; doing gym; painting*
Laura: *painting; singing (a little)*

This key represents the minimum information. Many students will extract other activities not mentioned in the SB, e.g. art, English, P.E. etc.

3. TAPESCRIPT

Listen to Karen talking about her family. Complete the family tree in your book and the ages of the children.

Karen. Could you tell me a bit about your family?

My mother is Lynne. My daddy is Chris. My oldest brother's Paul.

How old's he?

He is thirteen and David is three. James is four.

And how old are you?

Nearly eight.

So really how old are you?

Seven at the moment.

KEY

Lynne (mother)	Chris (father)

| Paul aged 13 | Karen aged 7 | James aged 4 | David aged 3 |

Writing

Students write about a family they know for homework.

4. Puzzle it out!

TAPESCRIPT

You are going to hear seven short scenes. Each time you must guess which shop or which place you are in. Write the name of the place each time in the spaces in the word puzzle. When you've got all seven places you'll find the name of one more place or shop. Are you ready? Here's scene number one.

MAN: Yes, can I help you?

WOMAN: Can I have a service, please?

MAN: Not today, I'm afraid. We're very busy. Let's see ... is next Wednesday OK?

WOMAN: Yes, that's fine. And can you check the lights when you do the service?

MAN: Yes, of course. Do you want some petrol now?

WOMAN: Yes, 30 litres, please.

So where were they? Write the word in the spaces next to the number one. Now listen to scene two.

WOMAN: Jean, can you shampoo Mrs Howard, please? Now, do you just want a trim?

GIRL: Yes, can you cut about three centimetres off all round?

WOMAN: Right. Lovely weather, isn't it?

GIRL: Yes, it's just like spring today.

WOMAN: There, how's that? Your hair's very thick.

GIRL: Mmm. Can you cut a bit more off? I don't like it when my hair falls into my eyes.

WOMAN: Like this?

GIRL: That's lovely. Thank you.

Now listen to scene three.

WOMAN: Good morning.

MAN: Oh, good morning. I have a room booked. The name's Jones.

WOMAN: Jones ... Ah yes, Room 103. Can you sign here, Mr Jones?

MAN: Certainly.

WOMAN: And here's your key.

MAN: Thank you.

Now scene four.

(singing by a cathedral choir; final prayer and blessing; organ voluntary)

Now scene five.

WAITER: Would you like to order now, madam?

WOMAN: Yes, please. Er ... Can we have a big mixed salad to start with, and then I'd like some sea food. Is the scampi nice?

WAITER: Everything is nice in San Martino's, Signora!

MAN: I think I'll have a canelloni followed by veal in tomato sauce.

Now listen to scene six.

GIRL: I'm afraid this book is overdue, sir.

MAN: Oh, is it?

GIRL: Yes, it's a week late. That's twenty pence, please.

MAN: Oh, right. Here you are.

GIRL: Thank you.

MAN: Erm ... I wonder ... have you got the latest book by Desmond Morris. You know, the man who wrote *The Naked Ape* ...?

GIRL: No, I'm afraid it's out. But you can fill in a card here and we'll let you know when it comes in.

And now for the last scene. Scene number seven.

MASTER: Come on, hurry up, everyone. The bell's gone. Lee, don't run in the corridor.

BOY: Please sir, I can't do games today. My mum's sent this note.

MASTER: Right. Can you take it to the school secretary after assembly? Now get to your classroom quickly. Come on, Janice. You're late!

Did you get them all? Now you can read the name of another place or shop. It's a word going downwards not across.

KEY

1. *garage* 2. *hairdresser's* 3. *hotel* 4. *cathedral* 5. *restaurant* 6. *library* 7. *school*

The 8th word is *grocer's*

Reading

This is based on an authentic magazine article. It has been edited and simplified.

NOTES

read the papers: public libraries in Britain provide daily newspapers as part of their services

25 pence worth: 25 pence would only buy a very small piece of cheese

Big Meal of the day: the capital letters means that Peter has given ironic emphasis to this. Really his meal is rather humble and thus not very big. Traditionally, for working people, the evening meal is the big meal of the day. The fact that Peter is unemployed adds to the irony

'lunch': The inverted commas imply that Peter doesn't think that he has had a real lunch

the heater: a self-standing heater

Exercise 1

KEY

1. *Have you got a job?*
2. *What time do you get up?*
3. *What do you usually have for breakfast?*
4. *Where do you go after breakfast?*
5. *Why do you go to the library?*
6. *Which parts of the paper do you read/always read/read first?*
7. *What do you do after the library?*
8. *What do you (usually) have for lunch?*
9. *What do you do after lunch?*
10. *When do you go to carpentry classes?*
11. *What do you do on the other days?*
12. *When do you start preparing the evening meal?*
13. *What do you do after supper?*

14. *Do you watch TV very much?*
15. *When do you go to bed?*

Exercise 2

Tell students to use the questions they constructed in Exercise 1 to roleplay an interview with Peter Maxwell. The student taking the part of Peter uses the reading text to provide the answers to the questions. Encourage the students to make the interview as realistic as they can.

Students' Book pages 80, 81

Reading for information

These authentic advertisements are taken from a London evening newspaper.

NOTES

West End: (c.f. page 66) the area of central London where there are many cinemas, theatres, shops, restaurants and nightclubs, etc.
Classic 123: as in many countries, British cinemas have been converted into 'multiples' (i.e. small cinemas) so that they can show more films to smaller audiences
Haymarket: the name of a street
progs: programme, i.e. the times of each programme
'U', 'A', etc.: Note the certificates of the films here are: U = children can go to see the film without an adult; A = children must be accompanied by an adult; AA = young people under 14 are not allowed; X = adults over 18 only are allowed.
Since publication these certificates have changed slightly. They are now: U = (as before); P.G. = parental guidance (some scenes may not be suitable for children); 15 = young people over 15 only are allowed; 18 = adults over 18 only are allowed
County Hall: the administrative centre of the city of London situated on the south bank of the River Thames, almost opposite the Houses of Parliament

KEY

Exercise 1

4 (The Classic 3 in Oxford St. has a double programme)
3
2 are named (although Flash the Teenage Otter is a Walt Disney production as well)
4 times and 5 times on Fridays and Saturdays
all of them – 6

Exercise 2

12.50
9.05
2.10
11 p.m.
7.45

Exercise 3

From the Westminster Pier Booking Office SW1
It starts at 8.15 p.m. and finishes at 10.00 p.m.
It passes St Paul's Cathedral and Southwark / 's k/ Cathedral
4: Waterloo Bridge, Blackfriar's Bridge, Southwark Bridge and London Bridge
The nearest underground is Westminster Station
£1.00

Exercise 4   Plan a day out

SSR

1. *Time Bandits at 5.55*
2. *We can first go and see the Great Muppet Caper at 2.35 and have something to eat in a restaurant after the film. Then we can take the underground from Piccadilly Circus to Westminster, do a little sightseeing and then catch the boat at Westminster Pier at 8.15*

Exercise 5   Advertisement for the house in Hadley Common

NOTES

As with other advertisements in this book, this contains special stylistic features, e.g. abbreviations and sentences without verbs. The nature of small advertisements – the more you say, the more you pay for – means that they are always short.

Barnet/Herts: Barnet is a town in Hertfordshire, north of London
reception rooms: i.e. sitting rooms
p.w. inc.: per week inclusive of all costs like heat, light and the telephone
Taylor and Clegg: the name of the estate agents

Students complete the letter with information from the advertisement either in class or at home.

SSR

Dear Tom,
Thank you for your letter. I hope you are well. We are still looking for a house. We saw another one yesterday. It was quite nice. It's in Barnet. It's a detached house and there are three bedrooms, a bathroom and two reception rooms and a beautiful kitchen which is also a breakfast room. There is also a garage for the car.
It costs £100 a week to rent. Dick says it's too expensive, but I'm trying to persuade him.
See you soon,
Much love,
Julie

Students write a similar letter for homework.

Students' Book pages 82, 83
Language focus

KEY

1. Which is correct?
1. *a*) 2. *a*) 3. *b*) 4. *c*) 5. *c*) 6. *b*) 7. *a*) 8. *c*) 9. *b*)

2. Fill in the right form of the verbs

ANN: Hello, *is* that Jackie?

J: Yes, *speaking*.

A: Jackie, this *is* Ann. Listen, *are* you free on January 21st?

J: You mean on Saturday? Yes, I *am*. Why?

A: Well, I've *got* tickets for the Haircut 100 concert at the Hammersmith Odeon. *Would* you *like* to come?

J: Yes, I'd *love* to. I *like* Haircut 100. What time *does* the show *start*?

A: At 7.30. *Shall* we *meet* outside the Odeon?

J: No, *let's meet* at my house first. There *are* always so many people outside the Odeon.

A: OK. I'll see you at your house at about 7 on Saturday then.

Students can either work on their own or in pairs completing this conversation, or ask them to complete it orally in class and to write out the conversation in full for homework.

3. Complete the conversation

Students work on their own or orally in pairs. They write out the conversation for homework.

KEY

WAITER: *What would you like?*

FRIEND: I'd like a steak and a salad, please.

WAITER: And you, sir?

YOU: *I'd like roast beef, with roast potatoes and peas.*

WAITER: Yes. One steak and salad, and one roast beef with roast potatoes and peas.

FRIEND: Mmm. This steak is good. Is your beef all right?

YOU: *Yes, it is.*

FRIEND: Oh good. By the way, do you like Warren Beatty?

YOU: Warren Beatty? He's all right.

FRIEND: Well, there's a good film on at the ABC cinema with Warren Beatty in it. It's called *Reds*. Would you like to see it?

YOU: *Yes, I'd love to.*

FRIEND: Oh, good.

YOU: *What time does it start?*

FRIEND: I think it starts at 8.30.

YOU: Well, let's go then.

FRIEND: Waiter! Can I have the bill, please? Thank you.

YOU: *How much is it?*

FRIEND: £5 each.

YOU: OK. Here's my money.

4. Put the sentences in the right order

Students arrange and write the sentences in a logical order.

NOTES

Systems analyst: a computer worker who plans subjects for study by using sets of figures

KEY

Peter Gibbs is a systems analyst. He works for a company in Swindon, a big town in the south of England. Here is a typical day for Peter. He gets up at 7 o'clock, reads the paper and has breakfast. Then he goes to work. He goes to work by car. He starts work at 9 o'clock. In the summer he starts work at 8 o'clock. He usually has lunch in the office canteen. He finishes work at 5.30. Then he goes home and has supper. After supper he usually reads the paper and watches TV or sees his girlfriend. He sometimes goes swimming or plays squash. He goes to bed at about 11.30.

Students use the paragraph as a model to write about their own daily lives for homework.

5. Puzzle

KEY

colours:	rooms of house:	shops or buildings:	family relations
blue	bedroom	bank	sister
brown	toilet	cinema	father
red	kitchen	chemist	son
green	hall	post office	daughter

Homework

Choose from:
1. Language focus exercises 1, 2, 3, 4 or 5 as time and situation allows.
2. Unit 10 Workbook exercises.

Unit 11 Shopping

Presentation and practice	Set title	Language use	Examples
Dialogue: Part 1			
Set 1	Plans for the near future	Ask and talk about plans for the near future	*What are you doing this afternoon?* *What is she doing this afternoon?* *I'm going to the conference.* *She's going to the conference.* *Are you going to the conference?* *Is she going shopping?* *Yes, I am./No, I'm not.* *Yes, she is./No, she isn't.* *We're leaving this morning/on Saturday/next week, etc.*
Dialogue: Part 2			
Set 2	Shopping for clothes	Admire Ask permission in a shop Give permission Comment Ask people to do things Ask about cost and size Ask and talk about ways of paying	*What a lovely sweater!/lovely sweaters!* *Can I have a look at it/them?* *Can I try a sweater on?* *Yes, of course/certainly. Here you are.* *It's/They're nice, but it's/they're a bit too big.* *Can you give me a size 10?* *How much does it cost?* *What size are you?* *How would you like to pay?* *I'll pay cash.* *Can I pay by credit card?*
Spoken transfer: Cued roleplay		Combined	
Skills development: Listening Reading Writing	**Description** Joy tries to arrange a business meeting on the phone. Students work out point and duration of time. Sarah writes to Diana about her life in Rio. Students answer questions. Students use a diary entry to write a letter about plans during a holiday.		
Oral exercises: 1 2 3 4		Ask about plans Talk about plans (Open exercise) Ask permission in a shop (1) Ask permission in a shop (2)	Joanne isn't going to the conference. *Oh, is she going shopping?* Yes, she is. Vince and Kelly aren't going to a concert. *Oh, are they going to the theatre?* Yes, they are. What are you doing this evening? *I'm staying at home.* We've got lots of T-shirts. *Can I have a look at them, please?* Yes, certainly. This is a good camera. *Can I have a look at it, please?* Yes, certainly. Do you like this sweater? *Yes. Can I try it on, please?* Yes, of course. These jeans are your size. *Can I try them on, please?* Yes, of course.

Grammar focus	Active vocabulary and expressions		
	stay	*That's a good idea.*	
Present continuous tense (future reference) – positive, negative and interrogative Time adverbials with future reference: *tomorrow afternoon, next week*, etc. Preposition of time: *for* (duration)	*airport* *coach* *dinner* *fortnight* *lunchtime* *rest (of the time)* *tour* *trip*	*bring*	*marvellous* *tomorrow* *Have a nice time!*

	medium
	size
	cost
	have a look at
		pay
		suit
		try (on)
			large *Can I help you?*
			a bit *Here you are.*
			  It suits you.
			  Yes, certainly/of course.

Exclamations: *What a...! What...!* Modal verb: *can* (permission) *Yes, certainly/of course.* Modal verb: *can* (request) Qualifier: *a bit* + adjective Question words: *How much? What size?* Modal verb: *will* (decision)	*cash* *cheque* *clothes* *coat* *dress* *handbag* *jeans* *shirt* *skirt* *trousers*	*pretty* *smart* *tight*	
	mountain *learn* *pleased* *everything*		

Unit 11 Shopping

Students' Book pages 84, 85

Check homework from Unit 10.

Set 1 Plans for the near future

Work through Exercises 1 and 2 before doing the dialogue. Introduce the concept of future time and future plans with questions relevant to the students' own lives, e.g. ask: *What are you doing after the class/this evening/at the weekend?* Say also what you are doing so that they can hear the present continuous being used for future use.

Exercise 1

Refer the students to the language box which presents a substitution table. Point out that the tense is the same as the present continuous in Unit 7, but it is accompanied by a future time adverbial. Students roleplay the characters using the notes given, changing parts each time.

Exercise 2

In pairs, students talk about each of the characters, using the 3rd person singular.

🔲 Dialogue: Part 1

Active words and expressions:	stay That's a good idea.

Exercise 3

Active words and expressions:	airport coach dinner fortnight lunchtime rest(of the time) tour trip bring marvellous tomorrow Have a nice time!

Refer students to the extract from the holiday brochure. Ask a few check questions about the location of each hotel, e.g. *Where is the Half Moon Bay Hotel? (In Antigua.)* etc. Do not worry about the pronunciation of the names. Check some of the departure dates. Point out that holidays can last for one, two or three weeks in each place. Work T-S with the dialogue first, with one of the students taking the part of Doug. Students work in pairs, reading the dialogue. They change parts.

Students use the chart to roleplay similar conversations. They can choose different places, hotels and departure dates each time. Ask two or three pairs to perform their conversations for the class.

Students' Book pages 86, 87

Exercise 4

Draw the students' attention to the language box with the list of future time adverbials, and the use of *on* and *at* in time phrases. Spend some time on this before doing the exercise. One way of practising the time adverbials is to set up a guessing game in groups. One person chooses one of the times listed, e.g. *on Tuesday evening*, but does not tell the rest of the group which one. The others must simply ask *yes* or *no* questions to guess which one, e.g. *Are you leaving in the morning? (No, I'm not.) Are you leaving next week? (No, I'm not.)* and so on.

Refer students to Vince's diary and work T-S1, S2, S3, etc. asking a few check questions using the structure, *What is/are ... doing in the morning/afternoon/evening... ?* Students work in pairs completing the dialogue orally. Ask them to write the complete version for homework.

NOTES

Cats:	a musical with music by Andrew Lloyd-Webber. It is based on a collection of poems about cats by T.S. Eliot
Simpson's:	a restaurant which serves traditional British food such as roast beef and roast lamb
Panam:	Pan American Airlines
Euston:	a main London station which serves Scotland and the north-west of England

SSR

DIANA:	When are your family arriving, Vince?
VINCE:	*They're arriving (at Heathrow) tomorrow at 8 p.m.*
DIANA:	Oh, are they? Are they going sightseeing in London?
VINCE:	*Yes, they are. They're going on a coach tour of London on Thursday.*
DIANA:	Oh, that's good. Those tours are quite good, I think. Are you going on any trips outside London?
VINCE:	*Yes, we're going to Scotland.*
DIANA:	To Scotland! How lovely! When?
VINCE:	*We're going on Sunday.*
DIANA:	How are you travelling?
VINCE:	*By train./On the night train./We're going on the night train from Euston Station.*
DIANA:	And how long are you staying there?
VINCE:	*We're staying there for two days./We're coming back on Tuesday.*
DIANA:	Great! And then are you staying the rest of the time in London?
VINCE:	*No, we're not. We're going to Stratford-upon-Avon.*
DIANA:	To Stratford! How are you getting there? By train?
VINCE:	*No, we aren't going by train. I'm renting a car.*
DIANA:	That's a good idea. And have you got tickets for the theatre?

VINCE: *Yes, We've got tickets for 'A Midsummer Night's Dream'.*

DIANA: They say it's very good. And you must see the musical *Cats,* too. It's marvellous.

VINCE: *We're seeing 'Cats' on Friday./this Friday, in fact.*

DIANA: Oh, are you? When are you going back to the States?

VINCE: *We're leaving Heathrow Airport on Saturday morning at 10 a.m.*

DIANA: Well, enjoy your stay. It sounds fun.

Exercise 5

Students ask around the class about plans. Then work in pairs and ask one or two people to report back to the rest of the class.

🔘🔘 Dialogue: Part 2

Active words and expressions:	medium size cost have a look at pay suit try(on) large a bit Can I help you? Here you are. It suits you. Yes, certainly. Yes, of course.

Students' Book pages 88, 89

Set 2 Shopping for clothes

Active words:	cash cheque clothes coat dress handbag jeans shirt skirt trousers pretty smart tight

Exercise 1

Students work in pairs identifying the clothes and the accessories. Ask random students what they are wearing with the question: *Joachim. What are you wearing today?* and a few more with the question: *Anna. Are you wearing shoes or boots today?*

Exercise 2

Practise the exclamations in the box chorally and then the request in the same way. Show students how to make up exchanges from the two boxes. Ask them to work in pairs.

Exercise 3

Work T-S with one student. Ask all students to go through the conversation in pairs, changing parts afterwards. Refer them to the charts showing the clothes sizes on the previous page (87). Ask them all to find their own size in its British equivalent for general clothing and for shoes. Ask male students to find their shirt collar size in its British equivalent. Students then roleplay shopping for clothes.

Exercise 4

This exercise practises ways of paying. Students practise the exchanges in pairs.

Roleplay

This roleplay combines all the sections in this set. Go through the cues given in the guide, eliciting example exchanges. Students choose two different items to buy and change parts. Notice that only the customer's guide is presented.

SSR

CUST: *What lovely/smart shoes!*

ASST: *Can I help you?*

CUST: *Yes. Can I have a look at those shoes, please?*

ASST: *Yes, certainly. Here you are.*

CUST: *Can I try them on?*

ASST: *Yes, certainly. What size are you?*

CUST: *Size . . . I think.*

ASST: *Here you are. These are size . . . .*

CUST: *They're nice but they're a bit . . . . Can you give me a size . . . ?*

ASST: *Certainly. These are size . . . .*

CUST: *Yes, I'll have them. How much are they?*

ASST: *They're . . . . How would you like to pay?*

CUST: *I'll pay cash./I'll pay by American Express.*

ASST: *That's fine. Here you are./Can you sign here, please?*

CUST: *Thank you. Goodbye.*

ASST: *You're welcome! Thank you. Goodbye.*

Students' Book pages 90, 91

🔘🔘 Listening

NOTES

Oxford: a university city in the south of England, to the west of London

TAPESCRIPT

Joy is trying to arrange a date for a business meeting with Liz Kennedy. Listen and then answer the questions in your book.

LIZ: Hello? Liz Kennedy here.

JOY: Liz, it's Joy here. Listen, can we fix a day for that meeting?

LIZ: Sure. Let me get my diary . . . here we are . . . Mmm, I'm a bit busy but let's see. What day suits you?

JOY: What about Wednesday, May 5th?

LIZ: Sorry! I'm going to Oxford on the 5th.

JOY: Thursday then?

LIZ: No, I'm staying in Oxford for two days. I'm coming back on Friday morning.

81

JOY: Friday the 7th?
LIZ: Yes.
JOY: What about Friday afternoon then?
LIZ: (*doubtfully*) Yes ... the trouble is, my parents are coming to dinner on Friday evening and I really must do the shopping in the afternoon ... so I'd rather not ...
JOY: You are difficult! Perhaps one evening then. Let's see. What about Tuesday evening? Tuesday, May 11th?
LIZ: Sorry. Doug and I are going to the theatre that evening.
JOY: Wednesday the 12th?
LIZ: (*cautiously*) Yes ... I'm seeing a business contact from Paris in the morning but the afternoon is OK. Shall we say 2.30 in the afternoon?
JOY: Fine! At last! So ... (*writing in her diary*) 2.30 on Wednesday, May 12th. See you then.
LIZ: Yes, OK.
JOY: And Liz ...
LIZ: Yes?
JOY: Don't ring me and say you can't come after all!
LIZ: (*laughing*) No, I won't. I promise! Bye, Joy.

KEY

Wednesday, May 5th
Two days
On Friday evening
Tuesday, May 11th
Wednesday, May 12th, in the morning
2.30 p.m. Wednesday, May 12th

Reading

Active words:	mountain learn pleased

Ask students what they know about Rio de Janeiro. Can they name any famous places there?

NOTES

Copacabana beach: one of the most famous beaches in the world
Sugarloaf Mountain: there is a funicular railway/cable car to the top of this landmark in the harbour of Rio de Janeiro
Ipanema: a suburb of Rio, also with a famous beach

KEY

Sarah and the family are living in Rio de Janeiro in Brazil.
Yes, they do. They're enjoying it very much.
It's very hot.
On Copacabana beach.
Robert is learning to surf and the children are swimming.
They're meeting Robert's new boss in a smart restaurant in Ipanema./They're going to a restaurant in Ipanema.
They're going up the Sugarloaf Mountain.
She's going shopping.
He started his new job last Monday.
Yes, he does. He's really pleased with it.

Writing

Active word:	everything

SSR

The Tower Hotel
Monday 17th May

Dear Shirley,
    Everything is going just fine here! Kelly and the kids are arriving *at Heathrow tomorrow at 8 p.m./on Tuesday evening.*
    We have lots of plans for the next two weeks. On Thursday, Kelly and the kids are going on a coach tour of London. On Friday we're seeing the musical 'Cats' at the New London theatre. On Sunday we're catching the night train (from Euston) to Scotland. We're staying in Scotland for two days and coming back to London on Tuesday evening. Then we're going to Stratford-upon-Avon to see 'A Midsummer Night's Dream'. We're leaving London at 10 o'clock on Saturday 29th. We're flying with Panam on Flight 125.
    We are looking forward to seeing you on Sunday.
                    Love from Vince.

Homework

Choose from:
1. Set 1 Exercise 4 Open dialogue, page 86. Write out the missing part.
2. Writing, page 90.
3. Unit 11 Workbook exercises.

🔊 Oral exercises

1. Ask about plans

Joanne isn't going to the conference.
Oh, is she going shopping?
Yes, she is.
Vince and Kelly aren't going to a concert.
Oh, are they going to the theatre?
Yes, they are.

Now you ask about people's plans in the same way.

Joanne isn't going to the conference.
Oh, is she going shopping?
Yes, she is.
Vince and Kelly aren't going to a concert.
Oh, are they going to the theatre?
Yes, they are.
Diana isn't going to the conference.
Oh, is she going to Cambridge?
Yes, she is.
Vince isn't going shopping.
Oh, is he going to the conference?
Yes, he is.
Vince and his family aren't going to Cambridge.
Oh, are they going to Stratford?
Yes, they are.
Vince and his family aren't going by train to Stratford.
Oh, are they going by car?
Yes, they are.

2. Talk about plans (Open exercise)

Talk to Paul about your plans for the week.

What are you doing this evening?
I'm staying at home.
What are you doing tomorrow?
I'm coming to class.

Now you talk to Paul in the same way. Tell him about your plans for the coming week.

What are you doing this evening?
....
What are you doing tomorrow?
....
What are you doing tomorrow evening?
....
What about Saturday? What are you doing then?
....
What are you doing on Sunday?
....
What are you doing in the summer holidays?
....

Really? Well, I hope you enjoy yourself, anyway. I'm going on a walking tour in North Wales. I love mountains, don't you?

3. Ask permission in a shop (1)

Listen to two shop assistants talking to customers.

We've got lots of T-shirts.
Can I have a look at them, please?
Yes, certainly.
This is a good camera.
Can I have a look at it, please?
Yes, certainly.

Now you go into some different shops and ask to see things.

We've got lots of T-shirts.
Can I have a look at them, please?
Yes, certainly.
This is a good camera.
Can I have a look at it, please?
Yes, certainly.
We have very nice Italian shoes.
Can I have a look at them, please?
Yes, certainly.
This is a French handbag.
Can I have a look at it, please?
Yes, certainly.
We've got some new designer jeans.
Can I have a look at them, please?
Yes, certainly.
This tie is from Yves St. Laurent.
Can I have a look at it, please?
Yes, certainly.

4. Ask permission in a shop (2)

Here are some more customers.

Do you like this sweater?
Yes. Can I try it on, please?
Yes, of course.
These jeans are your size.
Yes. Can I try them on, please?
Yes, of course.

Now you ask permission in the same way.

Do you like this sweater?
Yes. Can I try it on, please?
Yes, of course.
These jeans are your size.
Yes. Can I try them on, please?
Yes, of course.
These ski boots are very good.
Yes. Can I try them on, please?
Yes, of course.
This jacket is very nice.
Yes. Can I try it on, please?
Yes, of course.
Do you like these shoes?
Yes. Can I try them on, please?
Yes, of course.
These trousers are American. They're very smart.
Yes. Can I try them on, please?
Yes, of course.

Unit 12 Back from Cambridge

Presentation and practice		Set title	Language use	Examples
Dialogue:	Part 1			
	Set 1	Orders: direct and indirect	Give orders and tell others to give orders	*Get down!* *Tell her/him to get down.* *Don't do that!* *Tell her/him not to do that.* *You mustn't smoke.* *You must fasten your seat belts.*
Dialogue:	Part 2			
	Set 2	Past activities	Ask and talk about past activities	*Did you have a nice weekend?* *Yes, I did. It was lovely.* *It wasn't too bad.* *It was all right.* *What did you do (last weekend)?* *Where did you go last summer?*
Dialogue:	Part 3			
	Set 3	Offers of help	Offer and accept help	*Would you like a lift/to borrow my umbrella?* *Oh, thank you. That's very kind of you.*
			Offer and refuse help with a reason	*Would you like a lift?* *It's all right. I can go by underground.*
Spoken transfer: Cued roleplay			Combined	
Skills development: Reading		**Description** Rules for a party game. Students answer questions and play the game.		
Writing		In pairs, students write instructions for a simple party game.		
Listening		A person talks about a recent holiday. Students make notes in chart form.		
Oral exercises:	1		Respond to orders	Get down! *I don't want to get down!*
	2		Explain orders	That sign says, 'Please don't touch the models'. What does that mean, Jason? *That means we mustn't touch the models.*
	3		Give orders	I don't want to brush my hair. *But you must brush your hair.* I want to play in the street. *But you mustn't play in the street.*
	4		Ask about past events (1)	Ask Jason if he had a nice half-term. *Did you have a nice half-term, Jason?* No, I didn't. It was boring.
	5		Ask about past events (2)	Ask where he (Vince) stayed in Rio. *Where did you stay in Rio?*
	6		Answer about past events	Did you go to Greece? *No, we didn't go to Greece, we went to Italy.*

Grammar focus	Active words and expressions
	drop dangerous everyone down Don't worry. pick up loudly everywhere else quietly someone out of

Imperatives – positive and negative
Tell him/her to/not to + verb
Modal verb: *must/mustn't* (obligation and prohibition)
	hair brush main great (=marvellous)
	hand hit quiet so (near)
	road keep
	        stop
	        touch
	        wash

	lose wet more Oh dear! Never mind.
Past simple tense: regular verb *stay*; irregular verbs *have*, *go, see* – positive, negative and interrogative Mixed *Wh-* questions	nightclub special also relative sea(side)

	car park borrow short That's very kind
	lift find of you.
	                 mind
	                 run

Would you like a + noun? *Would you like to* + verb? Modal verb: *can* (possibility)	homework help difficult notebook paper word
	ill
Adverbs of manner: formation with *ly* Quantifier: *each*	answer question win clearly game person choose wrong count

Unit 12 Back from Cambridge

Students' Book pages 92, 93

Check homework from Unit 11.

🔲 Dialogue: Part 1

Active words and expressions:	drop pick up dangerous loudly quietly everyone everywhere someone down else out of Don't worry.

Draw students' attention to the pronouns *everyone*, *everywhere* and *someone*, and practise in other contexts.

Set 1 Orders: direct and indirect

Active words:	hair hand road brush hit keep stop touch wash main quiet great (=marvellous) so (near)

Exercise 1

Show the relationship between the indirect order (*Tell him to get down*) and the direct order (*Get down!*) – and draw attention to the position of the object pronoun. Also point out the position of *not* before the infinitive in the negative indirect order. Give some indirect orders round the class. (The students shouldn't make the direct orders sound too aggressive or rude.) Ask students to give the corresponding direct order. *Tell Paula to open the window. Tell Giorgio not to look out of the window. Tell Maria not to write in her textbook. Tell Juanita to stand up.*

Explain the context of the exercise – that of giving orders to a child. Act, with different facial expressions each time, the short exchanges 1 and 2.

Students work in groups of three.

Exercise 2

Practise the two sentences with *must/mustn't*. Indicate the weak form of *must/məst/* in the declarative sentence. Refer students to the first two signs and tell them what each means. e.g.
1. *This means that you mustn't walk across the road when the light is red.*
2. *This means that you must fasten your seat belt.*

In pairs students work out what each of the signs mean. Ask them to write the complete sentences in their exercise books.

KEY

This means you:
1. *mustn't* walk across the road when the light is red.

2. *must* fasten your *seat belt* when the sign is on.
3. *must* keep this entrance clear.
4. *mustn't* drop *litter* in the park or on the road.
5. *must* keep to the speed limit.
6. *mustn't* take photographs in the theatre.
7. *mustn't* go down this street because the sign says, '*No entry*'.
8. *must* give *way* to other drivers.
9. *mustn't* swim in the river.
10. *must* stop when you see this sign.
11. *mustn't park* between 8.30 a.m. and 9.30 a.m.
12. *mustn't* do a U turn in this main road.
13. *mustn't* bring sandwiches into the classroom.
14. *mustn't feed* the animals.
15. *must* keep *left*.

Exercise 3

This could be done together with the class contributing ideas, or as group work. Students may start their rules with *You must/mustn't* or *No . . . ing*.

Students' Book pages 94, 95

🔲 Dialogue: Part 2

Active words and expressions:	lose wet more Oh dear! Never mind.

NOTES

Cambridge:	a university city in the east of England
King's College chapel:	a beautiful chapel in King's College, one of the many university colleges in Cambridge
Star Trek:	a long-running science-fiction TV series from which films have been made
school again:	Jason's school has a week's holiday every term. This is the half-term holiday

Set 2 Past activities

Active words:	nightclub relative sea(side) special also

Exercise 1

BLACKBOARD

Did you have a nice	*weekend?* *holiday?* *evening?* *birthday?* *summer?* *Christmas?*

Students ask you questions S-T from this table. Reply, using the range of replies given in the language box. Students work in pairs as instructed. Ask questions T-S to random students.

Exercise 2

Go through the conversation yourself, acting both sides. Then go through it again with the students practising the question forms only. Then ask students to read it in pairs, changing parts.

Refer students to the chart about the different people's holidays. Help the students with the pronunciation of the proper names: Kirstin/kɜːstɪn/, John/dʒɒn), Felicity/fəˈlɪsɪti/, Frederick/ˈfredrɪk/, Lesley/ˈlesli/.

Ask questions from the following substitution table:

BLACKBOARD

Where did	Kirstin	go for	her	holiday	last	summer?
	John		his			winter?
	Felicity					
	Frederick					
	Lesley					

Students reply using the 3rd person singular and the relevant information from the chart.

Ask a student to take the part of Kirstin and ask the questions S-T down the left-hand side of the chart. Students work in pairs asking and answering about the other people, using the printed conversation at the bottom of page 94 as a model.

Exercise 3

Refer students to the model paragraph about Kirstin Brown and ask one of them to read it aloud. Ask questions about the other people in the 3rd person singular to prepare the work. Students then write about the other people for homework.

Exercise 4

Either ask general questions or ask students to talk briefly in pairs about things they have done. They can write a paragraph in class or for homework.

Students' Book
pages 96, 97

🔘🔘 Dialogue: Part 3

| Active words and expressions: | car park lift borrow find mind run short That's very kind of you. |

Set 3 Offers of help

| Active words: | homework notebook paper word help difficult |

Exercise 1

Take a few objects at hand such as a dictionary, pen, pencil, book, and make offers to one or two students, like this: *Jaime, would you like to borrow my dictionary? Silvia, would you like to borrow my pen?* Ask the students to repeat chorally. Students now work in pairs matching a situation and an offer from the two columns. Check at random when they have finished.

KEY

I haven't got a notebook. Would you like some paper?
I must catch the 9.30 plane. Would you like a lift to the airport?
I haven't got any money. Would you like to borrow £5?
This exercise is difficult. Would you like some help with it?
It's very cold in here. Would you like to borrow a sweater?
It's raining. Would you like to borrow my umbrella?
I don't understand this word. Would you like to borrow my dictionary?

Exercise 2

Students now complete the exchange by adding a polite acceptance to the offer.

Exercise 3

Here the students practise making a refusal. Practise the exchange yourself. Change your expression and voice for each speaker. Use the pictures to give the context to the situation. Go through the reasons for each refusal.

SSR

It's raining.
Would you like a lift?
It's all right. I'm going to the cinema.
OK.
Would you like a lift?
It's all right. My sister is meeting me. etc.

Roleplay

| Active word: | ill |

SSR

S1: *(dials number)*
S2: *Hello. . . . speaking/here.*
S1: *Hello, ... How are you? This is . . . .*
S2: *I'm fine, thanks. Why weren't you in class today?*
S1: *I'm ill/not very well.*
S2: *Oh, I'm sorry. Can I help you with anything?*
S1: *Yes, you can. You see I can't do my homework because I haven't got my textbook.*
S2: *Would you like to borrow my textbook?*

87

S1: *Oh, thank you. That's very kind of you. Can you bring me the book. I live at . . . . / My address is . . . .*
S2: *Fine. I'll come this evening with the book. Bye!*
S1: *Bye! And thank you very much.*

Students' Book pages 98, 99

Reading

Active words:	game person question choose
	count answer win clearly

For further games see Index 5, Selected further reading. The object of the game from a language point of view is to practise *yes/no* questions in the present and past simple tenses. The instructions are presented as a reading text with check questions on how to organise the game. The game can be saved for a suitable occasion if you wish. Help students with the names of possible pairs before you start the game. Here are some suggestions:

1. from your country – comedians, entertainers, famous married couples, etc. who are alive or who are dead
2. Mickey Mouse and Minnie Mouse – two Walt Disney cartoon characters
3. Starsky and Hutch – two American TV detectives
4. The Lone Ranger and Tonto – a cowboy and his Indian companion from a newspaper strip cartoon series, film serials and a film
5. Miss Piggy and Kermit the frog – TV puppets (The Muppets – see page 30)
6. Peter Pan and Wendy – from the children's story by J.M. Barrie
7. Fred Astaire and Ginger Rogers – American film stars, famous in 1930's films as a dance partnership
8. Simon and Garfunkel – American singers, famous for many songs, including *Bridge over Troubled Water*
9. Dr Jekyll and Mr Hyde – really one character from the story by Robert Louis Stevenson. Dr Jekyll transforms into the evil Mr Hyde after taking a certain drug
10. Tom and Jerry – two cartoon characters, a cat and a mouse
11. Prince Charles and Princess Diana – The Prince and Princess of Wales, the future King and Queen of Great Britain
12. Scarlett O'Hara and Rhett Butler – the main characters in the novel and subsequent film, *Gone with the Wind* (see page 120)
13. Diana and Paul; Vince and Joanne – characters in this book

Writing

Encourage the students to think of simple games. They work in pairs and make notes for the written instructions. They write the instructions for homework.

🔘 Listening

Active word:	wrong

TAPESCRIPT

Listen to Meg talking to a friend about her recent holiday in the States. Note down the information to complete the chart.

Did you have a good time in America?

Oh, we had a fabulous time. It really was a holiday of a lifetime for us.

Where did you go?

Well, we started off at Los Angeles and then we went up to San Francisco. Had a look in at Lake Taho, Vegas, Grand Canyon and made our way back to Long Beach and then eventually home.

And where did you stay on holiday?

We stayed in a hotel for the first two nights we were in America, but then we hired a camper. Fabulous trip it was with the camper. It really is the right way to see America. We had a couple of . . . erm, happenings there, if you like. We hired a car because we couldn't take the camper around because of the hills and, erm . . . we couldn't find the car when we went back for it. (Oh no! *laughs*) We eventually found it after a while but it took quite a time.

What else went wrong on your holiday?

Well, while we were in Disneyland, my husband was using his ciné camera and filming away quite happily and it broke down. We didn't realise it but – right, straight away – but, unfortunately, we lost a film out of it. And also, when we got back from our holiday, when some of our ciné film was sent away to be developed, a particular company made a mess of three of them. So we lost out again. They didn't do a very good job on them.

What was the most special thing you did on the holiday?

The most special thing for me was visiting San Francisco and I achieved a lifetime's ambition. I crossed the Golden Gate Bridge. Not once but six times!

How long were you in the States for altogether?

A total of fourteen days and twelve days we were travelling around in the camper.

KEY

Places visited:	*Los Angeles, San Francisco, Lake Taho, (Las) Vegas, The Grand Canyon, Long Beach*
Where she stayed:	*hotel (2 nights); in a camper*
Special occasion:	*visiting San Francisco; Meg crossed the Golden Gate Bridge six times*
Things that went wrong:	*couldn't find the car; ciné camera broke down (ciné films developed badly)*

Length of holiday: *fourteen days*
Her opinion of holiday: *fabulous – the holiday of a lifetime*

Homework

Choose from:
1. Set 1 Exercises 2 and 3, page 93.
2. Set 2 Exercises 3 and 4, page 95.
3. Roleplay, page 97. Write out the conversation after oral preparation in class.
4. Writing, page 98.
5. Unit 12 Workbook exercises

🔊 Oral exercises

1. Respond to orders

A parent is telling his child what to do.

Get down!
I don't want to get down!

Now you can respond to orders in the same way.

Get down!
I don't want to get down!
Sit still!
I don't want to sit still!
Eat your cornflakes!
I don't want to eat my cornflakes!
Wash your hands!
I don't want to wash my hands!
Talk quietly!
I don't want to talk quietly!
Brush your hair!
I don't want to brush my hair!

2. Explain orders

A teacher is taking some children round a museum.

That sign says, 'Please don't touch the models'.
What does that mean, Jason?
That means we mustn't touch the models.
Good boy! Now that sign says, 'Please don't talk loudly'.
What does that mean, Jason?
That means we mustn't talk loudly.

Now you can explain the signs for the teacher.

That sign says, 'Please don't touch the models'. What does that mean?
That means we mustn't touch the models.
That sign says, 'Please don't talk loudly'. What does that mean?
That means we mustn't talk loudly.
That sign says, 'Please don't drop litter'. What does that mean?
That means we mustn't drop litter.
That sign says, 'Please don't run'. What does that mean?
That means we mustn't run.
That sign says, 'No eating or drinking'. What does that mean?
That means we mustn't eat or drink.
That sign says, 'No smoking'. What does that mean?
That means we mustn't smoke.

Good Jason. You don't smoke, do you? So that's all right. Come along everyone, let's go and have a look at a model of the first railway train. Now remember—don't touch anything ...

3. Give orders

You are looking after a small child.

CHILD: I don't want to brush my hair.
YOU: *But you must brush your hair.*
CHILD: I want to play in the street.
YOU: *But you mustn't play in the street.*

Now you give orders in the same way.

I don't want to brush my hair.
But you must brush your hair.
I want to play in the street.
But you mustn't play in the street.
I don't want to go to bed.
But you must go to bed.
I want to play with the telephone.
But you mustn't play with the telephone.
I don't want to go to school.
But you must go to school.
I don't want to wash my hands.
But you must wash your hands.
All right then. But after, can I have some chocolate? Pl-ea-se?

4. Ask about past events (1)

Ask Jason if he had a nice half-term.
Did you have a nice half-term, Jason?
No, I didn't. It was boring.

Now you ask people questions about past events in the same way.

Ask Jason if he had a nice half-term.
Did you have a nice half-term, Jason?
No, I didn't. It was boring.
Ask Diana if she had a good day at Cambridge.
Did you have a good day at Cambridge, Diana?
Yes, I did. It was very interesting.
Ask Joanne if she had a good day at the shops.
Did you have a good day at the shops, Joanne?
Yes, I did. I bought a lovely sweater.
Ask Vince if he had a nice weekend.
Did you have a nice weekend, Vince?
Yes, I did. I went for a walk in Kensington Gardens.
Ask if Paul had a nice evening at the theatre.
Did you have a nice evening at the theatre, Paul?
Yes, I did. I went to see *Pirates of Penzance,* the musical. It was marvellous.
Ask if Liz had a nice holiday in Scotland.
Did you have a nice holiday in Scotland, Liz?
No, I didn't, actually. I was ill. I stayed in bed in the hotel all the time.
Oh, never mind. You had a good rest anyway!
I certainly did. *And* I read *Gone With the Wind* in three days!

89

5. Ask about past events (2)

Ask Vince about his last trip to South America.

Where did you stay in Rio?
I stayed in a hotel near Copacabana beach.

Now you go on. You ask Vince questions about his trip.

Ask Vince where he stayed in Rio.
Where did you stay in Rio, Vince?
I stayed in a hotel near Copacabana beach.
Ask Vince what he saw in Rio.
What did you see in Rio, Vince?
Well, it was Carnival time you see, so, well, I didn't see
very much.
Ask Vince where he stayed in Brazilia.
Where did you stay in Brazilia, Vince?
I stayed in a very nice hotel.
Ask Vince how long he stayed in São Paulo
How long did you stay in São Paulo, Vince?
I only stayed there for three days.
Ask Vince how he travelled to Manàos.
How did you travel to Manàos, Vince?
I flew with a domestic airline.
Ask Vince who he saw in Salvador.
Who did you see in Salvador, Vince?
I saw some business friends.
And did you have a nice time in Brazil?
I certainly did. I had a marvellous time.

6. Answer about past events

A girl is talking to her friend about her holiday.

Did you go to Greece?
No, we didn't go to Greece. We went to Italy.

Now you go on.

Did you go to Greece?
No, we didn't go to Greece. We went to Italy.
Did you stay for a week?
No, we didn't stay for a week. We stayed for two weeks.
Did you stay in a villa?
No, we didn't stay in a villa. We stayed in a hotel.
Did you go to the seaside?
No, we didn't go to the seaside. We went sightseeing.
Did you go to Florence?
No, we didn't go to Florence. We went to Rome.
Did you see the Coliseum?
No, we didn't see the Coliseum. We saw the Vatican.

Unit 13 Trouble at the hotel

Presentation and practice	Set title	Language use	Examples
Dialogue: Part 1			
Set 1	Past time	Ask and talk about the past day	*Where did you go? I went to Cambridge. When did you leave? I left at eight o'clock. Who did you see? I didn't see anyone.*
Dialogue: Part 2			
Set 2	Surprise and interest	Show surprise and interest to keep a conversation going	*My colleague was here at the conference. Oh, was he? I'm English. Oh, are you? She's a teacher. Oh, is she? I like playing football. Do you? Yes, I play for the local team.*
Set 3	Confirmation	Ask for and give confirmation	*Isn't Diana Trent a film director? That's right, she is. And doesn't she work for Focus Film and Video? Yes, she does. Didn't she go to Bristol University? That's right, she did.*
Dialogue: Part 3			
Set 4	Requests	Ask people to do things Agree to do things Ask others to make requests	*Can you answer a few questions, please? Yes, of course/certainly. Can you ask him to come and see me, please? Can you ask them not to leave? I want you to tell me about Mr Roberts.*
Spoken transfer: Open dialogue Roleplay		Surprise and interest Past activities	
Skills development: Listening	**Description** A policeman questions two teenagers about a break in. Students listen and analyse the questions.		
Reading	A middle-aged woman remembers when she was young and the first time she met her husband. Students answer a range of questions.		
Writing	Students refer back to the reading text on page 58, (about a family's Sunday outing) and use answers to questions as the basis for writing a similar paragraph, but this time in the past tense.		
Oral exercises: 1		Ask for and give past details (1) (Open exercise)	When did you get up today? *I got up at 6 o'clock.*
2		Ask for and give past details (2) (Open exercise)	Where did you go last weekend? *I {went to see my grandparents. / didn't go anywhere. / stayed at home.}*
3		Express surprise and interest	Some burglars broke into the school. *Did they? Yes, they did.*
4		Ask people to give instructions	They must fasten their seatbelts. *Can you ask them to fasten their seatbelts.* They mustn't smoke. *Can you ask them not to smoke.*
5		Ask people to make requests	Where do you want the students to meet? *Ask them to meet at the railway station.*

Grammar focus	Active vocabulary and expressions			
	detective	trouble	spend (time)	Is anything wrong?
	police		anyone	What's the matter?
Past simple tense: mixed regular and irregular verbs Question words: *Who? What else?*	wear	between	What else?	
	colleague	break (into)	hope	alone	no one	Oh no!
	be missing	find out	show	perhaps	into
			take		
Eched questions (present and past simple tenses) with auxiliary verbs: *be, do, have*	neighbour	come from	favourite	
	university			
Negative questions				
	Perhaps not.		*Just one moment.*	
Modal verb: *can* (request) *Yes, certainly/of course.* *Can you ask him/her to/not to* + verb *I want him/her to* + verb	cream	clear up	repair	
	carton	cut	shut	
	group	post	take away	
	luggage	put	Can you do me a favour?	
	know (somebody)			
	hard			
	break	steal		
She asked/told me to/not to + verb	boyfriend	get married	embarrassed	
	corner	go out with somebody	shy	
		marry	surprised	
		wait		

93

Unit 13 Trouble at the hotel

Students' Book pages 100, 101

Check homework from Unit 12.

🔲 Dialogue: Part 1

Active words and expressions:	detective police trouble spend (time) anyone Is anything wrong? What's the matter?

Set 1 Past time

Active words and expressions:	wear between What else?

Exercise 1

Practise the exchanges in the box chorally and individually. Refer students to the questionnaire. Choose some questions from each of the questionnaire sections which require the use of verbs with regular past tense endings, i.e. *start, finish, talk, travel, play, visit, watch.* Point out how the regular past tense is formed by adding *-ed.* Draw attention to the spelling of *travelled.*

Now ask questions which require the use of verbs with irregular past tense endings, i.e. *get, have, leave, go, see, sit, come, take, do, wear, buy.*

Help the students to form their answers and write correct examples on the blackboard. (See SB, page 128 for a more complete list of irregular verbs.)

Point out to the students that in the section marked *Time* students can use *What time* or *When* in their questions.

Exercise 2

Ask the students to work silently noting down their answers. They can now work in pairs, changing parts after each section. For homework, students can write out answers to three questions from each section.

Exercise 3

Set this piece of work for homework. Students in fact have to provide an alibi – they must be able to account for their whereabouts during a certain time of the day. If time allows, act the situation orally in groups in a later lesson.

Students' Book pages 102, 103

🔲 Dialogue: Part 2

Active words and expressions:	colleague be missing break (into) find out hope show take alone perhaps no one into Oh no!

NOTES

my film: Diana is referring to the film she is going to show in competition at the conference

Set 2 Surprise and interest

Active words:	neighbour university come from favourite

Exercise 1

Say both parts of the exchange yourself making sure that you have a rising intonation on the short form echoed questions. To give thorough practice, go through all the echoed questions in the chart. Explain that these echoed questions are very helpful when you want to keep a conversation going, because they show that you are interested in what the other person is saying.

Exercise 2

Refer to the Conference Bulletin extract on the right of page 103 and do question and answer work. Ask one student to take the part of A and work S-T with the model conversation. Ask students to run through it in pairs and to change parts. Students then use the information from the Conference Bulletin to make similar conversations.

Exercise 3

Refer students back to the third column (Say something else) of the language chart on page 102. Show how these sentences add information to the initial statement. Work with one student T-S talking about some of the things you like and like doing. Add a reason or some extra information each time.

Make sure the students are familiar with the topics listed in the left-hand column and that they have something to say about some of them. Draw attention to the initial phrases listed under 'Begin like this'. Monitor each pair as they work. At the end of the task ask two or three pairs to repeat some of their conversations for the whole class.

Set 3 Confirmation

This set practises negative questions with short form positive answers. Refer back to the question in Dialogue: Part 2: *Doesn't your colleague go into your room sometimes?* Now refer the students to the exchange in the box. Work T-S, S-T and S-S. Students use the information from the Conference Bulletin from Set 2 Exercise 2 to write negative sentences. Check these first before the students begin pair work.

KEY

Paul Roberts
Isn't Paul a cameraman?
That's right, he is.
Doesn't he work for Focus Film and Video, too?
Yes, he does.
Didn't he go to Wolverhampton Technical College?
Yes, that's right, he did.

Vince Hall
Isn't Vince a sound technician?
That's right, he is.
Doesn't he work for Sight and Sound Company?
Yes, he does.
Isn't he married with three children?
Yes, he is.
Didn't he go to night school in Detroit?
That's right, he did.

Joanne Tessler
Isn't Joanne a film assistant?
That's right, she is.
And doesn't she work for Sight and Sound Company, too?
That's right, she does.
Doesn't she come from California?
Yes, she does.
And doesn't she live in Los Angeles?
That's right, yes, she does.
And didn't she go to the University of Southern California?
That's right, she did.

Your knowledge of the class will be important here for transfer work. If possible, ask questions about students and their families, e.g. *Isn't your brother a student in America? Doesn't your father work for Fiat? Didn't you go to England last year?*

Explain that the students should confirm or correct your questions.

Students' Book pages 104, 105

🔘🔘 **Dialogue: Part 3**

Active expressions:	Perhaps not.
	Just one moment.

KEY

He wants Diana to answer a few/some more questions.
He wants her to tell him about Paul.
He wants her to ask Paul to come and see him.
He wants her to tell Vince and Joanne not to leave the hotel.

The inspector wants to see Paul and the Americans because they knew that Diana was in Cambridge and he wants to ask them about the film.

Set 4 Requests

Active words and expressions:	carton cream group luggage clear up cut post put repair shut take away Can you do me a favour?

Exercise 1

Refer students to the pictures and the first request: *Can you close the window, please?* and practise it chorally with the response, *Yes, of course.* Students work in pairs with the other situations. Ask them to change parts.

Exercise 2

Practise the request in the box, explaining that here you are asking someone else to make a request. Refer students to the short conversation between Paul and Diana. You take the part of Diana and work T-S with one student and S-T with another. Ask students to read the conversation and change parts. Students roleplay, using the characters and the messages given in the chart.

Exercise 3

Refer students to the note that Liz Kennedy writes to her husband, Doug. Ask the following questions:
What time will Liz be back? (At 7.)
Why is Doug staying at home? (Because it's his day off.)
How many pints of milk does she want? (3)
(NOTE: milk and dairy produce are delivered to people's homes in Britain. One pint is about ½ litre.)

Students now write the answers to the questions printed in the book. Check these orally when the students have finished writing.

KEY

She wants him (the milkman) to leave 3 pints of milk and 2 cartons of cream.
She doesn't want him to leave anything on Saturday.
She wants them (the builders) to clear up in the evening and take away their tools.
She wants him to take away the VCR and bring back a new model.
She doesn't want the gardener to cut the roses.

Students write the instructions out again using indirect requests either in class or at home. Refer them to the models at the end of the exercise.

SSR

Doug,
Just a few things for you to check. I'll be back at 7. Hope you enjoy your day off!
Can you ask the milkman to leave 3 pints of milk and 2 cartons of cream today, but ask him not to leave anything on Saturday.
Can you ask the builders to clear up in the evening and take away their tools and ask them not to smoke in the bathroom!

Can you ask the video hire man to take away the VCR and bring back a new model.
Can you ask the gardener to repair the gate but ask him not to cut the roses.
Have a nice day!
Liz.

📼 Open dialogue

> **Active words:** know (somebody) hard

SSR

Talk to Liz

LIZ: Oh, hello. Don't I know you? Aren't you from Lyon in France?
YOU: *No, I'm not, I'm from . . . in . . . .*
LIZ: Oh are you? Sorry! Tell me, when do your classes finish this term?
YOU: *They finish in (July).*
LIZ: Oh, do they?
YOU: *Yes, they finish (at the end of the first week of July).*
LIZ: Well, aren't you pleased with your English now?
YOU: *Yes, I am. Very.*
LIZ: Do you know anyone English?
YOU: *No, I don't./Yes, I do, I know someone called . . . .*
LIZ: Keep working hard! Bye for now!
YOU: *Bye.*

Roleplay

This is similar to Set 1 Exercise 3, page 101. The students who are roleplaying the teenagers need to work out exactly what they did during the evening. The parent's job is to try and find out if they are telling the truth or not. Therefore, their answers must be the same. The parent must ask the same questions to each of the teenagers in turn. One of the teenagers must be out of earshot while the first one is being questioned.

Students' Book
pages 106, 107

📼 Listening

> **Active words:** break steal

TAPESCRIPT

Listen to Police Constable Mackenzie questioning two young people about a break in at their sports centre. Listen to the whole conversation once. Then listen again and pay special attention to the questions the Constable asks. Do they start with *When, Where,* or *Who?* Answer the questions in your book afterwards.

PC: Now, there's nothing to worry about. I want to see everyone who used the pavilion yesterday. Let's start with you two. Can you come in here, please?

JANET: Who . . . us?
PC: That's right. You and your friend. Now, tell me . . . when did you come in here yesterday?
JANET: About 2.30.
MARK: Yes, about then.
PC: About 2.30. And did you notice the windows?
MARK: No, why?
PC: Someone broke them, that's why. And were the cups and silver in the cupboard then?
MARK: Yes, I remember looking at the swimming trophy.
PC: The cupboard is always locked, I understand.
JANET: Yes. Well, I suppose it is.
PC: Where is the key to the cupboard?
JANET: I haven't a clue.
MARK: No, I don't know. Ted knows.
PC: And who is Ted?
MARK: Ted's the caretaker.
PC: Ah. Now, when did you leave the pavilion in the afternoon?
JANET: About 4. Wasn't it, Mark?
MARK: Yes, it must have been about then.
PC: And where did you go then?
MARK: We went to the caff (café) down the road.
JANET: Yeah, we had a coke in the caff (café).
PC: I see. And did you see anyone in the room where the cups are when you left?
MARK: No.
JANET: Yes, I did.
PC: Who did you see?
JANET: I don't know her name, a new instructor . . .
PC: I see. Where is she now?
JANET: Don't know.
PC: Right. That's all. Thank you.

KEY

When/What time?	*2 questions*
Who?	*2 questions*
Where?	*3 questions*

Reading

> **Active words:** boyfriend corner get married
> go out with somebody marry
> wait embarrassed shy surprised

This extract is adapted from a longer magazine article in which various people were interviewed about how they met the people they eventually married.

KEY

At a dance at the village hall.
She was about 19.
Her best friend, Marjorie.
Very pretty.
She was shy.
Because no one asked her to dance.
She told her to go and ask one of the boys to dance.
No, she didn't.

She told one of her boyfriends to go and ask Win for a dance.
A boy called Mick.
Yes, he asked her to go to the cinema with him.
He asked her to marry him.
Because they were too young.
On Win's 21st birthday.
Yes, they are.
She always says, 'You mustn't sit and wait for things to happen'.

Writing

Ask the students to look back at the reading text on page 58 which describes a Mexican family's Sunday in Chapultepec Park. Explain that they are going to describe their day as if it was last Sunday, i.e. in the past. First ask them the questions printed in their books to guide them through the text, and elicit the appropriate information. Ask them to write out a complete paragraph for homework.

SSR

On Sunday we got up quite early. We didn't have a big breakfast, only coffee and bread and butter. Then we went to church. After church we all went to Chapultepec Park. First we went boating on the lake. Then we sat under the trees and had our picnic lunch. The children played with their kites. In the afternoon the small children rode their bicycles. At about five o'clock we bought fruit and then we caught the bus home. We had supper at home and then the children went to bed.

Homework

Choose from:
1. Set 1 Exercise 1, page 101. Students answer selected questions from the questionnaire.
2. Set 1 Exercise 3, page 101.
3. Set 4 Exercise 3, page 105. Students rewrite the note.
4. Writing, pages 106, 58. Write about Chapultepec Park.
5. Unit 13 Workbook exercises.

🔲 Oral exercises

1. Ask for and give past details (1) (Open exercise)

When did you get up today?
I got up at 6 o'clock.

Now you answer the questions.

When did you get up today?
. . . .
When did you arrive here?
. . . .
Who did you see first today?
. . . .
What did you have for breakfast this morning?
. . . .
How much did you spend on food yesterday?
. . . .

2. Ask for and give past details (2) (Open exercise)

Listen to Joanne talking to Diana, Paul and Vince.

JOANNE: Where did you go last weekend, Diana?
DIANA: *I went to see my grandparents.*
JOANNE: And what about you, Paul?
PAUL: *I didn't go anywhere.*
JOANNE: Really? And where did you go, Vince?
VINCE: *I stayed at home.*

Now you say what you did in the same way.

Where did you go last weekend?
. . . .
And where did you go last Christmas?
. . . .
Where did you go last Easter?
. . . .
Where did you go last summer?
. . . .
JOANNE: I went to Bermuda. It was great. I went with a crowd of friends.

3. Express surprise and interest

Some burglars broke into the school.
Did they?
Yes, they did.

Now you respond to the statements with surprise and interest.

It was at the weekend.
Was it?
Yes, it was.
They stole the book money.
Did they?
Yes, they did.
It was about £500.
Was it?
Yes, it was.
I know one of them.
Do you?
Yes, I do.
He's my neighbour.
Is he?
Yes, he is.
And he's a very quiet man. He's always gardening.
Funny, isn't it, how strange people are?

4. Ask people to give instructions

You are a member of the cabin crew for BA flight 307. Read the list of instructions and then tell a new colleague what to do.

They must fasten their seatbelts.
Can you ask them to fasten their seatbelts.
OK. Fine.
They mustn't smoke.
Can you ask them not to smoke.
OK. Fine.

Now you ask people to give instructions in the same way.

97

They must fasten their seatbelts.
Can you ask them to fasten their seatbelts.
OK. Fine.
They mustn't smoke.
Can you ask them not to smoke.
OK. Fine.
They must put their seats upright.
Can you ask them to put their seats upright.
OK. Fine.
They must finish their drinks.
Can you ask them to finish their drinks.
OK. Fine.
They mustn't stand in the gangway.
Can you ask them not to stand in the gangway.
OK. Fine.

Ladies and gentlemen we are now approaching London Heathrow. The local time is 11.15 and the temperature is 17 degrees centigrade. The 'No smoking' sign is now on. Would you please extinguish all cigarettes and kindly return to your seats.

5. Ask people to make requests

You are a teacher in charge of a class outing. Tell your assistant teacher what to do.

Where do you want the students to meet?
Ask them to meet at the railway station.

Now you go on in the same way.

Where do you want the students to meet?
Ask them to meet at the railway station.
When do you want the students to meet?
Ask them to meet at 4 o'clock.
What food do you want the students to bring?
Ask them to bring some fruit for the journey.
How much money do you want the students to bring?
Ask them to bring about £5.
What clothes do you want the students to wear?
Ask them to wear a warm jacket, a sweater and jeans.
Fine. Is that all?
I always like a class outing, don't you?

Unit 14 Success!

Presentation and practice	Set title	Language use	Examples
Dialogue: Part 1			
Set 1	Predictions	Predict future events	*I'm (not) going to win.* *She's/She isn't going to win.* *We're (not) going to win.* *People aren't going to like it.*
Dialogue: Part 2			
Set 2	Identification	Identify belongings	*Whose is this pen? It's mine.* *Is this your book? No, it's Maria's.* *Whose are these gloves?* *They're hers/his.* *Whose are these books?* *They're ours/yours/theirs.*
		Identify and describe belongings	*Whose is the Cadillac?* *It's the Conways'.* *Which is the Conways' car?* *Theirs is the blue and red one.*
		Identify and describe objects you like	*Which running shoes (ones) do you like?* *I like the red ones.* *Which sports bag do you like?* *Well, I quite like the one with the Tiger label on it.*
Set 3	Recent activities	Ask and talk about recent activities	*Have you had lunch yet?* *Yes, I have.* *No, I haven't.* *I've (have) had lunch.*
		Ask and talk about length of time	*How long have you lived in this city?* *I've lived here for 16 years.* *Juan has lived in Mexico City for 16 years.*
Dialogue: Part 3			
Spoken transfer: Roleplay		Combined	
Skills development: Reading Writing 1 and 2	**Description** A holiday job advertisement followed by a letter of application with a curriculum vitae Students complete their own application form for a summer camp job and write a covering letter modelled on the one they have read.		
Oral exercises: 1	Predict the weather		What's the weather like today? *I think it's going to be fine.*
2	Talk about future events		Any news of your parents? *Yes. They're going to move to the south coast.* Oh, really?
3	Talk about uncompleted activities		Are you coming with me? *No, I haven't had breakfast yet.*
4	Talk about completed activities		Have you done your homework this morning? *Yes, I did it before breakfast.*
5	Identify belongings		Which is your hat? *This is mine.* Which is Paul's bag? *This is his.*
6	Describe clothes		Which dress do you like? *I like the white one with silver stripes on it.*

Grammar focus	Active vocabulary and expressions				
	success	*important*	*safe*	*topical*	*luckily*
	invite	*political*		*true*	*Whose?*
Future tense: *going to* + verb (prediction) – positive, negative and interrogative	*ball*	*catch*	*jump*	*romantic*	
	education	*change*	*score*		
	goal	*cry*			
	menu	*order*	*Congratulations!*		
Question words: *Whose? Which?* Possessive pronouns: *mine/yours,* etc.	*glove*	*shorts*	*gold*	*I quite like...*	
	label	*sports bag*	*silver*		
	rollerskates	*star*			
	running shoes	*stripe*			
Genitive plural ending *s'* Pronouns: *one, ones* Adjective phrases: *the one/ones with the...on it/them.*					
Present perfect simple tense (+ *yet*) – positive, negative and interrogative Preposition of time: *for* (duration)	*shower*	*make (your bed)*	*yet*		
	thing	*tidy*			
		wash up			
	strap	*Good luck!*	*Take care of yourselves.*		
	suitcase	*It's time to go.*			
	camp	*experience*	*hear from*		
	examination	*interpreter*	*outdoor*		

Unit 14 Success!

Students' Book pages 108, 109

Check homework from Unit 13.

🔵⚫ Dialogue: Part 1

Active words:	success invite important political safe topical true luckily Whose?

NOTES

Documentary section:	the section for films about real-life subjects. A silver star is awarded to the best film in each section
première:	a French word for the first public presentation of a film in a country or area, e.g. the European première of *Gone with the Wind*
They caught a man at the airport:	Diana's film is controversial. ('Yes, and it's political.') It questions the safety of nuclear power stations and sets out arguments for not continuing a policy of developing nuclear energy. Some 'important people' would prefer there to be no debate about the uses of nuclear energy. Someone has paid a thief to steal Diana's film so that it can't be shown to the public

Set 1 Predictions

Active words:	ball education goal catch change cry jump score romantic

Exercise 1

This set presents and practises the use of the *going to* future to express predictions, e.g. *I think it's going to rain.* *Going to* used to express future plans is introduced in *Building Strategies*, the second book in this series.

Go to the window, look out and say: *It's (not) a (very) nice day today. The sun is shining./It's raining.* Then ask: *Is it going to rain/be hot/be sunny today/tomorrow?* Get the students to say what they think the weather is going to be like.

Refer them to the language boxes at the beginning of the set. Ask students at random to read out a few sentences from each box to practise both the positive and the interrogative form. When the patterns have been established, ask the students to look at the first illustration in the set of pictures. Ask the whole class: *What do you think is going to happen in this picture?* Elicit the

reply: *The horse isn't going to jump the fence.* Ask the students to look at the remaining pictures and write captions for each picture. They should use the *going to* future and one of the verbs listed each time.

KEY

The horse/It isn't going to jump the fence.
They're going to get married.
He's going to cry.
He's going to catch the ball.
He's going to score a goal.
The baby/She isn't going to eat her food.

Exercise 2

Show students how to make the questions shown in the examples. Explain the meaning of *astrologer*. Establish the meaning of the topics and ask students to work in pairs asking appropriate questions about each of them. Check random students when they have finished.

SSR

Romantic life:	*Am I going to meet someone nice in the summer/get married/fall in love?*
Work:	*Am I going to get a good job/another job/work in another country, city/change my job/get more money?*
Money:	*Am I going to win the lottery/football pools/be rich?*
Home life:	*Am I going to move to a bigger apartment/flat/house?*
Education:	*Am I going to go to college/get good results/pass my exams?*
Travel:	*Am I going to travel to America/go to Britain?*

Remind students to choose only those topics they would like to ask the astrologer about.

Students' Book pages 110, 111

Set 2 Identification

Active words:	glove label rollerskates running shoes shorts sports bag star stripe gold silver I quite like . . .

Exercise 1

Practise the questions and answers in the box using some of the items listed in the rubric. It is best to collect your items from the students and have them all in one collection on your table. Hold each item up so that students can identify their owners. Refer students to the complete paradigm of the possessive pronouns on page 115.

Exercise 2

NOTES

Custom Car Club: the idea of painting your car with elaborate designs and decorative colours started in America and spread all over the world

Students should choose either the Volkswagen or the Volvo as their own. They first identify and then describe the other cars, following the examples in the book. They write sentences about each car for homework.

Exercise 3

Refer students to all the sports items. Explain that they are going to choose and describe the ones that they like. Show how the pronoun *one* becomes *ones* in the plural and can stand for all objects. Show them too, how the prepositional phrase *with the Tiger label on it/with the star on it*, etc. is very useful when you want to identify particular items from a collection, e.g. in a shop window.

Practise the exchanges chorally. Then set students to work in pairs talking about the sets of sports items. Ask some students to ask you S-T about the ones that you like.

🔘 Dialogue: Part 2

Active words and expressions:	menu order Congratulations!

Students' Book pages 112, 113
Set 3 Recent activities

Active words:	shower thing make(your bed) tidy wash up yet

Exercise 1

This set practises the use of the present perfect tense to talk about recent activities. It can be useful here to contrast the present perfect with the past simple tense. Practise the sentences in the box chorally, indicating how the *have* auxiliary verb is shortened to *'ve* in the 1st person singular. Ask random students to ask you questions S-T choosing from the questions in the chart. Students complete the questionnaire individually, then work in pairs, asking and answering.

Exercise 2

Students tell you about their partner's activities, joining the positive and negative statements with *but*.

Exercise 3

Students use the chart and their answers to write sentences for homework.

Exercise 4

Practise the exchange in the box chorally. Ask students to ask you the questions S-T. Give answers in the short form. Give the full (written) forms afterwards and write them on the blackboard. Students ask and answer the same questions in pairs, making notes as they do so. Check with random questions round the class. Students write about each other either in class or at home. Find out if any students have relatives away from home for any reason. Find out where and how long they have been there.

🔘 Dialogue: Part 3

Active words and expressions:	strap suitcase Good luck! It's time to go. Take care of yourselves.

Students' Book pages 114, 115
Reading

Active words:	camp examination experience interpreter hear from outdoor

NOTES

free board: free accommodation and food
work permit: foreign students need to secure official permission to work in Britain before taking up a job there

Refer the students to the layout of the letter but only mention it in passing. The date – omitted on purpose – comes under the writer's address. Concentrate on the content and the organisation of the letter.

Ask a few questions to guide the students through the main facts of the letter. Then ask them to read it again and copy and fill in the form for Sylvana. They can compare their notes with each other afterwards. Ask students to copy the form again into their notebooks and fill it in for themselves.

Show the relationship between Sylvana's letter and the notes on the form. Make sure the students use Sylvana's letter as a model for their own letters. See if the students can complete these letters in class so that you can round off the course by collecting in the finished pieces of work. Their performance will provide good feedback and a means of assessment of their ability to master key verb structures in English.

Homework

Choose from:
1. Set 2 Exercise 2, page 110. Write sentences.
2. Set 3 Exercise 3, page 112. Write sentences.
3. Writing, page 114. Write a letter of application for a job.
4. Unit 14 Workbook exercises.

🔘 Oral exercises

1. Predict the weather.

What's the weather like today?
I think it's going to be fine.

Now you go on in the same way.

What's the weather like today?
I think it's going to be fine.
What's the weather like today?
I think it's going to be wet.
What's the weather like today?
I think it's going to be hot.
What's the weather like today?
I think it's going to be cold.
What's the weather like today?
I think it's going to be warm.
What's the weather like today?
I think it's going to rain.
Oh dear, it always rains when I go on holiday.

2. Talk about future events

Listen to these two people.

Any news of your parents?
Yes. They're going to move to the south coast.
Oh, really?

Now you talk about future events in the same way.

Any news of your parents?
Yes. They're going to move to the south coast.
Oh, really?
Any news of Diana?
Yes. She's going to make a film in America.
Great! I hope she comes to L.A.
Any news of your brother?
Yes. He's going to change his job.
Really?
Any news of Mary and Simon?
Yes. They're going to get married.
That's nice. Are you going to the wedding?
Any news of Paul?
Yes. He's going to work in Los Angeles for a year.
Of course. He's got a friend there, hasn't he?
Any news of your sister?
Yes. She's going to have a baby.
Oh, really? What is she going to call it?

3. Talk about uncompleted activities

A teenager is talking to her mother.

Are you coming with me?
No, I haven't had breakfast yet.

Now you go on in the same way.

Are you coming with me?
No, I haven't had breakfast yet.
Are you coming with me?
No, I haven't got dressed yet.
Are you coming with me to the shops?
No, I haven't had a shower yet.
Are you coming with me to the swimming pool?
No, I haven't made the beds yet.
Are you coming with me to the park?
No, I haven't tidied the house yet.
Oh, all right. I'll help you. Then we can go out together.
Yes, that *is* a good idea. But first ask your brother to get up. He can help us, too.

4. Talk about completed activities

A parent is talking to his son.

Have you done your homework this morning?
Yes. I did it before breakfast.

Now you answer in the same way.

Have you done your homework this morning?
Yes. I did it before breakfast.
Have you done your exercises this morning?
Yes. I did them before breakfast.
Have you made your bed this morning?
Yes. I made it before breakfast.
Have you read the new lesson this morning?
Yes. I read it before breakfast.
Have you tidied your bedroom this morning?
Yes. I tidied it before breakfast.
Have you written the exercises this morning.
Yes. I wrote them before breakfast.
Oh, you are good.
Yes, I know. I want you to buy me a Pac-man video game.

5. Identify belongings

Which is your hat?
This is mine.
Which is Paul's bag?
This is his.

Now you identify belongings in the same way.

Which is your hat?
This is mine.
Which is Paul's bag?
This is his.
Which are our tickets?
These are ours.
Which is my umbrella?
This is yours.
Which is Liz's bike?
This is hers.
Which is the Conways' house?
This is theirs.

6. Describe clothes

Listen to two people in a clothes boutique.

Which dress do you like?
I like the white one with the silver stripes on it.

Now you describe the clothes you like.

Which dress do you like?
I like the white one with the silver stripes on it.
Which shorts do you like?
I like the green ones with the Ellesse label on them.
Which running shoes do you like?
I like the white ones with the black stripes on them.
Which sports bag do you like?
I like the red one with the picture of Snoopy on it.
Which sweatshirt do you like?
I like the blue one with the big star on it.
So do I. Let's get one each.

Unit 15 Consolidation

Skills	Description	Language use/topics/structure
Reading and speaking	A game: Famous lives Students use paragraphs about famous people to practise question and answer forms with a range of tenses.	Facts and personal information using *Wh-*question words: *Which? What? When? Why? Verb tenses: going to* future; past simple tense of verb *be*; past simple tense of other verbs
Reading	The story of the film *Gone with the Wind.* Students use the text to make questions for given answers.	Regular and irregular past simple tenses used for narration; comprehension and question formation using: *Who? Where? What?* and *Why?*
Speaking	Students discuss *Gone with the Wind* and other films.	
Listening and writing (authentic)	Two students studying in London talk about themselves, their studies, their stay in Britain and their plans. Students make notes under headings.	Mixed functions and structures to do with personal information and plans
Speaking	Students use notes to interview each other.	
Writing	Students write about themselves and their partner.	

Students' Book pages 116–119

Check homework from Unit 14.

Game: Famous lives

Make sure you understand the instructions yourself before trying to explain the game to the students. If necessary, try the game out with a colleague before the lesson so that you are thoroughly familiar with the rules. Do not worry too much if the students do not absorb all the instructions at once. It is often easier to pick up the rules while playing. Demonstrate how the game works by drawing your two charts on the blackboard and selecting a student to play with you. You may only need to play two or three rounds of the game to give the class an idea of how to play it and the language they will need.

Before the students start playing, refer them to the list of questions on page 117, which they will need to ask at each throw of the dice. Practise these chorally. Select one of the famous people from which you can provide sample answers to the questions. Go through some of the useful expressions (also on page 117) showing how they relate to the throwing of the dice, e.g. *Oh dear, I've got that./I need a 3/4.* and so on.

Do not ask the students to read about all the characters before they start. Ask them simply to look at their names and photographs, and select two whom they are interested in. Each pair should help each other during the course of the game if there are any difficult words, and, if necessary, ask you for an explanation. Dictionaries should be available if the students want to use them. It is not important that the students read or learn about *all* the characters, nor that they understand every word and are familiar with every structure. The game is simply to encourage reading for specific information.

Students' Book pages 120, 121

Reading: Gone with the Wind

Refer the students to the title of the film. Ask if anyone has seen it and what they thought of it. See if anyone knows who wrote the book and who starred in the film.

Ask the students to read the text and find the answers to these questions:

BLACKBOARD

Where did Margaret Mitchell live?
When did the story happen?
Who were the two main characters in the story?
Who played their parts?
How long was the film?
Did people like it?

Students' Book pages 122, 123

Ask the students in groups to study the text again and work out any words they do not understand individually. If the group as a whole cannot solve the problem, go round and help them. Ask them to work individually on the question formation exercise.

SSR/KEY

1. *Who was Margaret Mitchell?*
2. *Who was David O. Selznick?*
3. *Who was Clark Gable?*
4. *Where was Margaret Mitchell from?*
5. *Where did Selznick first meet Vivien Leigh?/Where did Selznick find someone for the part of Scarlett O'Hara?*
6. *Where was Vivien Leigh from?*
7. *How long did Margaret Mitchell take to write the book?*
8. *How long did Selznick search for someone to play the part of Scarlett O'Hara?*
9. *How long did the film last?*
10. *When did Margaret Mitchell start to write 'Gone with the Wind'?*
11. *When did Selznick first meet Vivien Leigh?/find an actress for the part of Scarlett?/When did the filming of 'Gone with the Wind' start?*
12. *When did Selznick finish the film?/send the telegram to his colleague?*
13. *What was the name of Vivien Leigh's fiance?*
14. *What is 'Gone with the Wind' about?*
15. *What did the journalists do after the end of the film?*
16. *Why did Selznick spend two and a half years searching for an actress to play the part of Scarlett?*
17. *Why did Vivien Leigh and Laurence Olivier come to the studios on the night of the filming?/on the night of December 10th?*
18. *Why didn't Scarlett love Rhett Butler?/ Why wasn't Scarlett happy with Rhett Butler?*
19. *Why did the Mayor of Atlanta close all the schools and public buildings in Atlanta?*
20. *Why was the novel 'Gone with the Wind' so popular/successful?/Why did it become the most popular novel of all time?*

Take in the students' work and check it. Allot one mark for correct comprehension and another for correct tense and question formation.

Now ask the students to look at the comments about *Gone with the Wind* in the bubbles. These are from people who have recently seen the film on television.

Check comprehension: *Who liked it? Who didn't like it? Why not?* Use these opinions as a bridge either to a discussion of a film which is popular at the present time, or towards a discussion on the lines suggested in the book. In either case ask the students to form groups.

🔘🔘 Listening

Direct the students' attention towards the headings in the left-hand column. See if they can suggest the questions which the interviewer is going to use. Play the tape and ask students to fill in the information for both the students. Elicit the answers in full form as a way of checking for comprehension.

TAPESCRIPT

Listen to two students, A and B, talking about their stay in Britain. Fill in the chart below with the information as you listen.

Would you like to tell me your name, please?

My name's Anna.

And which country do you come from?

I come from Poland.

Why did you decide to visit England?

I came here to visit my friends and then I decided to stay a bit longer to learn English.

Where are you studying?

I am studying at (the) Cambridge Language School.

And how long is your course? How long are you going to study for?

I'm going to study for about one year and I would like to take (a) special course to prepare to take First Cambridge Certificate.

What sort of things do you like to do in your spare time?

I like doing ... I think, a lot of different things. I like reading. I like going to the cinema, to the theatre, and I like knitting very much.

Could you tell me a little bit about your family?

I have parents and only one brother. He's older than me ... five years. He's married and he's got one child and he's seven now.

Could you tell me your present address, please?

It's High Road, Cambridge.

And how long have you been in England?

I've been here for ten months.

When are you going to go home?

I don't know yet.

What about your ambitions in life?

Now, I would like to speak English very well, and that's my biggest ambition.

Would you like to tell me your name, please?

OK. My name is Katsahiko. This is my first name. And my family name is Yamamoto.

And what's your country of origin?

I come from Japan.

Why did you decide to visit Britain?

Because I wanted to study English. I think English is the most useful language of the world. I want to learn it er, much ... more and more.

And where are you studying at the moment?

I'm studying English in the English school in London.

The name of the school is International House.

And how long is your course?

I'm taking (an) eight weeks course.

What sort of things do you like to do in your spare time?

Erm ... I like playing tennis, or swimming and skiing.

Could you tell me about your family?

I have father, mother and one elder sister and one younger brother.

How long have you been in England?

I've been in England six weeks.

And what date are you leaving?

Erm ... I'm leaving on 22nd September.

What are your ambitions in life?

Mmm ... I want to be a great businessman. Yeah.

Anything else?

Nothing special but I want to be happy, anyway.

KEY

	A	B
Name:	Anna	Katsahiko Yamamoto
Country of origin:	Poland	Japan
Purpose of visit to Britain:	to visit friends and to learn English	to study and learn English
Place of study:	the Cambridge Language School	International House in London
Length of study:	1 year, to take the Cambridge First Certificate	8 weeks
Present address:	High Road, Cambridge	doesn't say
Interests:	reading, going to the cinema and the theatre, knitting	playing tennis, swimming and skiing
Family:	parents, one brother 5 years older who is married with 1 child	father, mother, one elder sister, one younger brother
Length of time spent in Britain:	10 months	6 weeks
Date of return home:	don't know	22nd September
Ambitions:	to take the First Certificate; to speak English very well	to be a great businessman; to be happy

Leave out the follow-up to the listening exercise if the students are not resident in Britain, or adapt the questions so they apply to your students' own situation.

Homework

Choose from:
1. Page 122. Questions on *'Gone with the Wind'*.
2. Writing, page 123.
3. Unit 15 Workbook exercises.

Tests

Opening Strategies is accompanied by a test booklet containing three short tests. Test 1 covers Units 1–5 of the Students' Book; Test 2 covers Units 6–10; and Test 3 covers Units 11–15.

The tests fulfil three objectives:

1 they give the teacher and students valuable information concerning the students' progress
2 they give the teacher feedback on the effectiveness of his or her teaching
3 they give the students additional motivation to approach their studies seriously

Each test is divided into eight sections. The first three sections which form Part One cover structure and vocabulary. The remaining five sections which form Part Two cover the communicative use of language. By studying the scores achieved in the different sections teachers can see if extra work is necessary in any particular area.

The sections in each test are as follows:

Part One (45 minutes – 40 marks)

Section	A	Grammar recognition	20 marks
	B	Grammar production	10 marks
	C	Vocabulary	10 marks

Part Two (45 minutes – 60 marks)

Section	D	Listening	10 marks
	E	Reading	10 marks
	F	Skeleton dialogue	10 marks
	G	Writing	15 marks
	H	Oral	15 marks
		Total	100 marks

Test description

Section A (Grammar recognition)
This multiple-choice section in each test is presented in the form of a dialogue. Students are asked to select the correct forms from four alternatives. There is only one structurally correct and contextually appropriate response in each case, so alternatives cannot be accepted.

Section B (Grammar production)
This section has been included because it is seen as a natural step forward from being able to recognise a structure to being able to produce it. In almost every case there is only one acceptable form.

Section C (Vocabulary)
In the first two tests this section combines both vocabulary selection and production. In the third test, this section is devoted entirely to vocabulary production.

The sections do not test more than a small but important range of vocabulary items from Opening Strategies. Teachers will need to make spot checks on vocabulary at more regular intervals during the course of their teaching if they wish to keep a more comprehensive check on vocabulary.

Section D (Listening)
The recordings for this section of the test are available on the set of cassettes accompanying the Students' Book of Opening Strategies. Teachers should try to provide the best acoustic conditions possible for this section of the test. A language laboratory would be ideal. In the first test this section tests the students' general understanding of a short scripted scene. In the second, the students are expected to be able to extract more specific information from similar scenes. The third listening section is an extract from an authentic conversation and contains many of the features of authentic conversation such as hesitation, overlap, false starts, etc. Students are asked to identify true and false statements.

Section E (Reading)
This section is designed to test the students' ability to identify texts, and to read, search for and interpret information. In the first test the students are only required to recognise the form of each particular text. In the second and third texts they have to find and interpret more specific information.

Section F (Skeleton dialogue)
A number of different skills are tested in this section but all of them involve the testing of the students' awareness of the normal pattern and flow of conversation.

Section G (Writing)
This section tests the students' ability in communicative writing. This is necessarily fairly open-ended although some guidance is given. Teachers should try to assess each student's work as an attempt at *communication* rather than as a grammar exercise.

Section H (Oral)
In each of the three tests this section involves a structured conversation, between the teacher and each individual student. Although this procedure is time-consuming, it is the most effective way of assessing each student's progress in oral communication. If time is short, teachers may wish to conduct the conversations with individual students while the rest of the class are doing the other sections of the test. In either case, teachers should allow the students time to prepare for the conversation first.

Teachers who, for practical reasons, find it impossible to administer this section orally can convert the section to a written mode with the students writing one or both parts of the conversation. The scoring will have to be adjusted in this case.

Administering the tests

For successful use of the tests, the following points should be remembered.

a) They are tests, not teaching material. It would be wasteful of precious classroom time to use them for classwork or homework, and the results from their use in these ways would not be meaningful.

b) If students are allowed to have the test booklet for any length of time *without* strict supervision, future test results are likely to be affected! Even when using the booklets for formal testing sessions, make sure they are collected *as soon as the test is over.*

c) With achievement tests it is usually considered reasonable to give the students adequate warning of the test session so that they can revise.

d) Always tell the students how much time they have available for each part of the test.

e) Make sure that the students *do not write* in their test booklets. Make sure that all the students have enough paper for their answers.

f) Test instructions do not form part of the testing materials. Teachers may explain the instructions in the students' mother tongue if they wish.

Key

Test One (Units 1–5)

Section A (Grammar recognition)
One mark per correct response

1. C	11. D
2. B	12. B
3. D	13. C
4. A	14. A
5. A	15. A
6. C	16. C
7. B	17. A
8. C	18. B
9. A	19. D
10. B	20. D

Section B (Grammar production)
One mark per correct response
1. is
2. are
3. does
4. she
5. called
6. They
7. in
8. His
9. from
10. can't

Section C (Vocabulary)
One mark per correct response
1. French
2. very
3. cake
4. taxi
5. music
6. tickets
7. umbrella
8. map
9. type
10. writing

Section D (Listening)
Two marks per correct response
2. E
3. C
4. A
5. F
6. B

Section E (Reading)
Two marks per correct response
1. E
2. B
3. C
4. A
5. D

Section F (Skeleton dialogue)
One mark per correct response
1. C
2. F
3. K
4. I
5. B
6. D
7. G
8. A
9. H
10. J

Section G (Writing)
Teachers may use their own marking proportions but the following is suggested: out of a total of 15, score up to

5 for successful *communication* of ideas (this may include fluency, style and appropriateness)

3 for *coverage* of information (has the student included all the relevant information?)

3 for accuracy in *grammar* and choice of *vocabulary*

2 for accuracy in *spelling*

2 for correct *layout*

Section H (Oral)

Out of a total of 15, score up to

10 for *responding appropriately* to each question

5 for *pronunciation, fluency* and *accuracy*

Test Two (Units 6–10)

Section A (Grammar recognition)
One mark per correct response

1. C	11. B
2. B	12. C
3. B	13. B
4. D	14. D
5. A	15. B
6. A	16. B
7. D	17. C
8. A	18. C
9. D	19. B
10. A	20. B

Section B (Grammar production)
One mark per correct response
1. Can Andy play the guitar?
2. Does Jack live in Brazil?
3. Were Vince and Joanne at the conference this morning?
4. Did you like the concert?
5. Is Maggie Australian?

6. usually
7. always
8. never
9. sometimes
10. once

Section C (Vocabulary)
One mark per correct response
 1. fourth
 2. Friday
 3. September
 4. night
 5. west
 6. floor
 7. weather
 8. garden
 9. factory
10. flight

Section D (Listening)
Two marks per correct response
 1. C
 2. D
 3. A
 4. B
 5. C

Section E (Reading)
Two marks per correct response
 1. The Holyrood School
 2. The Newcastle Academy
 3. The Holyrood School
 4. English in the Sun
 5. The Tower Language School

Section F (Skeleton dialogue)
One mark per correct response
 1. How far do you run?
 2. How long does it take?
 3. How often do you run?
 4. When do you run?
 5. Where do you work?
 6. What do you do after work?
 7. Are you married?
 8. Does she run?
 9. How many children have you got?
10. What do you like doing in your spare time?
(NOTE: The above are suggested responses. Teachers should accept other reasonable responses.)

Section G (Writing)
Teachers may use their own marking proportions but the following is suggested: out of a total of 15, score up to

5 for successful *communication* of ideas (this may include fluency, style and appropriateness)
3 for *coverage* of information (has the student included all the relevant information?)
3 for accuracy in *grammar* and choice of *vocabulary*
2 for accuracy in *spelling*
2 for correct *layout*

Section H (Oral)
Out of a total of 15, score up to

10 for *responding appropriately* to each question
 5 for *pronunciation, fluency* and *accuracy*

Teachers may wish to use two or three prompt cards containing different information, names, etc. so that the oral tests may be varied.

Test Three (Units 11–15)
Section A (Grammar recognition)
One mark per correct response

1. A	11. C
2. D	12. D
3. B	13. A
4. A	14. B
5. C	15. D
6. B	16. C
7. C	17. C
8. D	18. A
9. B	19. B
10. B	20. C

Section B (Grammar production)
One mark per correct response
 1. Where did Tom go yesterday?
 2. When/What time does Mary usually have lunch?
 3. What is Susan writing at the moment?
 4. What colour is your coat?
 5. What size are you?
 6. When are you/we leaving?
 7. How are Tom and Susan going/travelling to Manchester?
 8. Which sweater does Colin want?
 9. How long have Keith and Mandy lived in London?
10. Whose car is that?/Whose is that car?

Section C (Vocabulary)
Score one point per correct response
 1. afternoon
 2. centre
 3. buy
 4. shop
 5. window
 6. expensive
 7. cost
 8. cash
 9. card
10. cheque

Section D (Listening)
Two marks per correct response
The following sentences are true: 1, 3, 5, 6, 9

Section E (Reading)
Two marks per *accurate* response
Suggested responses:
 1. a diplomat
 2. In 1962
 3. the British Spy Service in London
 4. 5 years
 5. James Bond

Section F (Skeleton dialogue)
One mark per *suitable* response
Suggested responses:
1. Good morning, I'm pleased to meet you.
2. Thank you.
3. Yes, I've worked with Mr Christopher for two years.
4. Yes, I worked with Mrs Stanford for two and a half years.
5. I didn't work. I was at college.
6. I was at Mountpleasant College.
7. Oh, have they?
8. Yes, I lived there for ten years.
9. Yes, I can speak Swahili.
10. Oh, do you?

Section G (Writing)
Teachers may use their own marking proportions but the following is suggested: out of a total of 15, score up to

5 for successful *communication* of ideas (this may include fluency, style and appropriateness)
3 for *coverage* of information (has the student included all the relevant information?)
3 for accuracy in *grammar* and choice of *vocabulary*
2 for accuracy in *spelling*
2 for correct *layout*

Section H (Oral)
Out of a total of 15 for each roleplay score up to

10 for *responding appropriately* to each question
 5 for *pronunciation, fluency* and *accuracy*

Select one of the four roleplays. In order to maximise the authenticity of the activity arrange chairs back-to-back so that there is no visual contact with the student.

Box A
You need to obtain the following information from the student: Name, car number, street where parked, time. You will then inform the student that the car was in a 'no parking' area and has been taken away by the police. Tell the student to come to the police station to collect the car. Adopt a formal and 'official' style on the telephone.

Box B
After collecting the information about where and when the umbrella was left at the restaurant inform the student that no umbrella has been found. Suggest that student telephone again next week because a customer may have taken the umbrella by mistake. Adopt a friendly and helpful style on the telephone.

Box C
Answer the telephone with the name of the hotel. Ask for *spelling* of the name *Nott*. Ask for room number. Find room number from hotel register and tell student that Mr Nott is out. Take message. Adopt a helpful and friendly style on the telephone.

Box D
Answer telephone with name of theatre. After request for tickets explain that cheapest tickets for Tuesday evening are £15 each. There are two tickets at £6.50 each for Wednesday evening. Take credit card number and name. Tell student to collect the tickets by 6 o'clock on Wednesday evening. Adopt a friendly and helpful style on the telephone.

Tapescript

Test One
Section D (Listening comprehension)
Look at pictures A to F in your test book. Listen to the dialogue and choose the right picture. Here's an example. Listen.

Number one
MAN: My name's Bassett. George Bassett.
RECEPTIONIST: Ah, yes. Mr Bassett. Room 623. Here's your key.
MAN: Thank you.
Now which is the right picture? Picture A? Picture B? No, you want picture D. You write 'one D' on your answer paper. Now here's number two.

Number two
WOMAN: I want a record for my daughter, Janet.
MAN: What sort of music does she like?
WOMAN: She likes pop music. She likes a man called Demis Roussos.
MAN: This is his new record. It's called *Wind of Change*.
WOMAN: How much is it?

Number three
MAN: This is my brother Tony. He likes tennis and cars.
WOMAN: Can he drive?
MAN: No, he can't. He's only sixteen.

Number four
MAN: Coffee?
WOMAN: No, tea, please. Can I have a piece of chocolate cake?
MAN: Here you are. Tea's twenty-seven pence, the cake's thirty-five pence. That's sixty-two pence.
WOMAN: Here you are.

Number five
OPERATOR: Number, please?
WOMAN: Can I have three-two-one, double six-four-seven.
OPERATOR: Yes, one moment, please.
(*ringing tone*)
MAN: Three-two-one, double six-four-seven?
WOMAN: Richard? This is Carol.
MAN: Oh hello Carol. How are you?

Number six
MAN: What do you like doing Mrs Brighton?
WOMAN: Well, I like sightseeing, you know museums and old buildings...but my husband...
MAN: Yes?
WOMAN: He likes swimming.

MAN: Greece is very beautiful, or Italy, or Spain?
WOMAN: Yes, Greece. I love Greek cakes.
MAN: So you want a holiday in Greece?
WOMAN: Yes, please.

Test Two

Section D (Listening comprehension)

Look at the example in your test book. Listen to the dialogue and choose the correct answer for this question: *What does she want to buy?*

MAN: Have a look at this one. It's quite new and it's near the station. *(rustle of paper)*
WOMAN: Yes, it's very nice, but I want one with three bedrooms and a garden.
MAN: *(sorting through papers)* Three bedrooms ... and a garden ... let me see ... Ah yes. Here's one ... it's in Pine Road, three bedrooms and a garden.
WOMAN: How much is it?

Well, what does she want to buy? ... a car? a shop? a house? a disco? Of course, she wants to buy a house. So the correct answer is 'C'. So you write 'C' on your answer paper.

Now listen to number one: *How many bedrooms are there in Tom's flat?*

MAN: What's the new flat like, Tom?
TOM: It's OK. It's very small. Of course Rosie and I have got our bedroom, but the baby sleeps there, too. Then the girls, Tina and Susie, sleep in another room.
MAN: What about Rosie's mother, Mrs Andrews?
TOM: Yes, there's a bedroom for her as well.

So, how many bedrooms are there in Tom's flat?

Number two: *What time does the supermarket close on Fridays?*

RADIO ANNOUNCER: Do you work in an office? Do you finish work at 6 o'clock? Is it difficult to do your shopping? Here's a special message for *you*! Crockford's supermarket at 28, The High Street is open until 6.30 every evening, but on Friday evening we're open until 8.30 in the evening – just right for your weekend shopping – Crockford's supermarket, 28, The High Street.

So what time does the supermarket close on Fridays?

Number three: *Where is this woman?*

MAN: Can I help you?
WOMAN: Yes. Have you got any red roses?
MAN: Red roses? Yes, over here, madam. Smell them. They have a beautiful perfume.
WOMAN: *(smelling)* Yes, beautiful.
MAN: How many do you want, madam?
WOMAN: A dozen, please.
MAN: Twelve red roses. That's six pounds, madam.

So where is this woman?

Number four: *What is the girl doing?*

MAN: How are you?
GIRL: *(breathless)*. I'm a bit tired and the water's very cold.

MAN: Yes, I know, but it's only two more miles.
GIRL: Can you see the coast?
MAN: Yes, I can. There are a lot of people. They're waiting to welcome you.

So, what is the girl doing?

Number five: *What does she want?*
WOMAN: I'm thirsty.
MAN: Would you like some coffee?
WOMAN: No, not coffee. I'd like something cold.
MAN: I've got some beer, or some milk ...
WOMAN: No ... no, I think I'd like some water.

So, what does she want?

Test Three

Section D (Listening comprehension)

NICK: Did you go to England at Christmas?
MARK: No, ... we went ... er, we went to the mountains. It was not bad ... it snowed, we did a little bit of skiing. No, ... er, quite honestly ... I think ... going back to Britain at Christmas is ... is ludicrous quite honestly, what with the Christmas traffic and everything.
NICK: What did you do in the mountains ... you went skiing ... ?
MARK: Yeah, ... it was nice actually ... so, we went skiing ... went to a few parties ... went to the cinema a couple-a-times ...
NICK: Mmm. What did you see?
MARK: We saw a ... couple of films actually ... we saw ... er, some 'Bond' film ... I can't remember which one now.
NICK: What ... the latest ... ?
MARK: I can't remember ... I think probably *For Your Eyes Only*. Yeah, that was it.
NICK: Ah, yeah.
MARK: We saw that one ... and then we saw ... oh, what was the name of that film? ... a very strange film ... ah, *The Sting*.
NICK: Yeah, that's good that film ... Anyway, what are you doing this summer?
MARK: Well, I'd like to stay in Torino for the Rolling Stones concert.
NICK: The Rolling Stones? Are they definitely coming?
MARK: Seems so, yeah ... that'll be the ... er, 'bout the 12th July.
NICK: Yeah, ... yeah.
MARK: How long are you st ... when does your holiday begin?
NICK: Probably mid ... er, I'm go ... I'm probably going to England ... erm, in the last week of July.
MARK: But they ... you're given ... your holiday's how long? Four weeks?
NICK: Well, I mean ... Well, I will take *five* weeks in fact ... I mean ... because we re-open the office at the beginning of September ...
MARK: Yeah ...

Index 1 Grammatical summary

Grammatical item		Example sentence	Unit reference (Unit number followed by set number or D (Dialogue), R (Reading), W (Writing))
I Sentence types			
1. Declarative	positive	*I live in London.*	throughout
	negative	*I don't like dogs.*	throughout
2. Interrogative	*yes/no*	*Are you Mrs Trent?*	throughout
	Wh-questions:		
	What	*What's your name?*	1:1
	Where	*Where are you from?*	2:2
	When/What time	*When/What time does it open?*	6:5
	Who	*Who's Brooke Shields?*	4:2
	Which	*Which film shall we see?*	9:4
	Why	*Why does she hate Scawsby?*	9:R
	Whose	*Whose film is next?*	14:2
	How	*How are you?*	3:1
		How do you get to work?	8:1
	How old	*How old is it?*	4:4
	How far	*How far is it?*	8:1
	How long	*How long does it take?*	8:1
	How often	*How often are you late for work?*	8:1
	How much	*How much is it?*	4:1
	How many	*How many are there?*	8:3
	negative questions	*Aren't you from Manchester?*	13:3
3. Imperative	positive	*Sit down!*	12:1
	negative	*Don't touch!*	12:1
4. Short answers	*be*	*Yes, I am./No, I'm not.*	1:1,2:2
	have	*Yes, I have./No, I haven't.*	7:3
	can	*Yes, I can./No, I can't.*	4:3
5. Echoed questions		*Oh, are you?*	13:2
6. Simple sentences			throughout
7. Compound sentences		*She likes cats but she doesn't like dogs.*	3:2
8. Complex sentences		*She doesn't like Scawsby because there's nothing to do there.*	9:R
II Verbs: main tenses			
1. Present tense *be*		*My name's Diana.*	1:1
2. Past tense *be*		*How was the film?*	6:1
3. Present simple		*Do you like cats?*	3:2
		I go swimming on Monday morning.	7:2
4. Present continuous		*He's doing exercises.*	7:1
5. Past simple		*Did you like the concert?*	9:5,12:2,13:1
6. *Have got*		*Have you got any children?*	7:3
7. *There is/are*		*Is there a bank near here?*	6:3
		How many rooms are there?	8:3
8. Present perfect:			
	with *yet*	*Have you had lunch yet?*	14:3
	with *for*	*I've worked here for 4 years.*	14:3
9. Future:			
	present continuous	*They're coming tomorrow.*	11:1
	going to	*They're going to win.*	14:1
10. *Let's* + verb		*Let's see 'Gone with the Wind'.*	9:4

III   Verbs: other forms

1. Imperatives:
in commands	*Sit down!*	12:1
in directions	*Turn left at the pizza bar.*	6:3
in parting wishes	*Have a nice time!*	11:1

2. Gerunds after verbs:
like	*I like reading.*	4:2
love	*I love skiing.*	4:D
hate	*I hate writing letters.*	4:2
go	*I'm going jogging.*	7:2

3. Infinitive + *to* with verbs:
want	*I want to buy some stamps.*	6:2
would like	*Would you like to go out?*	9:3

4. Object pronoun + infinitive + *to* with verbs:
ask	*Can you ask him to come in?*	13:4
	He asked me to dance.	13:R
tell	*They told us to wait.*	13:R
want	*She wants them to clear up.*	13:4

IV   Verbs: auxiliaries and modals

be		throughout
have	*Have you got any children?*	7:3
	I haven't had lunch yet.	14:3
do	*Do you like London?*	3:2
do (inversion)	*So do I./Nor do I.*	4:2
can (ability)	*Can you ski?*	4:3
can (request)	*Can I have two coffees, please?*	4:1
can (request)	*Can you give me a size 10?*	11:2
can (permission)	*Can I try this on?*	11:2
can (possibility)	*Where can I get some stamps?*	6:3
be going to	*He's going to cry.*	14:1
must (obligation	*You must talk quietly.*	12:1
and prohibition)	*You mustn't smoke here.*	12:1
shall (suggestion)	*What shall we do?*	9:4
will (decision)	*I'll phone back later.*	9:1
	I think I'll have it.	11:2
would (offer)	*Would you like a salad?*	8:2

V   Verbs: semi-copula

look	*It looks delicious.*	8:2
sound	*That sounds a good idea.*	14:3

VI   Verbs: voice

1. Active		throughout
2. Passive	*I'm called Georgina.*	3:R

VII   Nouns

1. Singular		throughout
2. Plural	*I like cats/children.*	3:2
3. Genitive *'s*	*I'm Diana's assistant.*	3:4
	It's the Conways' car.	14:2
4. Countable	*I want to get a film.*	6:2
	I want to get some stamps.	6:2
5. Uncountable	*I want to get some money.*	6:2

VIII   Adjectives

1. Attributive	*He's a good teacher.*	2:R
2. Predicative	*It isn't very big.*	2:R
3. Colour	*The walls are white.*	8:3
4. Nationality	*She's Italian.*	2:2

VIII Adjectives (continued)

5. Quality		throughout
6. Possessive	*my, your,* etc.	1:1,7:3
7. Demonstrative	*How much is this/that sandwich?*	4:1
	How much are these/those sandwiches?	4:1

IX Adverbs

1. Frequency	*He usually cycles to work.* (*sometimes,* etc.)	8:1
2. Degree		
very	*He's very nice.*	3:R
	I like it very much.	3:2
quite	*It's quite interesting.*	6:R
	I quite like the red one.	14:2
at all	*I don't like him at all.*	4:2
a lot	*They paint a lot.*	7:1
lots of	*I like doing lots of things.*	4:2
too	*It was too slow.*	9:5
a bit	*It's a bit big.*	11:2
a little	*I speak a little English.*	4:R
3. Manner	*Please talk quietly.*	12:1
4. Place	*Here's your key.*	1:D
	Here you are.	11:2
	It's here.	2:D
	It's over there.	2:D
5. Time		
past	*Where were you yesterday?*	6:1
present	*What are you doing now?*	7:1
future	*We're leaving tomorrow.*	11:1

X Pronouns

1. Personal		
subject	*I, you,* etc.	1:1,2:2
object	*me, you, him,* etc.	4:2
2. Possessive pronouns	*mine, yours,* etc.	14:2
3. Demonstrative pronouns	*What's this?/What's that?*	2:3
4. Distributive		
each	*Write each name clearly.*	12:R
every	*She goes jogging every day.*	7:2
everything	*Everything is just fine.*	11:R
everyone	*Everyone is looking at you.*	12:D
everywhere	*There are sweetpapers everywhere.*	12:D
5. Quantitative		
one	*There's one over there.*	6:3
ones	*I quite like the red ones.*	14:2
another	*There's another on the second floor.*	8:3
nothing	*There's nothing to do in Scawsby.*	9:R
anything	*There isn't anything to do here.*	9:R
something	*There's always something interesting to do,*	9:R
somewhere	*somewhere exciting to go.*	
someone(body)	*There's always someone new to meet.*	9:R
anyone(body)	*I didn't see anyone.*	13:D
no one (body)	*No one goes into my room.*	13:D
6. Reflexive		
yourselves	*Look after yourselves!*	14:D

XI Quantifiers

both	*We both work for S and S.*	3:D
many	*Many shops stay open late.*	6:R
most	*Most shops close at 5.30.*	6:R
some	*Some shops close early one day a week.*	6:R
all	*We're all good students.*	3:R

XII Determiners

Indefinite article	*It's a map.*	2:3
	It's an umbrella.	2:3
definite article	*I live in the north of England.*	3:3
zero article	*I like watching television at home.*	4:2
	I have lunch at work.	7:2
some	*I want to get some money.*	6:2
any	*Have you got any brothers?*	7:3

XIII Prepositions

1. Place

	in	1:W
	from	2:2
	on, of	3:2
	to, round	4:2
	at, near, opposite, next to, outside	6:3
	under	7:R
	between	13:2
	out of	12:D
	into	13:D

2. Time

	at, to, past, after, before, until	6:4,5:R
	on	7:2
	in	7:2,9:2,11:1
	for	14:3

3. Instrument

	by	8:1

4. Miscellaneous

with	*She's married with two children.*	3:R
	I like the ones with the stripes on them.	14:2
by	*I'm called Georgie by my friends.*	3:R
for	*I work for Fiat.*	3:2

XIV Conjunctions

and	*My address is . . . and my telephone number is . . .*	1:W
or	*Please write or phone.*	1:W
but	*I like cats but I don't like dogs.*	3:2

XV Exclamations

How . . . !	*How funny!*	6:D
What . . . !	*What a smart jacket!*	11:2
	What pretty sweaters!	11:2
Isn't it . . .	*Isn't it beautiful!*	7:4

Index 2 How to say it

Grammatical item		Example sentence	Unit reference
Ability	Ask about ability (in skills and sports)	*Can you ski?*	4:3
	Talk about ability (in skills and sports)	*I can ski.*	4:3
	Answer about ability	*Yes, I can./No, I can't.*	4:3
Accept	Accept an apology	*That's all right.*	4:D3
	Accept food or drink	*Yes, please.*	8:2
	Accept help	*Thank you. That's very kind of you.*	12:3
	Accept invitations	*I'd love to.*	9:3
	Accept something	*Thank you.*	1:D
Activities (see also Past events)	Ask about past activities	*What did you do yesterday?*	12:2
	Talk about past activities	*I went to Cambridge.*	12:2
	Ask about present activities	*What's she doing?*	7:1
	Talk about present activities	*She's jogging.*	7:1
	Ask about recent activities	*Have you had lunch?*	14:2
	Answer about past activities	*Yes, I have./No, I haven't.*	14:2
	Talk about past activities	*I haven't had lunch yet.*	14:2
Address	Ask for people's addresses	*What's your address?*	1:W
	Spell your address	*T-O-W-E-R H-O-T-E-L*	3:5
Admire	Admire things	*What a nice sweater! What nice sweaters!*	11:2
Age	Ask how old people and places are	*How old is he?/St Paul's Cathedral?*	4:4
	Say how old people and places are	*He's ten (years old). It's three hundred years old.*	4:4
Agree	Agree or disagree with people's likes and dislikes	*Yes, so do I. No, nor do I.*	4:2
	Agree to do things	*Yes, certainly/of course.*	13:4
Alphabet	Spell your name and address	*D-I-A-N-A T-R-E-N-T, etc.*	3:5
Answer	Answer the telephone	*5213. Hello. Yes, speaking.*	9:1
Apologise	Apologise to someone	*Sorry!*	4:D3
	Accept apologies	*That's all right.*	4:D3
Arrangement	Make an arrangement	*Are you free on Saturday? No, I'm afraid I'm not./Yes, I am.*	9:3
Ask	Ask people to do things (1)	*Can you show me a size 10, please?*	11:2
	Ask people to do things (2)	*Can you answer a few questions?*	13:4
	Ask others to make requests	*Can you ask her/him to come and see me, please?*	13:4
	Ask the time	*What's the time?/What time is it?*	6:4
Belongings	Ask people to identify belongings	*Whose pen is this?/Whose is this pen?*	14:2
	Identify belongings	*It's mine. It's the Conways' (car).*	14:2
	Identify and describe belongings	*Mine's the green one with the yellow flowers on it.*	14:2
Buy (see Get)	Ask where you can buy/ get things	*Where can I buy/get a film?*	6:2
	Say where you can buy/ get things	*At the chemist's. (You can buy/get some toothpaste at the chemist's.)*	6:2
	Say what you want to buy (or get)	*I want to buy/get some toothpaste.*	6:2
Choose	Ask about a choice of food or drink	*What is there? What sort of salad would you like?*	8:2
	Choose food or drink	*I'd like (a) green salad, please.*	8:2
Clock times	Ask the time	*What's the time?/What time is it?*	6:4
	Tell the time	*It's quarter past/to 7.*	6:4
Clothes	Ask permission to look at clothes	*Can I have a look at them?*	11:2
	Ask permission to try on clothes	*Can I try them on?*	11:2

	Ask for the right size of clothes	*Can you give me a size 10?*	11:2
	Comment on clothes	*They're nice but they're a bit big.*	11:2
	Give your size in clothes and shoes, etc.	*I'm size . . . .*	11:2
Colours	Ask about colours	*What colour are the walls?*	8:3
	Talk about colours	*They're white.*	8:3
Comment	Comment on clothes	*What lovely jeans!*	11:2
		They're nice but they're a bit small.	
Confirm	Ask for confirmation (1)	*Is your name Paul Roberts?*	1:1
	Give confirmation	*Yes, it is.*	1:1
	Ask for confirmation (2)	*Isn't Diana Trent a film director?*	13:3
	Give confirmation	*That's right, she is.*	13:3
		And doesn't she work for Focus Film and Video?	
		Yes, she does.	
Conversation	Show surprise and interest to keep a conversation going	*(I'm English.) Oh, are you?*	13:2
		(I live in Bristol.) Oh, do you?	
Correct	Correct information	*(Are you David Roberts?)*	1:1
		No, I'm not, I'm Paul Roberts.	
Cost (see, also Money; Pay)	Ask how much things cost (1)	*How much is a cheese sandwich?*	4:1
	Say how much things cost	*It's 30 pence.*	4:1
	Ask how much things cost (2)	*How much do they cost?*	11:2
	Say how much things cost	*They're £19.95.*	11:2
Count (see Numbers)			
Countries	Ask where people are from	*Where are you from?*	2:2
	Say where you are from	*I'm from Brazil.*	2:2
Date (see also Months)	Ask the date	*What's the date today?*	9:2
	Ask the date of people's birthday	*When's your birthday?*	9:2
	Give the date of your birthday	*It's on March 10th.*	9:2
	Give the month of your birthday	*My birthday's in March.*	9:2
	Make a date (Am.Eng.) (Brit.Eng = arrangement to meet)	*Are you free on the 3rd?*	9:2
Day (see also Greetings)	Say the days of the week	*Monday, Tuesday,* etc.	7:2
Describe (see also Identification)	Describe things	*It's blue with stars on it.*	14:2
		I like the ones with stripes on them.	
Directions	Give simple directions	*Turn left at the Pizza Bar.*	6:3
Disagree	Disagree with people's tastes	*Really? I do./Really? I don't.*	4:2
Dislikes	Ask about likes and dislikes (1)	*Do you like cats?*	3:2
		No, I don't. Not very much.	
	Talk about dislikes (1)	*I don't like cats.*	3:2
	Ask about likes and dislikes (2)	*Do you like writing letters?*	4:2
	Talk about dislikes (2)	*I don't like writing letters.*	4:2
		No, I hate it.	
Distance (see also Journeys)	Ask how far away places are	*How far is it to work?*	8:1
	Say how far away places are	*It's about 8 kilometres.*	8:1
Do (see also Jobs)	Ask what people do (for a living)	*What do you do? What does she do?*	3:4
	Say what people do	*She's a film director.*	3:4
		We work for Focus Film and Video.	3:4
Drink	Ask what people want to drink	*Do you want coffee or tea?*	4:1
	Say what you want to drink	*(I want a) Coffee, please*	4:1
	Offer drink	*Would you like some orange juice?*	8:2
	Accept an offer of drink	*Yes, please.*	8:2
	Refuse an offer of drink	*No, thank you.*	8:2

	Ask about a choice of drink	*What is there (to drink)?*	8:2
	State a choice of drink	*There's beer or wine.*	8:2
	Make a choice of drink	*I'd like some beer, please.*	8:2
Events	Ask about past events	*Were you at the conference this morning?*	6:1
		How was the conference?	
	Talk about past events	*I was at a meeting.*	6:1
		It was interesting.	
	Answer about past events	*Yes, I was./No, I wasn't.*	6:1
	Predict future events	*I'm not going to win.*	14:1
		People aren't going to like it.	
Family	Ask about the family	*Have you got any children?*	7:3
	Talk about the family	*I've got two sons and a daughter.*	7:3
Far away (see Distance)			
Fixed times	Ask about fixed times	*What time does the train leave?*	6:5
	Talk about fixed times	*It leaves at 5.30.*	6:5
Food (see Drink)			
Formal (see also Informal)	Greet people formally	*How do you do.*	2:1
	Introduce yourself formally	*How do you do. My name is Mrs Trent.*	2:1
		(I'm) Pleased to meet you.	
	Speak on the telephone formally	*Hello. Is that Mrs Pattison?*	9:1
Frequency (see also Routines)	Ask how often you do things (1)	*Do you ever cycle to work?*	8:1
	Say how often you do things (1)	*Yes, often./No, never.*	8:1
	Ask how often you do things (2)	*How often do you go out?*	8:1
	Say how often you do things (2)	*(About) twice/three times a week,* etc.	8:1
Future (see also Plans; Events)	Ask about plans for the near future	*What are you doing this afternoon?*	11:1
		Are you going to the conference?	
	Answer about plans for the near future	*Yes, I am./No, I'm not.*	11:1
	Talk about plans for the near future	*I'm going to the conference this afternoon.*	11:1
		We're leaving this morning/on Saturday/ next week, etc.	
	Predict future events	*It's going to rain.*	14:1
Get (see Buy; Want)			
Give (see also Orders)	Give confirmation	*Yes, I am.*	1:1
		That's right, I am.	13:3
	Give direct orders	*Get down!*	12:1
		Don't do that!	
	Give indirect orders	*Tell her/him to sit down.*	12:1
		Tell her/him not to do that.	
	Give names	*My name's Diana./Her name's Joanne.*	1:1
	Give opinions	*I didn't like the Brahms. It was too slow.*	9:5
	Give people things	*Here's your key.*	1:D1
	Give permission	*Yes, of course./Certainly.*	11:2
Goodbye	Say goodbye	*Well, goodbye./Goodbye!*	2:D3
	Make parting remarks	*See you later.*	4:D3
		See you soon. Bye.	6:D
		Have a nice day!	2:D3
Greet	Greet people formally	*How do you do.*	2:1
		Pleased to meet you.	
	Greet people informally	*Hello./Hi!*	2:1
		How are you?	3:1
	Greet people at different times of the day	*Good morning/afternoon/evening.*	1:2
Help	Offer help	*Would you like a lift?*	12:3
		Would you like to borrow my umbrella?	

	Accept help	Oh, thank you. That's very kind of you.	12:3
	Refuse help with a reason	It's all right I can go by underground.	12:3
		It's all right. I've got one.	
House and home	Ask about the rooms of the house	How many floors are there? Where's the study?	8:3
	Talk about the rooms of the house	There are three floors. The study's on the first floor. There's a big kitchen in the basement.	8:3
How often (see Frequency)			
Identification	Ask about objects	What's that? What's that in English?	2:3
	Identify objects	It's a key. It's an umbrella.	2:3
	Ask for identification	Whose is this pen? Is this your book? Which is the Conways' car?	14:2
	Identify belongings	It's mine./They're hers. It's the Conways'.	14:2
	Identify and describe belongings	Theirs is the silver and gold one.	14:2
	Ask people to identify objects they like	Which running shoes (ones) do you like?	14:2
	Identify objects you like/don't like	I like the red ones.	14:2
	Identify and describe objects you like/don't like	I don't like the one/ones with the Tiger label on it/them.	14:2
Informal	Greet people informally	Hi./Hello.	2:1
	Thank people informally	Thanks.	1:L
	Say goodbye informally	Bye!	4
		See you later.	4
		See you soon.	6
	Speak on the telephone informally	Hello. Is that Judy? It's Di here, Di Trent.	9:1
Interest	Show interest in a conversation	(I'm English.) Oh, are you? (He's a teacher.) Oh, is he?	13:2
Introduce	Introduce people	This is Mr Roberts.	2:1
	Introduce yourself	Good morning. My name's Diana Trent. How do you do.	1:D1 2:1
Invitations	Invite people to do things	Would you like to go out?	9:3
	Accept invitations	Yes, I'd love to.	9:3
Jobs	Ask what people do	What do you do?/What does she do?	3:4
	Say what people do	I'm a cameraman. She's a film director. He works for Fiat.	3:4
	Ask about people's jobs	How long have you worked here?	14:3
	Talk about jobs	I've worked in this school for four years.	14:3
Journeys (see Distance)	Ask how people get to work	How do you/does she get to work?	8:1
	Say how you get to work	I go/She goes by bus.	8:1
	Ask how far away places are	How far is it to work?	8:1
	Say how far places are	It's about 8 kilometres.	8:1
	Ask how long journeys take	How long does it take?	8:1
	Say how long journeys take	It takes about twenty minutes.	8:1
	Ask how often people do things	Do you ever go by car to work?	8:1
	Say how often you do things	No, never./Yes, sometimes.	8:1
	Ask about people's routines	Are you ever late for work?	8:1
Length (of time)	Ask about length of time (1)	How long have you lived in this city?	14:3
	Talk about length of time (1)	I've lived here for 16 years.	14:3
	Ask about length of time (2)	How long does it take to get to work?	8:1
	Talk about length of time (2)	It takes about 20 minutes.	8:1
Likes (see also Opinions)	Ask about likes and dislikes (1)	Do you/Does she like cats? Yes, I do./Yes, she does.	3:2

	Talk about likes and dislikes (1)	*I like cats./She likes cats.*	3:2
	Ask about likes and dislikes (2)	*Do you/Does she like writing letters?*	4:2
	Talk about likes and dislikes (2)	*Yes, I do./Yes, she does.* *I like writing letters.*	4:2
Live (see Places: location (1))			
Location (see Places)			
Money (see also Cost; Pay)	Ask how much things cost	*How much are those combs?*	4:1
		How much is that sweater?	11:2
	Say how much things cost	*They're 45p (pence) (each).*	4:1
		It's £19.95p (nineteen pounds, ninety-five pence.)	11:2
Months	Say the months of the year	*January, February, March, etc.*	9:2
	Ask about the seasons	*Which months are hot in your country?* *Which months are winter in your country?*	9:2
	Ask about birthdays	*When is your birthday?*	9:2
	Talk about birthdays	*It's in March.*	9:2
Names	Introduce yourself	*My name's Diana Trent.*	1:1
	Ask for names	*What's your name?*	1:1
		What's your surname?	3:5
	Give your name	*It's Diana Trent.* *It's Trent.*	1:1
	Confirm your name	*Yes, it is. It's Trent.*	1:1
	Correct people about your name	*No, it isn't Tessler, it's Trent.*	1:1
	Spell your name	*T-R-E-N-T.*	3:5
	Ask for the names of objects	*What's this/that?*	2:3
	Name objects	*It's a map.*	2:3
Nationalities	Ask about people's nationalities	*Are you American?*	2:2
	Say what nationality you are	*I'm American.*	2:2
Numbers	Ask for numbers	*What's your room number?* *What's your telephone number?*	1:3
	Give numbers	*It's 401.* *It's 38994.*	1:3
	Give numbers up to 10	*0 1 2 3 4 5 6 7 8 9 10*	1:3
	Give numbers in tens, hundreds, thousands and millions	*20, 30, 100, 1,000, 1,000,000*	4:1
Objects (see Identification; Names)			
Offer	Offer things – food and drink	*Would you like some salad?*	8:2
		Would you like a cup of tea?	8:2
	Offer help (see Help)		
Past events	Ask about past events (1)	*Were you at the conference this morning?*	6:1
	Answer about past events	*Yes, I was./No, I wasn't.* *Yes, they were./No, they weren't.*	6:1
	Talk about past events (1)	*I was at a meeting. They were in town.*	6:1
	Ask about past events (2)	*How was the meeting?*	6:1
	Talk about past events (2)	*It was interesting.*	6:1
	Ask for an opinion	*Did you like the concert?*	9:5
	Give an opinion	*Yes, I did./No, I didn't.*	9:5
	Ask about past activities	*Did you have a nice weekend?*	12:2
	Answer about past activities	*Yes, I did. It was lovely.*	12:2
	Talk about past activities	*It wasn't too bad.* *It was all right.*	12:2
	Ask and answer about the day	*Where did you go yesterday?* *I went to Cambridge.* *When did you leave?*	13:1

		I left at 8.	
		Who did you see?	
		I didn't see anyone.	
	Ask for confirmation about the past	*Didn't Diana go to Bristol University?*	13:3
	Confirm information about the past	*Yes, she did./No, she didn't.*	13:3
Pay	Ask about ways of paying	*Can I pay by credit card?*	11:2
	Say how you want to pay	*I'll pay cash.*	11:2
		I'll pay by cheque.	
People (see Age, Do, Family, Greet, Jobs, Journeys, Live, Nationality)			
Permission	Ask for permission (in a shop)	*Can I have a look at them?*	11:2
		Can I try them on?	
	Give permission	*Yes, certainly./Of course.*	11:2
Places: location (1)	Ask where people live	*Where do you live?*	3:3
	Say where people live	*I live in the south of England.*	3:3
		I live on the west coast of America.	
Places: location (2)	Ask where places and shops are	*Where's the post office?*	6:3
		Is there a bank near here?	
	Say where places and shops are	*There's one next to the post office.*	6:3
		Turn left at the wine bar and it's on your right.	
	Ask where you can get/ buy things	*Where can I get some stamps?*	6:2
	Say where you can get/ buy things	*At the post office. At the chemist's.*	6:2
Plans (see also Arrangement; Future; Suggestions)	Ask about plans for the near future	*What are you doing this afternoon?*	11:1
		Are you going to the conference?	
	Answer about plans for the near future	*Yes, I am./No, I'm not.*	11:1
	Talk about plans for the near future	*We're leaving this morning/on Saturday/ next week, etc.*	11:1
Predictions (see also Future)	Ask about predictions	*Are they going to win?*	14:1
	Answer about predictions	*Yes, they are./No, they aren't.*	14:1
	Predict	*It's (not) going to rain.*	14:1
		People aren't going to like it.	
Present (see Activities)			
Questions	About: age	*How old is he?*	4:4
	cost	*How much is this/that?*	4:1
	distance	*How far is it?*	8:1
	duration of time (=length of time)	*How long have you lived here?*	14:3
		How long does it take?	8:1
	frequency	*How often do you go out?*	8:1
	manner	*How do you get to work?*	8:1
	number	*How many rooms are there?*	8:3
	people	*Who's Brooke Shields?*	4:2
	places	*Where do you live?*	3:3
	point of time	*What time is it?*	6:4
		When does the train leave?	6:5
		When's your birthday?	9:2
	possessions (belongings)	*Whose is this bag?*	14:2
	reason	*Why didn't you like it?*	9:5
	specific things	*Which film shall we see?*	9:4
	things	*What's that?*	2:3
Reason	Ask for reasons (for an opinion)	*Why?/Why not?*	9:5
		Why does she hate Scawsby?	9:R
	Give reasons for an opinion	*It was too slow.*	9:5
		Because there isn't anything to do.	9:R
	Refuse help with a reason	*It's all right. I can go by bus.*	12:3

Refuse	Refuse food or drink	*No, thanks./No, thank you.*	8:2
	Refuse help with a reason	*It's all right. I can go by bus.*	12:3
	Request (Order) food or drink	*Can I have two coffees, please?*	4:1
	Make general requests (possibility)	*Can I speak to Judy, please?* *Can I take a message?*	9:1
	Request (Ask) permission	*Can I have a look at it, please?*	11:2
	Request (Ask) people to do things	*Can you give me a size 10?* *Can you answer a few questions?*	11:2 13:4
	Ask others to make requests	*Can you ask her/him to come and see me, please.*	13:4
Requirements (see Shopping)			
Routines (see also Frequency)	Ask about routines	*What time do you go to bed/get up?*	7:2
	Answer about routines	*Yes, I do./No, I don't.*	7:2
	Talk about routines	*My wife goes jogging every morning.*	7:2
Seasons (see Months)			
Shopping (see also Clothes)	Say what you want to buy	*I want to buy some stamps.*	6:2
	Ask where you can buy things	*Where can I buy a film?*	6:3
	Say where you can buy things	*(You can buy a film) at the chemist's.*	6:3
	Ask where places and shops are	*Where's the post office/newsagent's?* *Is there a shoe shop near here?*	6:3
	Say where shops are	*There's one next to the post office.* *Turn left at the wine bar and it's on your right.*	6:3
Size (see Clothes)			
Spell (see Alphabet)			
Suggestions	Ask for suggestions	*What shall we do this evening?* *Which film shall we see?*	9:4 9:4
	Make suggestions	*Shall we go to the cinema?* *Let's see 'Gone with the Wind'.*	9:4
Surprise	Show surprise and interest	*(I'm a teacher.) Oh, are you?*	13:2
Telephoning	Talk on the telephone	*Is that Judy? Yes speaking.* *It's Di here, Di Trent.*	9:1
Thank	Thank people informally	*Thanks.*	1:L
	Thank people formally	*Thank you.*	1:D1
Time (see Clock times; Fixed times)			
Titles	Greet people formally	*Good morning, Mrs Trent/Mr Hall/Miss Tessler.*	1:2
Want	Ask what people want (1)	*Do you want a coffee or tea?*	4:1
	Say what you want (1)	*I want a cheese sandwich.*	4:1
	Ask what people want (would like) (2)	*What would you like to drink?*	8:2
	Say what you want (would like) (2)	*I'd like some orange juice, please.*	8:2
	Say what you want to buy or get	*I want to buy some stamps/get some money.*	6:2
Weather	Ask about the weather	*What's the weather like?*	7:4
	Talk about the weather	*It's quite hot.*	7:4
	Comment on the weather	*Isn't it a lovely day?*	7:4
Work (see Jobs; Journeys)			

Index 3 Active words and expressions

The bold figure beside each word or expression indicates where it first appears as active vocabulary. The letter (v) indicates the verb form of the word.

A

a bit **11**
about **4**
abroad **8**
across **7**
address **1**
afraid (I'm...) **9**
after **6**
afternoon **1**
again **6**
air (fresh...) **9**
airport **11**
a little **4**
all **2**
all right **4**
alone **13**
along **7**
a lot **7**
already **7**
also **12**
altogether **8**
always **8**
and **1**
animal **3**
another **8**
answer **12**
anyone **13**
anything **9**
arrive (v) **6**
ask (v) **6**
assistant **9**
at home **4**
at (place) **6**
at (time) **6**
at all **4**
at home **4**
at the weekend **7**
at work **7**
autumn **9**
awful **7**

B

baby **3**
back (I'll phone back) **9**
bad **2**
bag **9**
ball **14**
bank **6**
bar **6**
bathroom **8**
(be) (v) **1**
beach **7**
beautiful **7**
because **9**
bedroom **8**
beer **7**
before **6**
be missing (v) **13**
between **13**
bicycle **7**
big **2**
biscuit **4**
black **4**
blue **8**

boat **7**
book **2**
book (v) **6**
boring **9**
borrow (v) **12**
both **3**
boy **3**
boyfriend **13**
box **4**
bread **7**
breakfast **7**
break **13**
break into (v) **13**
bring (v) **11**
brother **3**
brown **8**
brush **12**
bus **6**
busy **6**
but **2**
butter **7**
buy (v) **6**
by **3**
Bye! **6**

C

café **4**
cake **4**
called **3**
camera **6**
camp **14**
can (v) (ability) **4**
can (v) (request) **4**
Can I help you? **11**
canteen **7**
Can you do me a favour? **13**
car **6**
card **9**
car park **12**
carton **13**
cash **11**
cassette **6**
cat **3**
catch (bus) (v) **7**
catch (ball) (v) **14**
cathedral **4**
centre **3**
certainly **11**
change (v) **14**
cheap **8**
Cheers! **8**
cheese **4**
cheque **11**
child **3**
chocolate **4**
choose (v) **12**
church **7**
cinema **4**
city **7**
class **2**
classical music **3**
clearly **12**
clear up (v) **13**
clock **6**

close (v) **6**
clothes **11**
club **9**
coach **11**
coast **3**
coat **11**
coffee **3**
cold **7**
college **7**
comb **2**
come **2**
company **3**
concert **4**
conference **6**
Congratulations! **14**
cook (v) **4**
corner **13**
cost (v) **11**
count (v) **12**
country **2**
country (opp. town) **8**
cream **13**
cry (v) **14**
cup **3**
cut (v) **13**

D

dance **9**
dangerous **12**
date **9**
daughter **7**
day **7**
days of the week **7**
Dear... **4**
detective **13**
diary **2**
dictionary **2**
different **8**
difficult **12**
dinner **11**
disco **4**
do (v) **3**
doctor **3**
dog **3**
Don't worry. **12**
door **8**
double **1**
down **12**
dress **11**
drink **4**
drink (v) **9**
drive (v) **4**
drop (v) **12**

E

each **8**
early **6**
east **3**
easy **8**
eat (v) **8**
education **14**
else **12**
embarrassed **13**
end **9**

enjoy 9
England 3
English 2
even 7
evening 1
ever 8
every (day) 7
everyone 12
everything 11
everywhere 12
examination 14
exciting 9
Excuse me. 2
exercises 7
exercise book 2
expensive 9
experience 14

F
factory 9
family 7
far 8
fast 9
father 7
favourite 13
film 3
find (v) 12
find out (v) 13
fine 3
finish (v) 6
first 8
(see Ordinal numbers 9)
first name 3
fish 8
flag 2
flat 3
flight 6
floor 7
floor (=storey) 8
flower 6
food 3
football 6
for 3
fortnight 11
free (opp. busy) 9
fresh (air) 9
friend 2
from 2
fruit 7
fun 6
funny (=strange) 6

G
game 12
garden 8
get (v) 6
get married (v) 13
get to work (v) 8
get up (v) 7
girl 3
give (v) 9
glass 4
glove 14
go (v) 4
goal 14
go home (v) 7
gold 14
good 2
Good afternoon. 1

Goodbye. 2
Good evening. 1
Good luck! 14
Good morning. 1
go out with (somebody) 13
go to bed (v) 7
great (=marvellous) 12
green 8
ground (floor) 8
group 13

H
hair 12
half 6
hand 12
handbag 11
happen (v) 9
happy 8
Happy birthday! 8
hard 13
hate (v) 4
have (v) 3
have a look at (v) 11
Have a nice time! 11
have got (v) 7
hear from (v) 14
Hello. 2
help (v) 12
Here's your key. 1
Here you are. 11
Hi. 2
hit (v) 12
holiday (on...) 8
home 4
homework 12
hope (v) 13
hot 7
hotel 1
hour 7
house 3
housewife 3
How? 6
How are you? 3
How do you do. 2
How far? 8
How funny! 6
How long? 8
How much? 4
How nice! 9
How often? 8
How old? 4
hungry 8
hurry 6
husband 7

I
ice cream 6
identity card 2
I don't know. 3
I don't understand. 3
ill 12
I'm afraid. 9
I'm fine, thanks. 3
important 14
I'm very well, thank you. 3
in 1
in (+parts of the day) 6
in English 2
interesting 6

interpreter 14
into 13
invite (v) 14
I quite like... 14
Is anything wrong? 13
It suits you. 11
It's time to go. 14

J
jeans 11
job 3
journey 8
jump (v) 14
just 4
Just one moment. 13

K
keep (v) 12
key 1
kitchen 8
know (somebody) (v) 13
know (something) (v) 9

L
label 14
language 4
large 11
last (night) 6
late 4
learn (v) 11
left 6
Let's... 9
Let's go out. 3
library 9
lie (down) 7
lift 12
like (v) 3
listen to (v) 7
live (v) 3
look (v) 8
look after (v) 7
look at (v) 7
look forward to (v) 9
long (time) 9
lose (v) 12
lots of 4
loud 9
loudly 12
love (v) 4
lovely 6
luckily 14
luggage 13
lunch 7
lunchtime 11

M
main 12
make (v) 3
make your bed (v) 14
man 3
many 6
map 2
married 3
marry (v) 13
marvellous 11
match 6
meal 9
meat 8
medium 11

meet (v) 2
meeting 6
menu 14
message 8
milk 4
mind (v) 12
minute 8
Miss 1
Mr 1
Mrs 1
Ms 1
money 6
month 8
Months of the year 9
more 12
morning 1
most 6
mother 7
mountain 11
much 3
music 3
must (v) 6

N
name 1
Nationalities 2
near 3
need (v) 9
neighbour 13
never 8
Never mind. 12
new 2
newspaper 6
next 8
next to 6
nice 2
night 6
nightclub 12
No. 1
no one 13
Nor do I. 4
north 3
notebook 12
nothing 9
Not too bad, thanks. 3
now 6
number 1
Numbers 0–10 1
10–1,000,000 4

O
o'clock 6
of course 11
often 8
Oh dear! 12
Oh good! 1
Oh no! 13
OK. 3
on (+ days of week) 7
on (+ dates) 9
once 8
on holiday 8
only 7
open (v) 6
opposite 6
or 1
orange 4
order (v) 14
Ordinal numbers 1st–31st 9

other(s) 7
out 3
outdoor 14
out of 12
outside 7
over there 2
own 9

P
packet 4
paint 7
paper 12
parcel 6
park 7
party 4
past 6
pay (v) 11
pen 2
pence 4
pencil 2
people 3
perfume 9
perhaps 13
perhaps not 13
person 12
phone (v) 1
photograph 7
pick up (v) 12
piece 4
place 3
plane 6
play (v) 4
Please 1
pleased 11
Pleased to meet you. 2
police 13
polite 2
political 14
pop music 3
post (v) 13
postcard 6
post office 6
pound (£) 4
pretty 11
programme 6
pub 7
purse 2
put (v) 13

Q
quarter 6
question 12
quiet 12
quietly 12
quite 6
quite (I quite like…)14

R
rain 7
read (v) 4
Really? 3
receptionist 1
record 4
red 8
relative 12
rent (v) 6
repair (v) 13
rest (of the time) 11
restaurant 6

ride (v) 4
right 6
river 8
road 12
rollerskates 14
room 1
romantic 14
round 4
run (v) 12
running shoes 14

S
sad 9
safe 14
sandwich 3
say (v) 9
school 2
sea(side) 12
second 8
secretary 3
see (v) 4
See you later. 4
See you soon. 6
See you then. 9
send (v) 6
shirt 11
show 6
shop 6
short 12
shorts 14
show (v) 13
shower 14
shut (v) 13
shy 13
sightseeing 4
silver 14
sing (v) 4
sister 3
sit (v) 4
sitting room 8
size 11
skirt 11
sleep (v) 7
slow 9
small 2
smart 11
smoke (v) 4
snow 7
So do I. 4
so (near) 12
soap 6
some 6
something 9
sometimes 8
son 7
song 7
soon 4
Sorry! 4
sort 8
sound (v) 14
south 3
speak (v) 4
Speaking. 9
special 12
spell (v) 3
spend (time) (v) 13
sports 4
sportsbag 14
spring 9
stairs 8

stamp 6
stand up (v) 7
star 14
start (v) 6
station 9
stay (v) 11
steal (v) 13
stop (v) 12
story 7
stranger 6
strap 14
street 6
stripe 14
student 2
study (v) 3
study 8
success 14
sugar 4
suggest 9
suit (v) 11
suitcase 14
summer 9
supper 7
surname 3
surprised 13
sweater 9
swim (v) 4

T,
table 7
take (v) 13
take (a taxi) (v) 8
take (+ time) (v) 8
take care of yourselves 14
take away (v) 13
talk to (v) 7
taxi 2
tea 4
teach (v) 3
teacher 2
telephone 1
television 4
tell (v) 9
term 9
terrible 7
Thanks. 1
Thank you. 1
Thank you very much. 6
That's a good idea. 11
That's all right. 4
That's very kind of you. 12
theatre 4
then 7
There you are. 4
thing 14
think (v) 7
thirsty 8
this (morning) 6
three times 8
ticket 2
tidy (v) 14
tight 11
tired 9
to 4
to (quarter to...) 6
today 6
together 6
toilet 8
tomorrow 11
too (= also) 2

too (+ adjective) 9
toothpaste 6
top (floor) 8
topical 14
touch (v) 12
tour 11
tourist 6
town 3
train 6
travel (v) 8
trip 11
trouble 13
trousers 11
true 14
try (on) (v) 11
T-shirt 9
turn (v) 6
twice 8
type (v) 4

U
umbrella 2
under 7
underground 8
unemployed 3
university 13
until 6
usually 8

V
vegetable 8
very 2
very much 3
very well 3
video 6
visit (v) 7

W
wait (v) 13
wallet 2
walk (v) 4
want (v) 4
warm 7
wash (v) 12
wash up (v) 14
watch (v) 4
watch 9
water 4
wear (v) 13
weather 7
week 6
weekend 7
well 3
west 3
wet 12
What? 1
What about you? 8
What does that mean? 3
What else? 13
What's the matter? 1
What time? 6
When? 6
Where? 2
Which? 9
white 4
Who? 4
Whose? 14
Why? 9
Why not? 9

wife 7
win (v) 12
window 12
winter 9
with 3
woman 3
word 12
work (v) 3
write (v) 1
wrong 12

Y
year 8
years old 4
yellow 8
Yes. 1
Yes, certainly. 11
Yes, of course. 11
yesterday 6
yet 14
young 3

Index 4 Useful word groups

Adjectives & their opposites

good	– bad	fast	– slow
big	– small	well	– ill
young	– old	hard	– soft
new	– old	heavy	– light
tall	– short	early	– late
fat	– thin	black	– white
hot/warm	– cold	interesting	– boring
long	– short	lovely	– awful
high	– low	cheap	– expensive

Countries & nationalities

NOTE: These are grouped phonologically not morphologically. The groups have no political significance.

'an' ending
America	– American
Germany	– German
Mexico	– Mexican
Paraguay	– Paraguayan

'ish' ending
Britain	– British
Denmark	– Danish
Finland	– Finnish
Ireland	– Irish
Poland	– Polish
Spain	– Spanish
Sweden	– Swedish
Turkey	– Turkish

'ese' ending
China	– Chinese
Japan	– Japanese
Nepal	– Nepalese
Senegal	– Senegalese
Vietnam	– Vietnamese

'i' ending
Pakistan	– Pakistani

'ian' ending
Argentina	– Argentinian
Australia	– Australian
Barbados	– Barbadian
Belgium	– Belgian
Bolivia	– Bolivian
Brazil	– Brazilian
Canada	– Canadian
Czechoslovakia	– Czechoslovakian
Egypt (ARE)	– Egyptian
Hungary	– Hungarian
India	– Indian
Italy	– Italian
Norway	– Norwegian
Russia (USSR)	– Russian
Tunisia	– Tunisian
Yugoslavia	– Yugoslavian

irregular
Holland	– Dutch
France	– French
Greece	– Greek
Switzerland	– Swiss

Word fields

Sports
cycle	ride a horse
fish	rollerskate
hang glide	run
jog	sail
mountaineer	scuba dive
play baseball	ski
badminton	swim
football	walk
handball	waterski
hockey	windsurf
icehockey	
netball	
squash	
tennis	

Clothes and accessories
bag	shirt
bangle	shoes
belt	shorts
blouse	skirt
boots	socks
bracelet	stockings
cardigan	sweater
coat	sweatshirt
dress	tie
jacket	tights
jeans	trousers
jewellery	T-shirt
pullover	umbrella
raincoat	underwear
ring	vest
running shoes	waistcoat
sandals	

Spare-time activities
do ballet dancing	listen to music
ballroom dancing	play the piano
disco dancing	the guitar
jazz dancing	cards
go to the cinema	chess
to the theatre	read
to the opera	sing
to a ballet	watch television
to a disco	
to a restaurant	
to a bar	
to a nightclub	
to evening classes in…	

Colours
beige	pink
black	purple
blue	red
brown	white
green	yellow
grey	

Public buildings, places and shops
airport	hostel
antique shop	hotel
baker's	jeweller's
bank	launderette
bar	library
bookshop	museum
boutique	newsagent's
bus station	petrol station
butcher's	pizza bar
café	police station
car park	post office
cathedral	pub
chemist's	record shop
church	restaurant
cinema	school
club	shopping centre
college	station
department store	stationer's
drycleaner's	supermarket
embassy	taxi rank
factory	theatre
flowershop	tourist information office
garage	toyshop
greengrocer's	travel agent's
grocer's	university
hairdresser's	videoshop
hospital	wine shop

129

Index 5 Selected further reading

1 General theory and practice

Brumfit C J and Johnson, K (eds) *The Communicative Approach to Language Teaching* (Oxford University Press 1979)
Finocchiaro, M *English as a Second Language* (Regents 1974)
Harmer, J *The Practice of English Language Teaching* (Longman 1982)
Johnson, K and Morrow, K *Communication in the Classroom* (Longman 1981)
Littlewood, W *Communicative Language Teaching An Introduction* (Cambridge University Press 1981)
Wilkins, D A *Notional Syllabuses* (Oxford University Press 1979)
Willis, J *Teaching English Through English* (Longman 1981)

2 Grammar

Thomson, A J and Martinet, A V *Practical English Grammar* (Oxford University Press, new edition 1980)
Leech, G and Svartvik, J *A Communicative Grammar of English* (Longman 1975)

3 Aids

Ayton, A and Morgan, M *Photographic Slides in the Classroom* (George Allen and Unwin 1981)
McAlpine, J *The Magazine Picture Library* (George Allen and Unwin 1979)
Mugglestone, P *Planning and Using the Blackboard* (George Allen and Unwin 1979)
Wilkinson, J *The Overhead Projector* (The British Council 1979)
Wright, A *Visual Materials for the Language Teacher* (Longman 1976)

4 Oral development

Holden, S *Drama in the Classroom* (Longman 1981)
Wright, A *et al. Games for Language Learning* (Cambridge University Press 1979)

Longman Group Limited,
Longman House, Burnt Mill, Harlow,
Essex CM20 2JE, England
and Associated Companies throughout the world.

© Brian Abbs and Ingrid Freebairn 1983

First published 1983
Fifth impression 1985

ISBN 0 582 51688 9

Set in Times New Roman

Produced by Longman Group (FE) Ltd
Printed in Hong Kong